WHEN LIFE WAS WOW!

BOB BAKER

WHEN LIFE WAS WOW!

A Memoir of Surprise

BOB BAKER

Images are from the author's collection, unless otherwise noted.
Miss University photo courtesy of
the University of Connecticut archive.
Linc Hawkes photo courtesy of Marblehead Messenger.
"Barefoot and 12" Huck image, Advertising Club of Greater Boston.

First published 2019

Manufactured in the United States

ISBN-9781099875564

•

The information in this book is true and complete
to the best of the author's knowledge.
In some cases, names have been changed.

•

Cover concepts and design direction: Bob Baker

Book design: Mark Sutherland

•

Endless gratitude to God,
Mom, Dad, son Rich,
Pete and Mimi Hart,
Jack Connors,
Roland Merullo,
Peg who was Diana.

•

Life isn't about finding yourself.
Life is about creating yourself.

- George Bernard Shaw -

Contents

INTRODUCTION

The Age of Surprise

When Life Was Wow! is a memoir of my rambles in five vibrant worlds during the liveliest half century in American history, the 1940s into the '90s. It's a treasure chest of anecdotes and life stories aromatic with nostalgia, alive with surprise.

The second half of the 20th Century just kept on kicking up sparks -- with every spark a surprise. It was the Age of Surprise. Everything fresh-faced and happening-happening-happening. Depression ended, World War ended, economy booming. Individualism, creativity and the American Spirit flourishing. Confetti storms of new products, new trends and whole new cultures -- the Beats, rock and roll, the hippie revolution ... surprise at every bend in the road.

wow

No word more accurately *echoes* the Age of Surprise than wow. Wow is the very sound of surprise ... a relaxed gasp ... as reflexive and quick to the lips as an exhale. Proclaiming the upbeat mood of the nation throughout the Age of Surprise, wow was the catchword on everyone's lips: a positive expression of surprise that could range from a soft-spoken sigh of awe ("That eulogy was ... wow.") to a shoutburst of exultation ("D'ja see that *catch!? Wow!* I mean ... *WOW!*"). And then there was the no-emphasis everyday version ("Wow, what a beautiful day.") -- expressing surprise, but more as a statement of truth.

Wow was everywhere. It was as suddenly 'there' as the air. It was a happy kids expression, a cheer, a mantra, and lacking only Latin translation to become our national motto throughout the ever-surprising second half of the 20th Century.

The Worlds According to Me

Some background to set the stage for the life stories to come -- how and where I played the game of life in the Age of Surprise:

• Golden Age of the Imagination (the 1940s) -- Due to a life-threatening allergy to Catholics in Old Greenwich, Connecticut in the '40s, I didn't have a friend to my name till we moved to Greenwich when I was 13.

I take that back. I had one friend, a damn good one, too. Thanks to the miraculous concurrence of *three* mini golden ages in the 1940s -- radio drama, comic books and Hollywood movies -- and with the white-bright Perrot Memorial library just down the street, I powered up an imagination which has not only been a friend for life, it has -- literally -- *created* my life.

• Golden Age of Prep (the 1950s) -- Though I was on the wrong side of the social ladder, there in Greenwich of the 100-acre estates, capitol of the Kingdom of Prep in the '50s, visions of Gatsbyhood danced in my head. Some-improbable-inexplicable-how, I impostored my way onto the elite Vacation Dances circuit, where, at the Greenwich Country Club one Scott Fitzgerald night, Brooke Hayward, pal to Jane and Peter Fonda, introduced "dressing down" to the still embryonic culture of Cool.

At UConn, thanks to huge $ bestowals from a pair of toe-tagged aunts, I achieve a sorta-Gatsbyhood, a cottage on a lake, a backslapping claque of uni-buttocked (half-assed) friends, and an eleventh-hour meltdown of the Ice Queen of KKG.

In this same era I also succeeded in losing the magical Peggy. She who owned the word "wonderful." She, who -- in a poetic sense -- would never leave me.

• Golden Age of Publishing (1946 to late '70s) -- Take this Gatsby wastrel, miracle him into Assistant Publisher job at *Harper's Magazine*; then even-greater-miracle him onto *Harper's* masthead in "Thurber" position just a year later. Rent controlled West Village apartment, membership New York AC -- all the trappings of fast-track success in New York *Citee* ... the Mecca of Success in the '60s.

A thorn to conscience drives me to abandon "Success" in favor of *"He's an idiot!"* lifestyle move to Harvard University Press in Cambridge. Then, Little, Brown in Boston -- where I'm fired from an 'administrative' job, *with* the advisory that maybe I'm "meant for something more creative ... like advertising."

• Golden Age of Advertising (the '60s to the late '70s) -- I rocket to stardom in the kindergarten surreality of the Boston ad agency troupe of advertising's storied Creative Revolution -- the victory of Magic Marker-inspired creativity over the formulaic suits'-slick mindset of the *Mad Men* regime.

The move to advertising was a giant step backward -- thank God. All of a sudden the homogenized "he" I'd been *begins* to become the individualist "I" I am to this day. I regress *professionally* to the imagination-stoked loner kid in Old Greenwich. Not only that, I'm being paid exorbitant doubloons to play god and carouse with an asylum's worth of other party-hearty imagination-stoked loonie-tics.

The bad news was that as *punishment* for creative award accomplishments, I'm elevated(?) to Creative Director. The Creative Director job is only 10% creative ... 90% director. Director = *administrator*! No way. No *mas*. Time to bust *free* of The Box. Time to become Me.

• World called Freedom (November 1974) -- *Recessionary* 1974, yet. With a what-the-hey toss of my leonine mane, and to yet another chorus of *"He's an idiot!"* from the Conventional Wisdom gang, I a gossamer-winged creative coocoo, leap into the abyss to face the future on my own in -- (hysterically *shrieked* laughter) -- *business*!

I swapped the Corporate Box for Outside The Box to chase ideas of all description, run with real people, party plenty -- all at the whim of my trusty advisor, my mirror. All in the welcoming environs of an inspirationally intoxicating place, a rum squall fisherman's world disguised as a town called Marblehead.

The how-to manual for solo entrepreneurship and free-form lifestyle had already been written -- in my 'singular' boyhood. The imagination-loading from the '40s which fueled my creative career in Boston fuels the creative pursuits I engage in to this day. *Plus*, the guerrilla mode mindset I'd been forced to adopt in my boyhood, infused in me an ability to adapt, and always find a way -- a happy escape.

A sorta-parallel universe to mine came to existence in the 1980s when the Internet enabled everybody and his sister Sue to work on their own from home. Today, that way-hot career world is B-schoolishly called "Entrepreneurial Lifestyle" and has an estimated population of 27 million.

My world is still called Freedom -- with an estimated population of Me. (*And* Huck Finn, who you'll discover later. As did I.)

Anatomy of an Idea

This bar-style topic-based storytelling format is the byproduct of my favorite storytelling venue (bars) and my belief that biography or memoir in its purest, most engaging form is "the story of stories."

By ballpark estimate, from as early as age 16 on, I've spent significant parts of 2,500 nights and 10,000 days in bars, saloons, pubs, watering holes, dives, boites, etc. -- most of them in the Age of Surprise.

As a frequent frequenter of spirited establishments, it is my informed opinion that bar-style is the God-intended vehicle for the sharing of life stories. There, in the intoxicating ambiance of a bar, topics arise which inspire one life story after another, a string of them -- something in one story suggesting the next. They jump cut from one captivating yarn to the surprising next, with wanton disregard for segue, chronology or continuity. There's an energy about it ... a buzz.

Bar-Style Storytelling

This is a roundup of accounts of my escapades presented in bar-style format. Bar-style storytelling isn't stories about bars; it's stories told in bar-style mode -- i.e. one story reminding the storyteller(s) of follow up stories on the same topic.

The 150 or so life stories, anecdotes and vignettes (all true) which are the heart and soul of *When Life Was Wow!* will be told bar-style in seven 'topic' sections -- Kid Stuff, Girls Are Different, Moves, Ideas, Characters, Opened Gifts, A Surprise Sidekick.

Each story will have a title, and other than the occasional vignette which is mainly for color, each piece will tell a complete story, many with the surprise ending or twist as actually played out. There will be *no* "Which reminds me ... " lines bridging stories. Each piece is self-contained and free-standing: you can end with Story X one day and start with Story Y the next without needing a refresher course.

•

May the wows be with you.

• •

•

1

Kid Stuff

The things about me and before me made me feel
like a boy again -- convinced me I was a boy again,
and I'd simply been dreaming an unusually long dream.

Mark Twain

• • •

·

A Useful Gift

Killer Kane's was maybe the funniest gift I ever got. But that came later. The most useful was the one from God: an up-down-all-around imagination I can focus to a pinpoint in a blink. The heavens didn't part or anything, it just was there for me when I was a kid in Old Greenwich and needed it -- it's been my pal, paycheck and wild card ever since.

The need was bigtime. Seeing as I was an only child who went to parochial school in a town two bus rides and an hour away, and seeing as Catholics were about as welcome as bubonic plague in Old Greenwich in the '40s, I had no friends outside school.

I mean, what the hell, parents reasoned, nine-year old Norton might leave home a right-proud Protestant, only to return from hanging out with Bobby the Boy Pope, blithering Latin, peppering his head, shoulders and chest with Signs of the Cross and demanding fillet of sole for supper.

Lucky for me, though, I had that Golden Age of the Imagination going for me, the amazing congruence of *three* golden ages: comic books, Hollywood movies, and the imagination-juicer of all time, radio -- comedy, soaps, mysteries, thrillers, drama -- the incomparable Theater of the Mind.

Lacking other kids to play with, ideas became my friends -- *and*, a way of life I'd thrive on throughout my life.

The Imaginary Boy

My parents moved to Connecticut from New York in the late '30s when I was an infant: Dr. Collins said "the country" would be good for Mom's health. It's a hoot to think "the country" then was just 20 bird miles from Times Square.

The birthplace of my imagination was a vanilla bungalow at 9 Center Road in Old Greenwich, Connecticut, across the street from a kinda-sorta swamp alive with prickers, but lacking frogs. Despite the barren setting my imagination took root and took off -- proof that imagination is a mind of its own, with a will and ways of its own. 9 Center was the center of worlds for me ... worlds to explore, worlds to invent.

One of my worlds was reading. Mom lit the light there; she was a *reader* reader. Dad stuck to "the papes" and *Life* magazine.

Mom never just read a book. She lived it. Her view of life was romantic and idealized; a pretty world with polite people spreading coats across puddles and living by a -- God forbid -- code. A code of -- God forbid -- honor. Possessed by that perception of life, were she alive today, she wouldn't be alive tomorrow. Want it or not, a good deal of her romantic nature and commitment to code rubbed off on me. It's cost me some over the years; but when it works, it's the Fourth of July.

One of the proudest moments in my life was the day I got my first library card. A door the size of Kansas swung wide wide open, revealing the bluest blue sky I ever did see.

I read everything I could get my hands on.

I wasn't supposed to, but I read the true-crime cases the *New York Daily News* featured every Sunday. They ran four full pages that had muddy photos of whiter-than-white girls' legs projecting from the underbrush of Lovers' Lanes in Ohio or Michigan. They used colorful words like "torso" and "garrotte" in the text. "Grisly" was frequent. I even had to wash my hands afterward: the *Daily News* bled oily black ink.

From *Life* magazine I learned about the war, far-flung places, famous people and all sorts more; including the fact that Rita Hayworth in a satin nightgown was *Wow!* -- though I wasn't quite sure why at the time.

Then there was the world of radio. Excitement at my fingertips, a click away there on my bedside table. The million voices I have today came from radio.

The Lone Ranger! Click the switch, fiddle the dial ... the *William*

Tell Overture! No sound before or since has stirred me as did that anthem to adventure. My heart's a jackhammer. The music settles, a voice of God thunders: "Return with us now to those thrilling days of yesteryear! From out of the past, come the thundering hoofbeats of the great horse, *Silvair*! The Lone Ranger rides again!"

Boy, did I return with them now! Every hoofbeat of the great horse *Silvair* (Silver), I returned with them now. You bet your ass I returned with them now. Every Monday, Wednesday and Friday at 7:30 on the dot, and WXYZ on the dial, I returned with them now.

I totally identified with Lone. He was Lone, I was lone. It was the lone two of us against whatever or whoever needed againsting that night.

Saturday night was another story. I was "strictly forbidden to listen to *Gang Busters* ever again." The one time I had, it was a sheet-swimming night. *Gang Busters* had to be a radio-stuffed-under-the-covers operation. No nightmares, though. Never.

You can't have a nightmare unless you're asleep. I never slept after *Gang Busters*. The stories themselves weren't scary; I knew most of them already from *Crime Comics*. They were true stories, drawn from FBI files: Dillinger, Baby Face Nelson, Machine Gun Kelly, Mad Dog Coll. The close of the show was true, too. Which is what kept me up all night. After the sound effects guy rat-a-tatted the last tommy gun and slam-clanged the cell door on Mad Dog with a *KA-CLANNNG* to wake the dead, a voice from the dead comes on -- with the for-real 'WANTED' bulletin:

"Norville Elwood Scragg ... six-feet-five inches tall; weight, hundred thirty-nine pounds ... jagged scar, left eyebrow to upper lip ... missing left ear ... no left ear ... five gold teeth ... walks with shuffle ... SHRIEKING giggle ... shrieking giggle ... Norville Elwood Scragg, wanted, kidnapping and decapitation slayings three young boys ... "

Then, Colonel H. Norman Schwarzkopf of the New Jersey State Police (father of General Norman Schwarzkopf) -- in a voice from the tomb -- adds the chill note of authenticity: "If you have seen this man, notify the FBI or your local law enforcement agency ... at once!"

I don't have to tell you in which Bobby Baker's bedroom window in the bungalow at 9 Center Road, Old Greenwich, Connecticut, old Norville Scragg's five gold teeth gleamed every other hyperventilated heartbeat the rest of that Saturday night without end -- even through the World War II-mandated blackout shades, they gleamed. I could hear that shrieking giggle, too -- even over the wail of troop train whistles a mile away and the tree branch skittering the windowpane, I could hear that fucker's shrieking-assed giggle. He was out there all night, all right, right outside my scared-stiff, shivering-paned window.

Whenever I was home sick, I caught soap operas. They made me feel adult: I was eavesdropping on adults, learning their secrets, what they talked about, how they spoke.

My mother opened the door to movies for me, too.

For a runt of a city, Stamford had more than its share of movie theaters: the Avon, Plaza, Palace, Stamford, Strand, Rialto. Many a Friday afternoon during the school year, Mom would take a bus from Old Greenwich to Stamford and meet my bus from Riverside. Since St. Catherine's had the decency to let out at 12:30 on Fridays, Mom and I had time for a leisurely lunch before heading off to a matinee.

We always had lunch at the Davenport Hotel. I loved the Davenport. Mom called our Friday afternoons at the movies her "treat" for me. The Davenport was a treat in itself.

There was nothing pretentious about the Davenport, but there was a rightness about it. It was roomy and gleaming clean -- just right.

First thing I'd do when we entered the Davenport was check out the wall rack of travel brochures and maps. More great reading material. The brochures took me places. But the maps fascinated me more, involved me more. I could read the brochure on Maine, and feel pretty good about the place. But when I'd solved the folds and finally had the map open and spread out on the kitchen table, I could actually plot where I'd build that log cabin -- it would either be up there on Carr Pond Mountain, near Fish River Lake or Priestly Mountain, near Clayton Lake. Then again, Pleasant Mountain sounded pretty good, and the roads looked to be better, too. There was plenty of exploring and imagining in those maps, once I ever got them open.

The Davenport's dining room was cranberry-colored drapes, bright-white tablecloths, sparkling glasswear. The waitresses wore cranberry-colored skirts and starched white blouses. Caroline who usually waited on us always had something nice to say to me about Mom, and to Mom about me. I always had broiled scallops, mashed potatos and peas. The rolls came in a wicker basket. They were covered with a white napkin to keep them warm. I'd have a butterscotch sundae for dessert.

Then it was off to whichever double feature at whichever theater we'd decided on this Friday. I've nothing new to tell you about the actual movies we saw; you've seen them all yourself. The main thing I remember was the experience itself, and the sense of awe I had about it. Once the houselights dimmed to darkness, that theater, even the seedy Rialto, was a church; and when the images flicked by on the silver screen, a 'Mystery' -- as the Mass is called a Mystery -- was being enacted. I'd come away with more of a sense, a feeling, about what I'd seen, than what I'd actually seen. I'm like that with movies to this day.

The Father of Cos Cob

Michael Santora was a classmate at St. Catherine's. Though not big on book learning, Michael was fierce bright in tricks -- most notably the one he bragged about at recess, the one he played at his father's drug store in Cos Cob.

Michael put in a fair amount of time at the store when his body wasn't in school. He manned the soda fountain, swept the floors and put up stock after school, weekends and during summer vacation. He'd been doing this since third grade.

'Round about sixth grade it was explained to Michael by his older brother Nick that the contents of those squarish blue boxes labeled Trojans were rubbers, and rubbers were used to prevent people women, mainly from having babies. Immediately on hearing this, great light filled Michael's cranium.

Wouldn't it be something just special, Michael wondered one fine day, wouldn't it be interesting, to take a straight pin and pierce the center of those little blue boxes all the way through?

In the scarce light of the storeroom, Michael practiced his impish accupuncture on many hundreds of little blue boxes until he was eighteen when the US Army, recognizing his genius, required his presence at a higher calling, the snuffing out of the already born.

Thus, thanks to Michael Santora, there are many who first saw the light of day in Cos Cob, Connecticut in the '40's who would not have seen the light of day in Cos Cob, Connecticut in the '40's.

Or anywhere.

Lost Chord Found!

Until seventh grade at St. Catherine's, we were taught by the Sisters of Mercy -- though mercy wasn't their strong suit.

At the end of sixth grade school year, as we were about to be released for a summer happily devoid of Mercy, Monsignor Ganley came before us to make An Announcement. Now if the nuns held us in fear and trembling, Monsignor Ganley was the Right Hand of God and the Avenging Angel all in one. Without exception, his Announcements had to do with Darkness: death of parent or schoolmate; tumors; rabid Dobermans; downed power lines.

The Apocalypse was lurking around the corner of even his most promising sounding Announcement. Example: Announcement that we'll be given the day off tomorrow.

With bated breath, awaiting the other shoe.

Raspy Doomsday voice: "Michael Connors' father died Friday. An excruciatingly agonizing death, falling into a steaming vat of carbolic acid at his place of employ. You will all attend his funeral tomorrow. It will be a Requiem High Mass. You will form in the schoolyard at 9. You will march over at 9:15 to the church, where you will dwell on Mr. Connors' death and pray that he may be with God in Heaven and not writhing in the carbolic conflagration of Hell. Be sure your fingernails are clean."

What's today's announcement? "The Sisters of Mercy will be replaced by another order in September, the Sisters of the Presentation," Monsignor Ganley said."They are from Worcester, Massachusetts. Avoid evil companions, avoid the occasions of sin this summer."

What's around this corner?

Savoring each word: "We shall now offer a prayer for the repose of the soul of my niece, who with three of her companions was killed in an *horrific* accident when the emergency brake on their car failed and the car rolled off a cliff where they were *parked* on the night of their Senior Prom. I only *pray* she was in the State of Grace while the car was in the air, before it crashed in jagged *splinters* of metal, glass and young bones, flesh and blood and spewing *entrails* upon the rocks. The most frightening thought of all, she was *not* wearing her Miraculous Medal that night! My sister found it on her *dresser* and *sped* to the dance to try to give it to her ... BUT! ... she and her companions had left the dance ea*rrr*ly! Be sure you wear yours all the TIME!"

Thus came I to eighth grade, to be nourished by solid-of-stature, solid-of-person Sister John Marie. Despite the foreign ring of her Boston accent, there was instant chemistry. She liked me, I liked her. She rubbed her mind against mine.

I caught fire.

The good news was I won scholastic scholarships to Catholic prep schools: Iona, in New Rochelle, New York; and Regis, in New York City. The bad was that I was class valedictorian, having to deliver the valedictory address on graduation day.

It wasn't really a speech the nuns gave me to memorize, more like a sermonette. About a minute-and-a-half's worth, without racing.

"Religion, the Hope of America." That's all I remember now, the title. But those words will haunt me forever. Amazing, too, that that's all I recall; because I repeated and repeated and repeated the piece -- in rehearsal after rehearsal I intoned the words in my achingly pure soprano. (If I spoke German, I'd have been a first-round draft pick of the Vienna Boys' Choir.)

Came The Day, as I'd feared it would. A tropic June day.

I'm wearing the prescribed uniform: navy blue blazer, white shirt, dark blue tie, gray trousers. But since both blazer and trousers are flannel -- end of season sale in March -- it means I'm wearing what can only be called a ... sponge ... on The (tropic June) Day.

Comes The Hour. We process to the stage. Actually, my classmates process to the stage; I, socks asoak, shlop.

Though its capacity was about 300 max, it seemed for sure there were fewer people in China that day than were in that auditorium that day. (Including my 17,000 aunts and uncles who'd come in caravans all the way from New York to see their firstborn nephew, Bobby the Christ Child, do them proud.)

It began. Drone, drone, drone; sweat, sweat, sweat.

A song; then some kind of-torian; another song, next kind of-torian; song, next-torian.

Everybody doing pretty well, too. Even Nicholas Connelly, the Salutatorian, who screwed up at every rehearsal. Then comes Monsignor Ganley, who does about a 25 minute discourse on Hell which nobody needs to hear, inasmuch as by being here, they are all already there.

I'm not aware he finished, but somehow through my coma I hear a growl, "... ictorian, Robert F. Baker."

I bolt up as if shot. I shlop to center stage. The Crowd is, by now, not only restless and maddened; if it can't have out, it will at least have blood.

Hands clasped behind my back -- as instructed -- keep slipperying unclasped. Shoulders way back, as instructed. Look straight ahead at distant point in back of auditorium. As instructed. Title first. Loud, clear, slow, so they hear your every syllable as if it were a sung note.

No choice. Moment of Truth:

```
    li          Hope        mer
                 of
                  A
        gion,
  "Re         the                    ca"
                          i
```

The Creator, in His Infinite Wisdom, chose that exact rat's ass *instant* for my voice to change! I seek, and achieve, octaves high and low previously unknown to human ear, each and every note of which, is offensive to human ear.

Rusty laryngitis.

I somehow made it all the way through "Religion, the Hope" but could not hear my own voice. No one could hear my own voice. After the title not a word was heard. Nothing was heard except *yowls* of laughter, *shrieks* of laughter, ululating *wails* of laughter. The crowd is a writhing, seething, spastic-plastic mass, bobbing and bopping up and down, back and forth, sobbing on shoulders, pants-wettingly gasping for air, lurching towards doors.

I shlop shrunk-shouldered back to my seat, to be greeted by the sight of 26 wailing, bopping, *yowling* classmates. Afterwards, I'm surrounded by the gang of 17,000 aunts and uncles. The gang says how just plain *marvelous* I was. But its collective tear-streaked mick-red face and choked-back guffaws shouted the otherwise truth.

Dad was right: sometimes you can be too smart for your own good.

Honesty

Age three, Kate standing on back seat of the car looking out the window. One of my blood-pressure-skyrocketing peeves is tailgating; and Kate, despite her tender years had witnessed many of my shakings of fists and hurlings of oaths at megaton monster machines all but filling the rearview mirror.

As we're cruising along, I chance to glance in the rearview, just as she's shaking her little fist and shouting at the top of her lungs, "YOU BUSTARD! ... YOU BUSTARD!" at the mystery vehicle behind us. It had effect: he immediately swerved off the road and stopped I could see in my rearview that he was scratching his head.

&

Son Richard was the most selfless person who ever lived. Smart, strong of character, hardworking, funny and all that good stuff, but he had that one major flaw: He was selfless to the extreme.

We saw early evidence of the problem when he was only four. Rich had just come home from a birthday party, and wife Nancy called the birthday party mother to see if he'd behaved himself. The woman laughed and said he'd been terrific, and she had a "sweet" story to tell about him.

Seems the ten or so little boys and girls were getting set to play Pin the Tail on the Donkey. There's the donkey all nice and taped to the refrigerator door -- and the kids youngsters all nice and equipped with paper tails in hand.

And there they all are jostling and vying at squeaky-voiced-eardrum-piercing pitch to see who the damn shrieking heck is gonna go first.

"I'm first!"

"No, me!"

"*Me!*"

The jostling and vying approach pandemonium.

For some strange reason, there's a lull.

Filled almost immediately by this shy deep voice. Almost to itself it seemed, it said, "I'd like to be third."

Richard, looking down at the floor. Totally selfless -- as he was always.

Wow.

Bad Apple

Bob Corriveau, office manager at an ad agency I worked for in Boston , pops into the copy department the day after Halloween -- bursting to tell.

"A slew of kids came by last night. Around 7:30; it seems to be over ... the doorbell rings. Two ten-year-old boys just wearing masks, plus a cute little five-year-old kid with curly blond hair in an angel costume -- with wings, even.

"I tell them to hold on, I'll be right back. I'd given out all the candy I had, so I run to the kitchen and look around.

"Oh yeah, that bowl of apples. I grab three apples and ... back to the door. Plop, plop, plop an apple into each of the big kids' bags and then ... plop ... into the angel kid 's bag.

"The angel kid looks down into his bag ... then up at me. " *'Hey mistah!'* he squeals ... 'You just bwoke my fuckin' *cookies*!' "

Foolin' Around

April Fools' is my favorite day of the year: the one time the wacko I am the rest of the year is accorded a degree of legitimacy.

Jack's Joke Shop was a fools' paradise situated in the shabbier climes of Boston back in the '70s. Son Richard, daughter Kate and I would visit the shrine a couple Saturdays each year, there to wallow in the clutter of nuttery all but falling from the walls; to return home with our day's trove of plastic dog stuff, tabasco-laced chewing gum and squirt rings -- said treasures to be inflicted with manic glee on an innocent world as early and often as possible.

On our very first pilgrimage to Jack's Joke Shop, Jack himself was standing near the door as we entered. Jack casually pointed to the floor: "Sir, I believe you just dropped something." Sure enough, there it was, a dollar bill close to my feet. I bent to retrieve it -- only to have it *zipped* from my almost-grasp at mach speed and returned by means of transparent filament to the spring-mechanized button gizmo in fun-loving smirky faced Jack's wise-ass hand.

The kids screamed with glee; I had no choice but to join in. And I of course had to purchase a Dollar-Snatcher of my own.

I also vowed to one day beat fun-loving Jack at his own smartass game.

It would come to pass that April Fools' fell on a Saturday in 1978. The stars were in alignment. En route to Boston, I'm brazen enough to tell the kids I intend to nail fun-loving Jack on His Turf and on The Most Unholy Day of the Year -- even though I hadn't yet figured out how.

As we walk through the door, there stands Jack, smiling beatifically. He looks at the floor near my feet and points: "Sir, I believe you just dropped someth ... "

I did *not* look at the floor; I pointed to Jack's trousers instead. "I know," I said, "but *your* fly is open!"

As Jack looked down, I sang out, "April Fool!"

I'd just scored the coup of all coups: I nailed the owner of *Jack's Joke Shop* himself on ... *April Fools' Day* -- and with the oldest, dumbest gotcha in the book!

Good old fun-loving wise-ass Jack did not look exceptionally smirky-faced happy.

The kids went bonkers.

Lone Eagle

I had a number of imaginary worlds in my friendless grammar school years, but the Big Three were football, knighthood and Indians.

In all my worlds, I'm the hero, of course. I mean, what the hell's the sense of creating a world-class world in the first place, if you're just going to be a stupid-assed waterboy or armor polisher once the cameras start rolling. Might's well lay on your back and count the cracks in the ceiling, cup your armpits and make fart sounds instead.

In football, I'm Johnny Lujack, ace quarterback for Notre Dame back then. On the receiving end, Bill Swiacki, the slippery Columbia end who almost singlehandedly beat that legendary Army team with his impossible catches. I grab my football, stand at the foot of the back porch steps, throw a spiral straight up in the air, catch it. Next pass couple yards farther from steps. Next, farther still. Half-hour later, I'm making falling-down, ass-over-tea kettle grabs out there in the ruts and scrub of the field seven yards away. Though we (I) never had a for-real opponent, we (I) also never lost a single game -- we (I) always won. "I'm a winner" ain't an all bad attitude for a kid to have.

All to know about my world of knighthood is my respect for the knightly code of honor, and that my hero was Sir Galahad whose motto was, "My strength is as the strength of ten, because my heart is pure." I liked the sound of that, and I still shoot for it a lot. Mostly I miss.

Far and away the biggest of my Big Three was the world of Indians.

Now this generation of AmerIndian description has every right to want to be called Native Americans, if that's what they prefer. But my alter ego, Lone Eagle, was from the '40s. Lone Eagle was not a Native American in the '40s; he is not a Native American in this telling. Lone Eagle was -- and is -- an *Indian*. On that my heart is pure.

The name Lone Eagle is a composite.

First off, the name needed to be Indian-sounding. I had an all-consuming fascination with, and passion for, anything to do with anything Indian. Of all my worlds, this was the one I devoted myself to most intensely: me against the white man; me against civilization; me against Hitler, Tojo and all the other bad guys; me against organized-this and group-that.

The pain inflicted on my parents' ears as a result of my outbursts of war-whooping and blood-curdling yowls, both inside the house and from the hut of branches and reeds I constructed in the sorta-swamp across the street, was compounded by the hysterical phone calls of neighbors in pain -- one of whom I heard scream into the mouthpiece one time, "For God's sake, will ya clap a muzzle on that idiot! He's driving my bowels through the goddam roof! My wife has *asthma*, too!"

Therapy hadn't been invented yet.

The 'Lone' aspect of Lone Eagle derived from my favorite radio program, *The Lone Ranger*. I could identify like crazy with the stirring adventures of old Lone: after all, I was a *lone*, wasn't I? But Lone was a white guy, with a Hollywood white hat which probably went to the dry cleaners between shootouts with the Cavendish gang. I wanted to be an Indian, like Tonto. But Tonto was a copout, a white man's Indian.

To arrive at my name, I simply swiped the 'Lone' from the Lone Ranger and combined it with what I judged the ultimate symbol of adventure and freedom: the eagle.

There's no record of the date I was self-christened Lone Eagle. But that's who I was until we moved to Greenwich when I was thirteen -- where I soon shoved him into the deepest pinhole recess of my mind, along with all the other toys and trappings of boyhood.

With Lone Eagle successfully out of the way, I was now able to devote the next 26 years to becoming everything Lone Eagle was not. I tamed my imagination, joined the crowd: bowed the good bow, yessed the good yes -- within the good Box. Sold out to The Man. The Woman. The Groupthink. The Lemmings. The Box. Lone Eagle would surface now and then -- for a blink. But I'd repress him back to limbo and continue on my compromised way. Not a backbone to my name.

Finally/luckily, there came the day. In 1974. Lone Eagle, in war paint. Not gonna take it anymore. I had the guts to go out in business on my own, at a time when nobody in their right mind went out on their own. Lone Eagle reclaimed me. I returned to the essence of that boyhood me, the idea kid me -- guided by a set of principles called "Instincts." Though they were scarcely front of mind at age thirteen, they were there at the heart -- and soul -- of me even then.

Instincts

1. God has a sense of humor. It's good to think funny.
2. You are one of a kind. "One" is a verb.
3. Life is a game -- *play* it.
4. Simplify.
5. Dream big, live full, stay small.
6. *Dare* -- pounce.
7. Be *sure* of nothing: surprise is everywhere.
8. Time is the only currency -- spend it *your* way.
9. The center of the universe is between your ears.
10. Stay loose. Mind-travel: *in*-venture. Create worlds.
11. Help the good. Rock the smug. Abide not assholes.
12. The only wealth is friendship. The only place is home.
13. There is *always* a way. Adapt.

My boyhood was off the curve, if not the planet. I thank God for that ... now. But at the time, at age thirteen, how prepared was I for the *real* world?

Time would tell.

●●●

•

2

Girls Are Different

Women love men who love women.
And women *know* men who love women.
You, Beggah, love women.

Musique

• • •

•

Kisserama

Although lacking friends in those grammar school days, I had
acquired one social skill which might come in handy -- in a manner
of speaking -- in the future: girl-kissing.

The way to acquire a social skill if you have no-zero-nada friends is
to arrange to have parents who do have friends. And if their friends
the Higginbothams have a daughter who's a classmate of yours, and
she and some other kids form The Social Club in seventh grade,
maybe you'll get invited to some of their parties.

One Friday evening in November, my father and I arrive at the
Higginbothams. We're greeted at the door by Carol and her parents.
I follow Carol downstairs, to join the ten or so other kids in the rec
room.

I stand there by the munchies table drinking Coke, eating chips
and shuffling my feet, while the normal kids drink Coke, eat chips
and joke with each other, middle of the room. Few minutes go by,
someone says, "Spin the Bottle!"-- a cheer goes up. Next thing you
know, we're all sitting in a circle on the carpet, Carol 's standing in
the center. She bends over and spins the bottle on the carpet. When
it stops spinning, the mouth of the bottle is pointing at Billy Strada,
the most popular kid in our class. With no hesitation whatsoever,
Billy Strada stands up, goes over and rests his right hand on Carol
Higginbotham's left shoulder, leans forward and kisses Carol
Higginbotham full smack-dab on the lips.

I'm not sure you heard what I just said.

I said, Billy Strada, who-at-the-time-is-only-twelve-years-old-like-
me, and who is definitely not *married to* Carol Higginbotham who-
at-the-time-is-also-only-twelve-years-old-like-me, not to mention not
even *engaged* to her; the same Billy Strada, has the unmitigated

gall to, without hesitation, stand up, go over, rest his right hand on Carol Higginbotham's left shoulder, lean forward, and ... *kiss Carol Higginbotham full smack-dab on her -- only twelve-year-old, unmarried, not-even-engaged -- lips* !

Carol sits down. Billy spins the bottle. And so it goes.

Before you know it, Louise Murphy, who I have a crush on, spins the bottle, and it points at me. Luckily, I'm comatose. I don't even bat an eye. Reflexively, I stand, perform my lip-service duty, spin the bottle ...

Half an hour later -- three more at-bats later -- I'm getting the hang of it. An hour more, eleven more at-bats, my lips plumb puckered out -- Mrs. Higginbotham at the top of the stairs sings out, "Bob, your father's here for you."

I'd just spent two hours swapping lips with a dozen fellow kids: indirectly -- second-hand-kissing, you could say -- the boys who've kissed the girls I've kissed as well. Two hours swapping lips with a dozen kids I've never said anything more than "hello" and "goodbye" to.

Another Social Club kissfest in seventh grade and two more in the fall of eighth grade and I have become one champion kisser -- in the Sealed Lips Division, that is. We were all pretty pure about it. But/and I am still also a champion in the Sealed Lips Division when it comes to chatting up and befriending my kissmates ... er, *class*mates. The wall-to-wall kissathons at the parties don't present the opportunity to advance my KidSpeak vocabulary beyond the aforesaid "hello" and the aforesaid "goodbye."

Thus, though there are now at least a dozen kids in the world I've been in mad kisseramas with, I'm no closer to knowing them or how to even *begin* to relate to their breed.

Now let's kick this Theater of the Absurd a notch higher -- or lower, as the case may be. We've moved to Greenwich; we're living in apartment 301 in the Chateau Lafayette Apartments. It's April of my eighth-grade year. My birthday's in April. At supper the Monday before, Mom says, "Billy Strada wants to come by and take you to the movies at the Pickwick Friday night."

Huh?

Billy Strada wants to come by and take me to the movies Friday night? Billy Strada who's only the most popular guy in the class, who lives way the hell over in Stamford, wants to take a stupid bus all the way to Greenwich so he can pay money to take me, this dweeb kid who he's still never said two words to, to ... *huh*?

What am I gonna say to Billy Strada? On the way to the Pickwick? Huh? And, after the movie, back from the Pickwick? Huh? Maybe recite The Gettysburg Address which I know cold for him?

I'm worried sick all week. About what am I gonna say? About Billy seeing our apartment, which is very clean ... also very threadbare. Friday night, quarter of seven the doorbell rings. Billy, looking his popular best. My parents give him a big hello, I grab my jacket. We descend in the elevator, cross the Post Road, head towards the Pickwick, five minutes away.

So far, not a word's been said. Lucky, lucky, lucky. We're almost there ...

Billy says, "Oops. Forgot something. We've gotta go back to your apartment."

Not a word is said on the way back. Still lucky.

Billy gets off the elevator first, rings the doorbell. My mother opens the door, smiling at me. Billy nudges me into 301 ahead of him. I get to the living room, Carol Higginbotham and a half dozen others from The Social Club start scream-singing "Happy Birthday"at the top of their obnoxious, half-assed lungs.

To this day, I couldn't tell you who the others from The Social Club were who were there. I cannot remember a single detail about the rest of that night, except that we didn't play Spin the Bottle -- I don't think.

It was on a par with the story years ago in *The Enquirer* or such about the boy supposedly raised by kangaroos who emerged in a daze from The Outback. If The Social Club'd shrieked that sonuvabitch a surprise party, he at least had The Outback and freedom just a hop, hop, hop away. I'm shocked numb, trapped in cell 301, human hyenas yiping their stupid asses off.

My "Religion the Hope" graduation speech fiasco later that year would have been preferable. "Religion the Hope" was at least a form of release, a venting. 301 was a box.

Theater of the Absurd

I haunted the Pickwick Theater the first year we lived in Greenwich. It was a couple hundred yards from our apartment, just 20 cents to get in.

The 400-seat Pickwick was a palace built in the 1920s. Giant serpentine pillars guard either extent of the stage, a great burgundy curtain drapes the span of the stage. When the houselights dim and the theater fades to dark, the show about the show begins. With a start, the great burgundy curtain parts, lurches, stutters, wiggles, plods aside. An inner burgundy curtain parts and eases aside. And another. Now a white veil, through which frames of the MGM lion begin to play. The veil wisps aside and the movie roars to life.

Overhead, the blue velvet ceiling is transformed by pinpoint lights and dry ice vapors to a midnight sky of twinkling stars and drifting clouds. Even in the worst clinker of a movie, there's always the midnight sky to gaze.

I had a favorite seat in the Pickwick, just as I do anyplace I often, commonly, generally, typically, ordinarily, usually and frequently frequent. After site-testing varied locations, it homed in on third seat in from the aisle, first row of the lefthand side of the section behind the loge section. Don't ask how I arrived at that, it'd take forever.

•

A Sunday in March. Maybe twenty other people sprinkled throughout the vast of the Pickwick. I'm in my usual seat. A pretty, dark haired girl enters the opposite end of "my" row. She sits three seats to my right.

What have we here? I keep glancing over at her throughout the movie, but her eyes never veer from the screen. Comes "The End," we each exit "my" row by means of the route we entered: she exits right; I, left.

Next Sunday, as I descend the aisle, she's already there, where she sat last week. I bypass 'my' usual seat and sit two seats away from her. I repeat my sidelong glances throughout the movie -- her gaze is fixed straight ahead on the screen.

The following Sunday, I sit next to her. But ... I never look at her. We're both glued to the screen. I should say, our *eyes* are glued to the screen. My 'self' is two seats to the right.

Sunday next, I drape my arm over the back of her seat and ease my hand ever so lightly arest upon her right shoulder. A butterfly would've been more attention-getting. I elevate the fingers to give them a stretch every so often, but never move the palm from its place on her shoulder.

Sunday after, arm over back of seat, hand alights lightly on shoulder -- same as week before. I never made further move. We never once looked at each other. Not a word between us. Sunday after Sunday after Sunday.

Until the inevitable Sunday she wasn't there ... or ever after there.

This surreal Existentialist mating ritual, though severely lacking in passion, nonetheless gleamed hope. It was a bridge to humanity for me, connecting the kid who'd lived in his Lone Catholic outsider wonk imagination until now to a real live girl with an understanding shoulder.

Thank you nymph, whoever you were.

Theater Earth

It's Sunday, I'm in my usual seat. The movie: *The Snows of Kilimanjaro*, with Gregory Peck and Ava Gardner. My feet on the divider rail, titles starting to roll.

Giggling girls descending the aisle. Two of them. One bumping the back of my seat as they settle in behind me.

Clucking.

"I just love Clark Grable, don't you?"

"*Gable* ... besides, that's Gregory Peck."

"They never have enough salt on this popcorn ... I just can't catch it behind me back ... you're captain this year, you lucky!" says a girl with a raspy voice.

"First game is Bassick, they're always first. It's in dumb ol' Bridgeport," says a girl with a sweet voice. "I'm sa sorry," she adds, after something brushes the hair at the back of my head.

"We all botherin' you?" sweet-voice asks.

I turn to face the disturber of my peace.

Wow. Sandy Evans, head drum majorette at Greenwich High. She of the Southern drawl, cream-dreamy face, sleepy knowing eyes and blessed shape. All the more arousing because rumor has it she "puts out."

"Nah, you're not bothering me," I managed; though suddenly my mind is filled with the vision of her twirling herself and her baton on the 50-yard line, wearing just the white leather boots and fake-diamonds tiara. She forgot the silver-spangled leotard, I guess. Maybe it's still in the dryer.

"Whyn't y'all come back here with us?" she honeys.

"OK," I gargle.

I gather myself as casually as I can, pretending to be intent on *Kilimanjaro* as I clump and bump my way into their row.

"Hah, ah'm Sandy Evans. This is Somebody Somebody." .

I say my name, then, "Good picture."

"Yeah. Whyn't you put your lil ol' arm round me."

"Whuh?"

"Putcher arm round me."

I did.

"Do y'all like to French kiss?"

"All the time." Though I never had; in fact I'd never even heard the term. I had no idea what it involved.

Somebody Somebody is staring straight ahead, pretending to be lost in (or on) Kilimanjaro, humming to herself to phase out our courting palaver. Still humming, she rose and went to move off down the row: "I'm gonna go sit down front, I can't see from here so good."

She may have been a not-overly-blessed-by nature person with bad grammar, but she was a very considerate not-overly-blessed-by-nature person with bad grammar. Off and down the row and aisle she hummingly went.

Though I'd been granted a momentary reprieve from the French kiss puzzle, I now had it immediately and indulgently solved by Sandy.

"Boy, you're ... *goo*od," she gasps, at a brief pause in the festivities.

A hidden talent unearthed.

We were at it throughout the whole of *Kilimanjaro*, and frankly I was glad when the lights finally came up. As was my tongue.

"Y'all take me home?" she kittened, fluttering them ahs uh hers ... er, *eyes* of hers.

"Sure. Where y'all ... where do you live?"

"Riverside."

"I would, but I don't have my car. It's being fixed."

Not true. A cool dose of reality had kicked in. Not good to be seen with Sandy, what with her rep and all. I'd be a hero with the guys, all right. But what if any preppy girls saw me with her? It could kill any shot at Gatsbyhood.

"That's OK, we'll just take the train." What the heck. Rainy Sunday-afternoon, everybody's home putting up their stamp collection, nobody'll see me. What the heck. We exited the Pickwick, leaving Somebody Somebody to ponder the mystery of the leopard on Kilimanjaro.

Mine was becoming an increasingly hard predicament -- our half-mile journey to the station was often interrupted by a duck into an alley and an exchange of good feelings between us.

Somehow we made it to the station and onto the train, where our passion blazed unabated -- and to the evident disgust of all but two of the ten passengers in our car.

The exceptions were a pair of round, white-haired ladies with jolly round faces who were obviously sisters. They couldn't stop chuckling. They shared their delight at our adolescent fever with the old conductor. He'd wink at them each time he came by. They'd wink back. And chuckle all the more.

When we got off the train at Riverside, Sandy said, "Mah house is less'n a mahl straight ahead. But ah know an ol' barn on the way. It's on the Thaxter's property, and it's got a hayloft. Ah'll show y'all ... the ... way."

I thought I knew what she meant by that, and I panicked. So I told her I had allergies -- though I didn't say to what. She said she understood, but she didn't look like she did. I told her I'd give her a call if my car ever got fixed -- which must have sounded as fishy as it was, and I felt real bad about it all the way home.

The Whirl of Holden Gatsby

Greenwich in the Fifties was the bash uncorked by Scott and Zelda Fitzgerald in the Roaring Twenties. The Beautiful had simply moved the party from New York "out to the country" -- hundred-acre estates with English gardens and the crystal ballrooms of the Greenwich Country Club, Round Hill Country Club, Indian Harbor Yacht Club, Riverside Yacht Club and Belle Haven Beach Club.

The children of The Beautiful were assured they were a breed apart and above. The Beautiful Children were imbued with the knowledge they were *entitled*, because ... because they *were*. Beautiful Teens attended Ivy League prep schools, parties and dances on the vast estates, swirls of debutante cotillions and Vacation Dances held at the clubs during the holidays and throughout the summer.

un-Beautiful Teens attended Greenwich High or un-Ivy League prep schools. We un-Beautiful Guys attended the front steps of the Y on Friday and Saturday nights.

We were the Y Boys. We didn't choose the Y Boys designation; we came to be called that. We prefered it not, but, like Everest, it was 'there,' so we had to live with it. We were an integral part of the Fifties' nightscape of the Greenwich YMCA, a monumental edifice of brick and money which dominated the corner of Mason Street and the Boston Post Road, the main drag connecting Port Chester to the west and the city of Stamford to the east.

To be specific, we were the Y steps at the Post Road side entrance. In all but the howl of winter, it was virtually impossible for you to pass by the Post Road steps after sundown and not find one, three or a dozen of us gaping at you.

Most of us lived near the Y, and the White Diner was just across the Post Road, which meant there'd be frequent changings of the guard, frequent change of faces and number as we came and went. But not of kind: none of us were preppies in the serious Greenwich sense, though a good many of us dressed to that, aspired to that. Some serious preppies did use the Y upon occasion; guys from Brunswick, guys home for Christmas vacation from Choate, Exeter, Hill and such. We became friendly with some of them, by way of cigarettes and dirty jokes. But none of them found it worth their while to join us on the steps at night. They had preppy fish to fry.

Too bad for them, too; they missed out on a lot. Summertime was best. The regular Joes, in their sparkling-white Fruit of the Loom T shirts, clean khakis, white athletic socks, polished no-name loafers with shiny good-luck pennies in the slots, smoking Kools.

We pseudo-preppies, in our short-sleeve blue button downs, knife-edge-creased khakis, white athletic socks, spit-shined Weejuns with *no* pennies in slots, smoking Luckies. Our main activity, beside lolling about in cool poses, was seeing, being seen and hooting. In that regard, we hooted at our buddies with hot dates who drove by. They drove slowly, flipping us a by-the-way wave for effect. The ones with hot machines raced their engines for effect. We didn't hoot at people we didn't know. We just looked cool for that sort. Hoots were for friends, or people we needed to think we were great guys.

Above and beyond serving as a pedestal, the steps were a springboard. We'd hang out there between 7 and 9 trying to figure out what to do, where to go, *after* 9. Home was excused from any consideration.

Maybe just shoot over to Port Chester ...

•

There was virtually no direct fraternization between the "rill" (real) "Grunch" (Greenwich) preppies with lockjaw diction and the likes of us Y guys. Occasionally, you'd happen on some rills at a party thrown by a rill who was at Grunch High now because he'd been kicked out of Choate for swiping the headmaster's sherry. Even then, the rills would usually-mostly-90%ly hang with only their own and make out with only their own.

The only common meeting ground was The Land of Booze. Liquor was readily available to virtually anyone 16 or over. Greenwich, Connecticut was on the state line with New York. The drinking age in Connecticut was 21. But just over the border in Port Chester, you only had to be 18. Or look 18. Or have a fake ID which said you were 18. Or have someone over 18 buy it for you. It didn't matter whether you were a preppy or a Y guy. If you had that certain *je ne sais quoi* called 'cash money,' the booze was yours.

So we'd occasionally find ourselves in booths across from Grunch preppies at the Hilltop, Barge, Log Cabin, Wagon Wheels, Vahsen's or other New York jukebox joints and roadhouses. But that's usually as close as we got -- across the room from.

But I with aspirations to Gatsbyhood, lucked out: I was able to cross the moat. A summer job gave me a bit of an in with the preppy crowd, particularly those of the female denomination: lifeguard -- two summers at Rocky Point Beach Club in Old Greenwich and three summers at Riverside Yacht Club.

Double Trouble

I'm in the classic "Lifeguard: Motif #1" pose atop the guard perch at Rocky Point this summery summer's day. Left leg casually draped over arm of chair, right hand shading eyes Injun-style as I scan Long Island Sound for swimmers in distress, preferably damsel swimmers in distress.

Out of the corner of my eye I espy a pair of damsels not in distress -- but distressing me. As in, enticing. A matched set of wow-caliber raven-haired beauties of Sophia Loren configuration headed my way, in the company of oh-by-the-way Paige Powell.

Don't nobody light a match.

Paige, who's headed to Smith in September, says, "They want to meet you. These are ... this is Eva and Carla Montevideo. They're twins."

Twins. No shit. I mean, just because they look *exactly* alike. Who'd ever have guessed? And she got into *Smith*?

(I change names here in case the statute of limitations hasn't expired. The real-name twins were featured in a photo essay on debutante twins in *Life* magazine in 1954. Paige Powell is not the Smithie's name either. I value my scalp.)

I said hi, and added something half-assed clever -- I hoped.

It must've worked, because they all half-assed giggled back. The one who half-assed longest and loudest, Eva, sidewised to her sister -- and for my benefit, too: "He's cute!"

When they return from their swim in the Sound, Paige and the other twin proceed to the Sand Pit to grab some rays. Eva minces up the ramp to preen perchside and giggle up at me for half an hour. I swear there wasn't a single complete thought exchanged beween us throughout that eternal 30.

Deliverance occurs when Alan Erb, my replacement, shows up to give me my break. "Break" in every sense of the word; I'm running on empty in the giggle department.

But what the hell, she's a preppy goddess. So I ask if she'll go out with me. She allows as how that "sounds fun." She minces over to the Sand Pit, grabs a lipstick from her purse, mince-hastens back, writes her phone number in lipstick on my forearm -- to a fresh cascade of it's-been-torturously-too-long-since-I've-heard-those giggles.

That night I'm talking with Y buddy Skip, who says he heard about the Montevideo twins: "You got the wrong one."

I asked why. "Don't let the giggles fool you. The word is Eva's an ice box. Carla's the hot to trot one."

Hey, no big deal. I've got the phone number, I just call and ask Carla out instead. No big deal.

I hate phones. I dread phones. 7:30, next evening, I call. Girl answers.

Suddenly, I'm out of breath. Voice cracks: "Hi this is ... B-bob Baker. Is ... ?"

"Oh hi, Bob, how are you?" the girl says with enthusiasm -- *and* lacking any hint of giggle.

"Is this Carla?" (Please let it be Carla.)

"No, it's *Eva*, you little silly-billy! Giggledy-gig-gig-gig."

The best defense is a good offense. I don't even ask Eva how she is: "Is Carla there?"

The non-sound of held breath. The feel of February.

"You ... want ... you mean ... you want to speak to ... *Carla*?"

"Yep. She there?"

Phone slammed on hard surface. This could be going better.

I catch bits of conversation in the distance in the course of the next minute: at the beginning, and at the end.

The beginning: " ... aker ... talk to *you*!"

The end: " ... fix him!"

Footsteps. "Yes?"

"Carla?"

"Yes."

"This is B-b-b ... I was wondering ... I was wondering ... "

"I'm sure you were."

"I was wondering if you'd consider going out with me Sat ... "

"No."

"We could ... "

"No."

"Oh."

"And don't ever call here ever again ... ever. OK?"

"OK."

The bark-giggling in the background as the phone was slamming its way to the cradle was the icing on the icing.

An' a-one, an' a-two

Rocky Point Beach Club wasn't on the rill preppy map. The physical plant consisted ofpool, bathhouses and snack bar. No clubhouse. Which meant no bar, no ballroom. Which meant only a few members of the rill preppy class -- those living in Old Greenwich who did their serious socializing at the rill Grunch clubs on weekends, but took their kids to humble-but-handy Rocky Point for swimming, burgers and root beer during the week.

One of the rills my age was Tad Girdler. Tad's mother was a Binney. The Binneys were Old Greenwich aristocracy. Tad was a terrific swimmer who swam for the Hill School and later for Yale. At the time he was dating an attractive girl named Martha Chappelle.

I'd asked Martha out once, but she turned me down. Politely. It wasn't a repeat of the Montevideo twins calamity, though. I'd called with low-to-no expectations to begin with -- I wasn't a rill preppy, after all. Not hardly aristocracy; the only throne I occupied was the one adjacent to the bathtub in our apartment. I knew my place.

That was late June.

About a month later, guess what. I get a call from Martha. Guess what? She's just been named "Miss Teen Queen" by the *Greenwich*

Time, the local newspaper. Among her prizes are all-expenses-paid trips to the very elite Stork Club and the Astor Roof in New York, with the escort of her choice.

Why is she telling me all this?

Because, for reasons beyond even this imaginary kid's wildest imagination I am the escort of her choice. Me, the crown prince of Apartment 301.

Either Tad Girdler knew something I didn't know about the Astor Roof, or Tad Girdler had fallen out of grace with Martha Chappelle. No matter. It's a bit of a coup. An association of sorts with the Gatsby Set. A foot in the door and maybe about to enter the room. Maybe.

The day of the Astor Roof is a steam bath Saturday in August, made all the more tropic because the only suit I own is the flannelest of gray flannel.

The ride to the city on the train is excruciating. The temperature is a zillion above.

The Astor Roof turns out to be much cooler; easily a half-degree cooler. Only about ten of the 150 or so tables are occupied. Real New Yorkers are anywhere but here at the decidedly *anti*-social hour of 3 on a Saturday afternoon. The only ones to be caught in an un-happening sauna like the Astor Roof at this hour are a rookie Teen Queen, an idiot wearing a gray flannel suit in August and ten tables of piefaces who are either from Dubuque or a barnyard away.

An orchestra starts setting up on the stage. A guy plops an easel with a sign reading SWING & SWAY WITH SAMMY KAYE stage left. Same guy plops easel with sign reading DO YOU WANT TO LEAD A BAND? stage right.

Out comes Sammy Kaye. He has a pleasant, if bland, face, and his suit is bland, too. But at least it ain't flannel. He gives all 66 of us a friendly, "Hello, folks," turns to band, does a few flitty-twitty air twicks with his baton, leads band in a medley of tunes syrupy enough to whack a battalion of diabetics.

Mercifully, it ended.

Sammy turns to us: "And now we'd like one of you fine folks from the audience to come up and do what you've always wanted to do ... *lead a real live band*! Any volunteers?

(This band is *alive?*)

The Dubuques are enshrouded in dumb. A thunderous dumb enshrouds the entire Astor furnace.

A banshee shriek pierces the shroud: "*He'll* do it! He's always wanted to lead a band!" Martha is pointing at me and clapping maniacally.

The Dubuques are wildly applauding. Sammy Kaye is winking coyly and beckoning me like he's just invented sarsaparilla and "Oh boy, aren't we all just a'gonna have us a whole buncha Midwestern-assed fun!"

I hear nothing, see nothing, feel nothing. I am inexorably drawn on leaden feet toward the stage.

Kathumd. Kathumd. Kathumd.

On the way up the steps to the stage, one of the kathumds kastumbles me.

Restoring my hearing. Unfortunately.

The Dubuques are ecstatically guffawing and harr-harring. Her Queenship is shriek-laughing.

Sammy puts his hand on my shoulder: "Well, you're a fine-looking young man. What's your name, son?"

"Bob Baker," I manage.

"Nice. I have a cousin named Bob. He's not a *baker*, though; he's a *banker*. Heh (wink wink) heh heh. Where you from, Bob?"

"Greenwich."

"Greenwich, that's in Connecticut, folks."

"That's nice," is the expression on 64 piefaces.

"What do you do, Bob?"

"I go to Iona Prep."

"Let's have a nice hand for Bob from Connecticut who goes to Wyoming Prep, folks."

Nice hand.

"OK, Robert, are you all set to play 'Do you wanna lead a band?' "

This obviously wasn't a rhetorical question as I'd have hoped, because suddenly my right hand is wearing a baton.

"Robert, the song you're going to lead the band in is 'Babyface.' Do you know it?"

Of course I knew it. In fact, I used to really like it. I even had to go to confession over Teresa Brewer who sang it after I saw her picture in the *New York Post* once. She had a catch-me-fuck-me look -- so I sort of did.

Get it the hell done with. Turn, face the shitbird band. They sit there looking at me.

I look at them. So what. Whaddya want from me, shitbirds?

I raise the baton.

They bring their instruments to the ready-pounce position.

My hand feels pretty stupid hanging in the air calling attention to itself, so I bring it down.

So they play a note.

So I up the hand.

They toot-thwankle-thump another note.

Sometimes I speed it up, but then I get nervous because it sounds too fast. So I slow it back; and it's obvious these guys are getting more than a little urinated off at me because I'm making them sound like clowns. So they get even. When I bring the baton down, the trumpet section pops up ... then down. As the trumpets sit, the clarinetists pop up ... then down.

Ditto and ditto and ditto until -- Compassionate God! -- 4.7 eternities later, somehow it ends. The Astor Roof echoes with barnyard laughter.

I can care less if my jock is on fire. It's over.

Afterward, Sammy Kaye came to our table and made winking chit-chat for a minute. He was an OK guy. He even autographed the picture the Astor Roof photographer took of Martha and me. He also gave me a cheesy souvenir baton with his signature printed on it.

I still have the picture, I mourn the loss of the baton.

Clown Jacket

Brooke Hayward's 1977 memoir, *Haywire*, is a playbill of characters active on the rill preppy scene, narrated from the vantage point of a star player. Brooke's mother is Margaret Sullavan, the movie star, who'd *previously*-previously been married to Henry Fonda, the movie star. Henry Fonda, his wife and children moved to Grunch about the same time as the Hayward tribe. The families are "Best Friends" -- Jane and Peter Fonda go to school with, and hang tight with Brooke and her sister and brother. Anyone mentioned in *Haywire* is rill preppy elite, the Inner Circle.

My first brush with the Inner Circle comes to pass when Tad Girdler says he's got a date with Timmie Hekma and he wants me to double up with her prep school roommate visiting from Savannah.

I couldn't imagine why he deemed me worthy. Chances are he'd tried 47 rills and they rilly weren't up for a blind date. Maybe he figured I could 'pass' -- he'd seen me in the accredited blue button-down/khaki slacks/Bass Weejun loafers/no socks, summer-casual uniform. (Also: Top-Siders, wash-faded madras shorts -- *never* pre-faded, poplins, polo jerseys -- but *never* with those idiot crocodile logos that started showing up on wannabe preppies in the early Fifties. Grunch preppies nay-*never-frigging-ever* did logos!)

Whatever the reason, it don't matter to me. I may be on the wrong side of the Social Ladder, but, what-the-hey, Holden Gatsby's always up for climbing.

Tad picks me up at 7, and we head for the Hekmas'. (According to *The Great Estates: Greenwich, Connecticut*, the Hekma estate, "Semloh Farm (Semloh is Holmes, the original owners' name, Wasp-cutely spelled backwards), consisted of a 20-room manse and outbuildings on 320 acres. It required 30 groundskeepers to maintain bridle paths, plantings and gardens. The Hekmas kept six riding horses for family use.")

Though it's summer, I'm wearing my one and only sports jacket, the red-black-and-white houndstooth check *wool* number which served me faithfully all four years at Iona Prep.

Timmie Hekma's friend, Marge Blood, turned out to be a looker in the Grace Kelly mode. She was also fun, and we hit it off from the start. I still have a black-and-white Polaroid Timmie took: I'm perched on a garden table, casually gesturing with the gin and tonic in my 'baton' hand. Marge, seated on a bench, looks like something out of *Town & Country*.

Despite the fact I have every reason to feel like an *un*-preppy impostor in my *woolen* in-*August*-mind-you! Houndstooth Check

Clown Jacket, I'm in control. A calm-cool has settled over me. I've assumed the mantle passed on to me by my mother ... to the purple born. That clown jacket is *The Emperor's Clothes* jacket. Neither Tad, Timmie or Marge notice it. I don't know whether I distracted them with my footwork or blarney, but I feel very much at home on this 320-acre estate. I feel as if I belong; they give me no reason to feel otherwise.

After a couple-three gin and tonics, we shoot to Wagon Wheels, about a half hour up the road and over the border in New York, for three-four more g and t's and Lindying to a half-way lively combo. When we return to Semloh Farm, we make drinks, hit the den, douse the lights and mildly make out. Marge Blood was the first rill preppy I ever kissed.

(Semloh Farm was the site of another first. In *Haywire*, Brooke Hayward says, "My first kiss, after a Saturday night party at Jackie Hekma's, started innocently with Ping Pong and ended in the dark ... ")

On the ride home, Tad says that if one of the Hekmas *rilly* likes you, on the way home from a date, she'll tell you to take the dirt driveway before the main entrance to the house. "You go about ten yards, and there's a barn. She hops out, opens the barn door, beckons you to drive into the barn, but not too far ... because it's a *hayloft*. The damn barn's built on a hill ... the hayloft's at street level. She closes the barn door and hops back in the car with you."

Greenwich girls and haylofts.

A Foot Away

It's about one a.m. this Saturday in May and Skip and I have been deported from the Ro over in Port, so we're crashing the party he'd heard about in Riverside.

(Translation: The Rotisserie, a joint in Port Chester, had a serving policy which got you a pitcher of beer as long as you had a dollar and weren't wearing a Cub Scout or Brownie uniform.

The bad thing about the squat cinder-block Ro was it was *right next door to the* equally squat, equally cinder-block Port Chester *police station*. This coincidence probably has more than a little to do with the fact that at precisely 12:30 a.m. every Friday and Saturday, the bartender answers the bar phone, listens, hangs up, shuts off the juke box and bellows, "You ain't got proof, you ain't here! *They're* here in ten minutes!" This arrangement benefited the owner of the Ro by enabling him to make a few bucks and still get the kiddies out well before the 3 a.m. closing hour. It's not beyond the realm of possibility, either, that the owner of the Ro did find a way to reward the considerateness of the men in blue next door in some remunerative or similarly alike dollarwise fashion.)

I followed Skip to Club Road in Riverside. We park down from the big house with the lights ablaze. The front door's wide open. "Come on in!" the party says. So we do. Roaring. Rill preppies galore. Hi-fi cranking, keg in the kitchen pouring its head off. Parents either bound and gagged in the attic, or off partying in Grunch, swapping stock tips, lies and spouses -- or whatever old preppies do for fun.

Grab a beer and check out the living room.

All those good-looking girls. Yeah.

That one. And her.

And, *wow* ... the one.

Smooth is the only way to describe her. From the tip of her honey-haired head down five-feet-five to her smooth-tan feet she is smooth. Her smooth-tan feet are moving her smooth-tan body in an abandon which is even smooth. (I know, I know -- abandons are supposed to be wild. Take my word for it, this one was smooth. Think ice cream. Vanilla.)

She's smooth-abandon dancing with a 12-foot male of the wonk persuasion. She's wearing a modestly low-cut lime-green cocktail dress, and one of the straps has slid off one smooth-tan shoulder, which lowers the bodice some to reveal an area of one satinous breast where it is not tanned but is indeed milky white and Jell-O-ing syncopatedly to the smooth-abandoned rhythms of her -- I finally realize -- shamelessly *naked* smooth tan feet.

"Who is *she*?" I mutter to the air.

"Vicki de Castro," comes from a guy behind me.

She's near enough that she picked up on the drop of her name. She looks over her shoulder with a sly smile.

She catches me mid-gawk. A look of disgust replaces the sly smile. She looks away. I'd have wished to pretend the look was only garden-variety disdain, which was as common in Grunch then as "Hello." But it wasn't disdain. It was chemically active disgust.

She smooth-abandonedly steers the 12-foot wonk to the other end of the room. "Auf Wiedersehen" -- German for goodbye -- was playing. I can hear it to this day.

Don't make me no never mind; I'm gonna contrive an ingenious way to meet her -- on my terms.

The more I watch her, though, the more I lose: muscle, voice and mind. Numb I stand there. Gaping.

Better move. Somewhere the bludgeoned-ox face can watch her without her catching the bludgeoned-ox face watching her. There, that dark corner by the grand piano.

Oops, stumble. A shoe, its mate right there. A pair of lime-green high-heel shoes.

My computerlike mind processed the infinity of data and came up with the solution in a split second: Of the dozen or so girls in this room right now, only one is wearing lime-green, and only one, the same one, is not wearing shoes. The only one wearing lime-green *and* not wearing shoes is ... Vicki de Castro.

These are Vicki de Castro's shoes.

A plan is born: Cinderella. Make sure nobody's looking. Grab a shoe, stick it under my sweater, take it home.

Call tomorrow. Nice and cool: "Hello Vicki, you haven't met me, but as an incredible coincidence of lucky-you Fate would have it, I maybe might have your shoe. It appears to me to be the left one."

So I did stick a lime-green high-heel left shoe under my sweater and take it home. And I hid it in the back of my closet, in a Jack Purcell sneaker box -- with the real Purcells on top.

But I didn't call her tomorrow, because I wanted the mystery to deepen. Let her cool her heel a little. Yeah, heel. Heh.

Besides, I wasn't immediately up for the possibility of that look of disgust again. Even over the phone.

Matter of fact, I allowed the mystery to deepen a bunch of tomorrows'worths, simply by not calling. Freshman year at UConn, I suspended the shoe from the ceiling by a thread, over my dorm room bed. I hadn't even heard about mobiles or Alexander Calder, either. An early example of me being ahead -- or, in a manner of speaking, a *foot* ahead -- of my time.

If anyone asked, I said it was a token of movie goddess Rita Hayworth's gratitude for certain intimacies I'd granted her after she'd seduced me to her suite at The Plaza under the pretext of showing me her extensive collection of postcards from around the world.

Naturally, I took grief for the shoe. But that's OK, because as long as it was there, the fantasy was alive -- no matter how remote, there's always a possibility.

The mobile lasted until my junior year, when some depraved tool went and swiped it.

Lotta weird people out there.

Impostor vs. Cool

Brooke Hayward talks about "a dance given by Miss Vicki de Castro" in *Haywire.* Not that I was aware at the time, but in one sense or another, I was beginning to work the room, the fringe of the Inner Circle.

I did finally get into "the room" with rill preppies. As in "ballroom" -- Vacation Dance ballrooms.

The Vacation Dances were held during the Christmas holidays and summer months at the rill preppy clubs. The girls wore gowns; guys, tuxedos. Nine times out of ten the music was 'Society Bandleader' Lester Lanin, with his coffee-grinder music and cheap-o felt beanie giveaways. The signature dances were the Charleston and the Lindy, the bouncy swing dance named after iconic aviator Charles "Lucky Lindy" Lindbergh. Both dances originated in -- no surprise -- the Roaring Twenties. There was no liquor served *at* the dances; but there was *plenty* available at pre-parties, and laced into cups of punch at the dance -- poured from Dod's (Dad's) 'borrowed' silver flask which traced back to Dod's Dod who'd pluck it from an inner pocket of his raccoon coat to share with his flapper date at the Yale-Brown game back in the, you guessed it, Roaring Twenties.

The ticket for admission to the Vacation Dances was the Vacation Dance list. If you had rill-preppy credentials your name was on the invitation list.

If your 'estate' was a 4 1/2-room apartment in an apartment house adjacent to the sixteen-wheeler, air brake-farting traffic light on the Boston Post Road, and the 'prep school' you went to was a *day school*, mind you, *and* bloody well *Papist*, mind you, and it was attended, mind you, by sons of *working class people*, mind you, many of whose surnames began with O' or ended in *vowels*, mind you, and your 'affiliations' were limited to membership in 'Guardians of the YMCA Steps,' the St. Mary CYO basketball team and a dishonorable discharge from the Teresa Brewer Fan Club ... you not Rill Preppy ... so sorry.

With qualifications like mine, I'm, if anything, the *Anti*-Rill Preppy. Making it even more amazing when the phone's ringing as I walk into the apartment, spring of my junior year. A woman whose name goes right by me because her operatic voice is totally "Society Matron," says she's calling "in reference to the Vacation D*ahn*ce Committee" and wants to "*ah*sk" me a few questions, if she might.

I have zero recollection of any of her questions or my answers. All I know is the same calm-cool that came over me at the Hekmas comes over me now. I'm cloaked in *The Emperor's Clothes* again -- every negative I utter is guaranteed to be perceived as a positive. Honesty has (almost) always been one of my major shortcomings, and it certainly was then. But Mrs. Whatever-her-name would hear only what she wanted to hear. I was in the magic zone again, and I knew it.

As a result, I wasn't drop-dead surprised when I received the engraved invitation to the Vacation Dance at the Riverside Yacht Club at the end of June. The thing that mystifies me to this day is, *Who would have proposed most-unlikely me as a candidate for an invite to the Vacation Dances in the first place?*

I rented a tuxedo from a place in Stamford. White jacket, black pants; but *not* the cufflinked shirt the guy wanted to foist on me. Rill preppies 'dressed down' -- white button-down shirts, I knew that. My bow tie was *not* a, God forbid, clip-on. Later on, when wearing a bow tie and someone had the stones to ask if it was a clip-on, I'd sometimes undo it, and re-tie it before their very eyes, without benefit of mirror.

So I hit the Vacation Dance at the Riverside Yacht Club in June. And one at the Greenwich Country Club in August, and another at Indian Harbor in December.

With one small-but-telling exception, all three Vacation Dances followed pretty much the same why-am-I-yawning script. I went stag, hoping to maybe happen upon, or be happened upon by my rill preppy princess there.

Uncool me would arrive at the dance, which supposedly began at 8, at 8:15. Lester Lanin's band would still be tootle-thwank warming up. In the course of the next half hour, it's me off to the side, half a dozen stag nerds wearing glasses or acne (or both) hanging around the punch bowl, and a few couples on the dance floor. More couples straggle in.

Suddenly, from nowhere, at 9:45, they *all* blast in. From the pre-parties, and blasted, they all blast in. Phalanxes of shitfaced preppies, fresh from guzzled booze at parties thrown by parents seeking to rekindle Flaming Youth -- by way of their Smoldering Young.

Mussed-up hair, lipsticked collars, straps slid from shoulders, zombie eyes, sidling stride.

Let the Dance Begin!

Pandemonium, instant frenzy: hands flailing, feet kicking, the brass glare of Dixie concussing the room.

The Mysterious Gatsby is more than a little out of his element *and* out of synch here. He is not only an impostor, an intruder, at this rill preppy party; he is boringly unshitfaced.

Over the next hour or so, I ask three or four girls to dance. A 'dance' consists of moving with, and Lindy-quickstep-spinning a girl throughout the echo chamber blare of a seven-tune set, shouting information, questions and witty remarks at her at the top my lungs -- none of which she hears -- and trying, unsuccessfully, to lip-read her un-shouted response. At the end of the dance, I return her -- anonymous, uncommunicated-with and unviolated -- to her date.

Somewhere between 11 and midnight, I'd wear out and go home. What the hell. They were them, and I wasn't. No sense trying to force it.

The single but significant exception to that monotonous script occurred around 11 at the Vacation Dance held at the Greenwich Country Club in August. Despite the fact that Lester Lanin's halfassed band has just polished off a set with its trademark scrang-dee-bing-boop-bw*aaa*ng and is taking a break, the crowd is still at full shout.

Incredibly, suddenly -- the shout goes ... hush. All eyes are gaga on the couple in the entry to the ballroom.The absolutely *shocking* couple in the entry to the ballroom.

The girl, a lithe, pretty brunette, is wearing a confident smile, a mellow tan, a light-blue Peter Pan-collared shortsleeve blouse, blue-and-white madras Bermudas and black Capezio flats. The guy, sinewy, darkly handsome, is wearing a politician's smile, a tan, a blue button-down shortsleeve, knife-creased khakis, highly polished Weejuns, no socks.

Standard rill preppy casual wear for summer.

Casual wear. I try to ESP these two jerks a message that this is a damn *formal* event and they better hit the trail before they get the boot.

Obviously, *they* don't get *my* message, because obviously *I* didn't get the *crowd's* message. You could *feel* the *awe* in the room. Acclaim lacking only applause. Daring of all daring. Flaunt of all flaunts.

They mingled, danced, made themselves right at home. No chaperone challenged, no sheriff cuffed them.

They don't *act* Above It All. They simply *are*. I asked a guy next to me who they were. "Brookie Hayward, Ken Towe," he said.

I'd just witnessed The Official Birth of Cool.

(I didn't know who Brooke Hayward was at the time, but in gathering background for this memoir, I came across the June 1, 1953 issue of *Life Magazine* featuring "Daughters of the Stars," with ponytailed teenager Brooke on the cover. The caption beneath a photo of her in a strapless gown and high heel shoes on page 101 says, "She wears shorts most of the summer but dresses up for country-club dances in pin-dot organdy." Yeah, sure.)

How I Spent My College Vacation

After 13 years doing hard time in Catholic schools -- the last four years, all boys -- with the exception of anything in *any* way related to textbooks or classrooms, UConn was a terrific learning experience for me.

My first week on campus, I learned a lesson in girls.

Barbara Nando was 5' 2" -- an incendiary device in a small package. I struck up a conversation with her as we waited to register for courses. It was immediately apparent we had a lot in common: she spoke English, I spoke English; she had dark hair, I had dark hair. Come to find out we both liked movies. Her favorite ice cream flavor and mine? Amazingly, the very same, coffee. More amazing, but also true, same second favorite: vanilla. Her favorite number was seven. I nodded my head when she said that, but I didn't lie that mine was too.

With that kind of karma zapping the ozone, it's no wonder that an hour after we met we're on the grass at Mirror Lake necking like mad fiends. Like we're Bonnie and Clyde and the cops got us pinned down, but no way they'll ever take us alive. We'll welcome convulsive death in each other's arms under a bodies-lurching hail of molten Tommy gun lead rather than suffer the arctic Hell of separation in the slammer.

Or something like that. Let's just say it was intense.

Later, goodnight time at the doorway of her dorm: she asks how I feel about going steady. I said I'd never gone steady before but it always sounded pleasant enough. So she said we were.

The next day, I must have parted my hair wrong, because in the middle of a greaseburger at the Blue & White, Barbara says she's decided we're no longer going steady. I asked why, but she said she'd have to let me know some other time.

The first person I bump into as I'm coming out of the Blue & White is Ben Brandon, another guy from Greenwich. I'd introduced Ben to Barbara the day before. I blurted out my sob-wracked tale of woe.

Ben, tall, blue-eyed, easygoing guy that he was, allowed as how he'd "be willin' to act as a go-between" and try and get old long-lost

Barb and I back together -- predestined lovers for the ages that we were.

I said I'd really appreciate that.

The next few days as I'm dithering about in a moped-up funk, poor noble Ben is negotiate-busting his ass off for me with Barbara.

There they are at the Blue & White, the Student Union, at Mirror Lake, Swan Lake, sitting side by side ten rows up in the empty stadium, on the library steps, in front of her dorm on South Campus. All the while, poor noble Ben negotiating, negotiating, negotiating. Selflessly, unstintingly, unsparingly negotiating. And all for me. Wow.What a guy.

At the cafeteria a week later, a guy foghorns across the room, "Hey, Baker, I hear Ben Brandon's going steady with *Ba-rrr-bara*! You Greenwich guys really stick together, huh?"

Existential Girl?

Any kind of an excursion in a car was called a road trip, or a "shoot." The serious shoots were adventures. A serious shoot required consumption of multiple frosty-foamy roadies whilst coursing significant miles over corroded backroads, most typically in a vehicle of questionable life expectancy, and, more often than always, in quest of those who wear perfume. And dresses and skirts -- girls still wore such, and every day they wore such.

I made maybe a dozen shoots. The one to Bennett Junior College in Millbrook, New York, with Dave Leslie, was in a car we rented from an upperclassman for 10 bucks.

We get there late Saturday morning, settle down in the common room of the residence hall waiting for our dates. A girl in the common room makes the wait a treat. She's a knockout: jet hair, flapper-style bob, cameo face, bee-stung lips. She could easily have been one of the Laidlaw sisters, patrician beauties all; one of whom, Peggy, was easily the most beautiful girl in Greenwich, if not the world. I never met Peggy Laidlaw; I just filled the last pew in St. Mary's with drool every Sunday, worshipping both God and her from afar -- though not necessarily in that order.

This Bennett girl was a rebel: invoking the Twenties, inspiring the

Sixties. There she is, sitting on the floor. Girls didn't sit on floors; girls sat in chairs, if not thrones. Especially, crosslegged, girls didn't sit on floors. Nowhere and at no time would a girl of good breeding ever-ever *dare* to sit crosslegged. She's wearing a baggy black Shetland crewneck, no blouse. Her skirt's a green-tartan kiltie, shorter than short -- such never before seen, not to be seen again for the good part of an unenlightened decade or more. Her perfectly formed legs are bare, her perfectly formed feet are bare. She sits with her back mostly to us, writing in what appears to be a journal, disdaining us, despite intrusion now and then by one of our clumsy attempts to get her attention. Occasionally, she'll cease writing, absentmindedly withdraw a cigarette from the pale blue pack, consider it, light it, take a lazy draw, funnel the smoke from her nostrils, infill the room with the gutter incense of those frog Gauloises. She stands once, stretches like a cat. A Persian cat. Girls didn't stretch. Not in front of boys, should or would a girl ever stretch like that. My heart races: her face in profile, my Existential mystery girl from the Pickwick Theater! But not. Maybe?

The ultimate gamin, the kind they name perfumes after. The kind you wish have bad breath or a cheesy accent or such, so you can forget about them on the spot. The fewer the unattainable goddesses in my life, the better.

Our dates walk in before I can figure out her tragic flaw.

F. Scott Girls

The best shoots ever were to Greg Merrick's house in Enfield, Connecticut.

In looks and dress alone, Greg was as Grunch preppy as they come. Tall, Cary Grant looks, easy smile. *Every*thing Brooks Brothers: from the BrooksCloth shirts with the goofy long tails on down to the calf-high black socks which called for garters.

Two things kept Greg from being a pure Grunch preppy: 1) Though he'd gone to Canterbury, a high-ticket *boarding* prep school, it was still a *Catholic* boarding prep school; 2) Greg was just plain nice. He'd last two seconds max in the Grunch piranha pool. They'd eat him alive.

Those shoots to Enfield! Ever and always, Gatsby's in the air.

While the Merrick place was no Greenwich estate, it bespoke affluence. Sizable-enough property for lawn fete or touch football. Comfortable manse accommodating mom, dad, seven kids and party after party after party.

And the Merrricks did love to party. From the moment the sun's over the yardarm, the hi-fi's a-playing, the bar she's open, the fridge she's open. Mr. and Mrs. party right along with us through the early hours of the bash. But when the lights in the living room and the dining room and the den would chance to one-by-one happen their way out, Mr. and Mrs. would just happen to happen their way out ... to the kitchen.

One singularly memorable Enfield shoot came to pass the time Greg and I experienced a shared case of party fever during a school week. Greg called Carolyn Barnard middle of the night, knowing her parents were away in Bermuda. It took Greg all of 46 seconds to get Carolyn to agree that a party with us and her friend Karen Bloom was a better idea than Plato or an isosceles triangle that day.

Carolyn and Karen stepped full-blown from Gatsby: thoroughbred blondes, good-looking as hell. They went to The MacDuffie School, the girls' 'finishing' school in nearby Springfield, Massachusetts, riding together in Carolyn's MG-TD. *Usually.*

We four hooky players convened at the Barnard's house that Wednesday at the uncivilized party hour of 10:30 a.m.! We descended the stairs to the Barnard's rec room. As we all stood there in the how-do-we-get-started? moment, Carolyn pulled the trigger.

"Oh my God! ... I almost forgot my lunch!" she yelped. She runs back up the stairs, returns carrying a thermos, proceeds to pour us each a share of the *martini* "lunch" she was to have enjoyed at MacDuffie that day.

Let the games begin!

The rest of that day-becomes-night is a mix of martinis, scotch, beer, grilled cheese sandwiches, games of pool, dancing, the making of out -- all to the bright of Carolyn's dad's mint collection of Louis Armstrong, Fats Waller, Bix Beiderbecke and other Twenties and Thirties giants. It's a miracle none got broken.

When we surface from the basement rec room at 9 p.m., we are giddy.

Them two equal party.

Next time we get together, you and I, we'll have lunch at The MacDuffie School. The marts are on me.

Gatsby at State U

My ascent to Gatsbyhood at UConn was mounted on the bones of two dead aunts.

The stage was set from the outset. In the community of 5500 students, stereotypes ruled. One of the stereotypes held that kids from Greenwich, whether or not their fathers worked construction or drove cabs or had a medical equipment store like my dad, all kids from Greenwich were "preppies."

I wasn't just a "preppy from Greenwich"; I even graduated from Iona Prep, a place with "prep" in its name, making me all the preppier. Kick it up another notch when somehow it became known I'd worn a tux once or twice and attended a Vacation Dance or two -- which other Greenwich kids validated as the ultimate preppy scene.

Preppy was 'it' in Fifties' youth culture as far as the Then-known Civilized World was concerned -- the Golden Age of Prep. And imperial Grunch was undisputed World Capitol of The Kingdom of Prep.

Sophomore year I'd joined a fraternity, SAE: jut-jawed guys with perfect teeth (myself disincluded) who were campus leaders in every category save humility.

Major outsider-type me went along with fraternity routine junior year, but/and after living illegally off campus in a cottage on Echo Lake the next year, courtesy of a $2000 inheritance from Mom's sister Aunt Helen, I was back living on campus at SAE. I'd completed the fall semester and officially graduated (by a hair'sbreadth). Plus, thanks to professor/friend Ken Wilson, I'm now even doing a semester of graduate work in English.

Out of the chute, astride a black stallion kickin' cinders left, right and center, her billowing white gown and white-streaked hair flailing the air, my deceased Aunt *Edith* waving a check from her estate in the amount of *$3000* with my name on it. (From David Halberstam's book, *The Fifties*: "The average person would expect to buy their first home for $5000.")

This time I take up illegal off-campus residence in a cottage at Andover Lake, about ten miles from campus.

I threw a party of some sort three or four times a week from March, 1958, through graduation week in June. The cottage itself was a worse-for-wear lakeside bungalow, with pine-paneled walls and the linoleum kitchen floor debating whether to start peeling today, or possibly hold off till next Tuesday. But it was well heated; it had a working fireplace; there was an excuse for a dock and even a canoe.

The furniture was mostly stick stuff, in residence from the '30s, probably. But that overstuffed tattered couch served admirably for the making of out, and even the sitting of down upon. Then there was the *piece de resistance*, the four-poster brass bed which all but consumed the bedroom. The place could have been a pup tent and I'd have rented it, if only for that brass seduction.

The view was picturebook. Andover Lake was a long vertical extent and green-fringed. On a clear day you could barely make out the cottages snugged into the pines on the far shore.

Wow!

Spring at Andover Lake was Easter morn and the Hallelujah Chorus. With that $3000 inheritance I'm one of the richest guys on (or off) campus: even certified prepsters at UConn were light years removed from my kind of 'disposable' income. I had money to burn, parties to throw, booze to share, girls to flirt with, guys slapping my back, pandering praise at every turn of my overstuffed ego.

New car: mint-condition used ('51) Lincoln Capri. Closetful of the good brothers Brooks' haberdash. Brand new Webcor hi-fi, 40-plus albums -- classical, pop, jazz. *The Great Baker* doesn't have the same ring as *The Great Gatsby*, but that's who I was. I had the kingdom -- Greenwich North.

Joan Weatherley was a mystery I couldn't be bothered to solve. No question she was a knockout. Blonde beauty, bedroom bod.

Her reputation preceded her -- unfortunately. She's a loner; stuck-up and cold. That was the word. The 'cold' rep came from the few guys on campus she'd gone out with once ... just once: "I mean she's good looking as hell. But she's so damn smart, you can't talk with her about normal things. She wants to talk about serious stuff ... life, and all that sorta shit. You're never gonna make out with her, either. I mean, yeah, you'll get a kiss g'night at the Kappa door, all right. But I mean, do y'know what it feels like to kiss a *bird*? Ever kiss a fucking *bird* goodnight? I mean, beakity-beak. That's what it's like."

Honor Roll grind. Off to New Haven weekends to be with this Yale guy. Adding to the loner image: last summer she'd cycled around Europe -- by herself -- staying in these things called youth hostels.

"Big deal," you say. "All kinds of people bicycle around Europe."

Put it in perspective: hardly any Americans in the Fifties doing that. None-to-zero American *girls* all by themselves *alone* doing that. There was even an article about her European summer cycle cycle in *The Daily Campus*.

Being a loner myself, I was more than ready to like someone for that. But, 'cold' was a squelch. Her attraction to a guy of the Yale persuasion was another turnoff.

In April, a sorority sister clues me I should ask her out; she's on leave of absence from the Yalie. Hey, y'never know. So out I ask her.

Saturday night party at my place at Andover Lake. Jumping good night. For everybody else: bird-kiss in the Kappa doorway for me.

If at first you don't succeeed: I ask her out again. Another jumping night at Andover. For everybody else -- another beakity-beak for me.

I happen to like ice as much as the next person. In my drinks. Once more ... once more. Maybe a miracle. If not: three strikes, she heads for the dugout.

To compound the problem, a picture of her in a white evening gown, front page of *The Campus* the Monday before her potential next at-bat. The headline above the picture: "Joan Weatherley Named Miss University." (As per tradition, she was one of one of six coeds nominated earlier in the semester in what was, essentially, a beauty contest poll.)

Great. She's not arctic enough to begin with, now she's a queen to go with it. Now I get beaked by an empress penguin 'stead of a sparrow. Nevertheless, I call and ask her out for Saturday. To her credit, her "Yes" didn't sound any more disinterested than usual since her coronation.

Saturday at Andover was going about as expected. The half-dozen other couples were dancing or otherwise actively engaged in having a good time. The Queen and I were actively sitting side-by-side on the tattered couch. She was actively keeping to herself, despite my occasional attempt at conversation. I couldn't think of anything else, so I asked if she wanted to canoe the lake for a while. She said yes. We slid the canoe into the water and paddled for twenty minutes or so. It was a star-sparked night. It could've been real romantic -- if it were anyone other than "Stone Cold Dead in the Market" weighing down the bow up there.

When we got back in, the couch was still available. I'm sitting there thinking I only have an hour or so before I have to take her back to campus for my last beaking. I plan to be a gentleman about it and not tell her it's the finale.

"I'm so crazy in love with you, I don't know what to do about it."

A voice said that. A voice beside me said that. At least I thought it was a voice beside me. And I thought that's what it said. I turned to the only possessor of a voice beside me and did the only sane, logical, intelligent thing a rational human being would do in that situation.

I said, "Huh?"

She's looking straight ahead, her speech throaty: "I said, 'I'm so crazy in love with you, I don't know what to do about it.' That's what I said."

How could I have prepared for that? How could I have *been* prepared for that? The arrow had been pointed due bye-bye South. She grabs the damn arrow and skewers my heart. Who's *ever* ready for a *total* flip-flop? Dumbstruck. I don't know who I am or where I am. The party doesn't exist. Nothing exists but her.

I kept asking her to say it again. And she kept saying it again.

And then I said I loved her too.

And you know what? As impossible as it may be to believe, I meant it. It was like those deathbed conversions you hear about, I guess. This 'thing' just came over me, and I thought to myself something like, "Hey, this proud creature cold as Nome just melted herself before my very eyes. Because of me. Wow."

We went into my bedroom and lay on the brass four-poster and kissed long full kisses and said "I love you" a hundred times to each other until it was time to drive her back to campus and the opposite of a bird kiss goodnight.

I didn't sleep at all that night, because I knew she probably didn't mean it -- that maybe it was the booze. But she'd only had two scotches and they were both real watery.

but but but but but but but

I was braced for the worst when the phone rang at 5 a.m.

"I couldn't sleep, Bob. I'm so crazy in love with you, I don't know what to do, Bob. What's the soonest I can see you?"

Gatsby at State U -- **The Movie Pitch**

"Myron, here's the pitch, Myron. Think big, Myron. Think 'Love Story', Myron. This loner kid from no money shit-lucks his way to the fringe of the 'in' crowd in Greenwich the capital of Preppy Woild in the Fifties. Then he jumps from a 'sorta' prep school taught by uptight Catlic guys in black dresses to the sudden freedom of State U with loose goils in tight skoits runnin' loose all ovah the campus.

"If the kid was a fish, he'd be a floundah. For three years he becomes somethin' he's never been before -- one of the crowd. He floundahs around, cuttin' classes, chasin' skoits, partyin' at the preppy fratoinity he joins, havin' not the slightest idea who the hell he is -- though everybody else tinks he's Mr. Prep.

"Then big money from passed away deceased aunts decides for the floundah that he will revoit to his true loner self. But this time he will be alone in a crowd -- even if it is a beautiful crowd. For the next two years the kid is The Great Gatsby at State U where the rest of the kids got only a buck-ninety-eight. He crescendo-ingly mates up wit a gawgeous previously-Antarctic-but-now-suddenly-hot-to-trot babe who is not only Miss Univoisity but comes from a father stuffed wit money ...

"So what's wit the pickle face, Myron?"

Voyeur

I found it in a junkshop near Jonesport, Maine, a place which had rewarded me with small treasures on previous visits. The appropriately tarnished and smudged brass sheriff'stype badge imprinted LICENSED JUNK DEALER in prominent display on my mantle. The MAINE RABBIT BREEDERS ASSOCIATION seal which I delighted to affix to letters of pseudo pretention until rust finally took it upon itself to suddenly settle in and rudely foreshorten the unsuspecting rabbits' ability to reproduce.

The black cardboardlike scrapbook projected from near the bottom of a pile of dusty books.

All of two dollars and I'm off with my trophy, feeling somewhat excited about the prospect of piecing together the story of a deceased person's life from this tableau of memorabilia (just as Werther Grue had spelled out a man's life in bank checks in *Vanity Fair* in 1932). But I'm feeling more than a little dirty at the same time.

I even waited until no one was around the house to pore through the scrapbook. When I opened it, a faint scent of lilac breathed through the years of must. The telling was of a girlhood through spinsterhood in coastal Maine from the late 1800's through 1949.

The scraps spoke little to me of her, just her world: friendly but joyless letters from the likes of Josie and Alice and Edna and Uncle John, some pressed wildflowers, her tasseled high school graduation program and firemen's dance programs and postcards from Josie (Atlantic City) and Alice (Philadelphia) and Edna (Boston) spoke to me of a life so contained and rote that I had to, out of some calledup sense of decency, cease my ferreting midway through and slam it closed forever.

Exhaling a least last gasp of lilac. The pale perfume of a heart gone by.

Pure Lust

Thanks to a series of minor miracles, my first real job was Assistant to the Publisher of *Harper's Magazine*. Although it was the business side of the magazine, and my ultimate ambition was editorial, located in that stately six-story red brick Harper & Brothers building at 49 East 33rd across the street from our offices, I was at least, geographically-speaking, close to my goal.

Rebecca in Personnel won my attention in the course of my *un*appointed rounds of 49. That's all I knew: Rebecca in Personnel. I'd yet to meet her. But her doe eyes and inspired packaging whet my desire to know her otherways, Biblical not excluded.

My arrival on the scene at *Harper's* couldn't have been better timed. I started at the end of October, 1960; the Harper Christmas party was a Thursday night in early December.

•

The liquor is hammering as hard in the ballroom of the Sherry-McAlpern Hotel as the rain is hammering the rooftop ballroom roof. Returning from a visit to the men's room, I glance into the outer parlor of the ladies' room. There's Rebecca, perched on the bench at the nose-powdering table, examining her unslippered foot.

What is it with me and unshod women?

"What matter?" I bumble-mutter in her direction.

"Shoes off dancing. Splinter."

" 'mon out, have look, OK?"

In front of me, looking up at me.

"I'm Bob ... Ba ... "

"I know." Naughty eyes.

"See tha foot."

"It's OK now."

My heart a jackhammer. "Wan' dance?"

Eyes.

No classic dance position. Instead, automatic head-on-my-shoulder-kissing-my-neck-hot-breathing-my-left-ear-crazy position. Kissing. A whole-lot kissing.

Predicament: 1) I'm a newly arrived seeker of The Grail in a place where those likely to rise to the top smoke pipes and wear tweed suits -- and behave that way; 2) I am not behaving that way; 3) The many smokers of pipes and wearers of tweed suits who are here cannot miss the fact that I am not behaving their way; 4) I am risking my entire *future* by not behaving their way; 5) She's driving me beyond crazy.

What to do?

No contest. My place or hers. "Where live?" I mutter.

"Here ... tonight. Took a room."

My nostrils as big as my eyes. Tell you whah ... god a idear. You go dow your room, I go drugstore lobby, geh merc- chrome your splinner boo-boo ... "

"Room 1144."

As I assertively plunk the box of Trojans on the drugstore counter, the promotionally minded clerk asks if there will be anything else. I reply, "Boddle merc-chrome," in the manner of *obvious* association. You know: love and marriage, salt and pepper, condoms and mercurochrome.

Knock on 1144. Door opens. Eyes.

She's wearing a yellow rain slicker. Yup, a yellow slicker.

Ballad of a Fox

Rebecca and I never did have a real date. We had lust fests, Orgies-for-Two.

One Friday night Dan Brooks and I went uptown to catch a flick, *Ballad of a Soldier*. We're standing in line for tickets and I feel a tap on my shoulder: "Hi."

Sly smile.

"Hi, Rebecca ... you with someone?" She gestures towards a guy in the back of the line who looks for all the world like Woody Allen. Woody is looking soulfully towards her. She is looking bodily at me.

"You like him?"

She shrugs.

"Idea, Rebecca. Meet me at the popcorn stand exactly 15 minutes after *Ballad* starts. Got a watch?"

We meet at the appointed minute, grab a cab to 16 Abingdon -- naughty, naughty, naughty all the way.

The cabbie had some close calls with sidewalks and lampposts along the way.

It's been said by many that *Ballad of a Soldier* is an excellent film.

•

Rebecca and I never did get to add a funch to our extensive repertoire. She only had from noon to 1:00 for lunch break. A "funch" was New York-speak for exactly what it sounds like.

Jayne, from the heart

My UConn friend Dan Brooks introduced me to Jayne. No sooner were we introduced than I blustered my importance as the Great New Guy at *Harper's Magazine*. It was immediately apparent it had no relevance whatsoever for Jayne, and I was succeeding only in *un*impressing her -- to the max. So, I changed tactics. Instead of trying to dazzle her with something *really* interesting, like me, I took a radically different approach. I asked her about herself.

She's going for her masters in psych at Cornell. She lives with a guy off-campus. She's just down for the weekend and she's staying with Dan's date, Barbara.The more I listen, the more I'm attracted to her. But for reasons that come from a part of me I'm unfamiliar with. She isn't New York-style -- from the intellect, from the ego. She's from the heart. She's the best friend of the sister I never had, who I can kid with, even as I'm falling for her. We're not out to out-dazzle each other, or out-cool each other.

I've no idea how I got her to leave the party and come to my place, because the longer I talked with her, the more she made clear she loves the guy she lives with. Maybe my momentary lapse into unphoniness had something to do with it.

I fixed drinks when we got to my apartment and we talked and we talked and we talked. And we got silly as kids and opened up to each other and told things deep inside and got silly as kids some more. And we kissed and felt each other with our clothes on, but before it went further, she said no. And it went no further.

But when morning came and I went with her by cab to Barbara's apartment, we knew something had happened. To each of us separately, to both of us together. Suddenly, magically, there was an "us" of some kind. Neither of us knew what. She said she'd have to think about it a lot, and she told me a time I could call her, and a place to write her.

Couple weeks later she writes back: she'll be driving down to stay at Barbara's in February and would love to get together if I'd like.

That stone-cold Saturday afternoon, Barbara suggested the three of us hit Glennon's, an Irish Third Avenue bar she'd heard was a "writer's place."

Glennon's was spacious and severe. Sawdust on the floor, bar-length mirror on the wall fronting the black-lacquered bar, maybe a dozen black-lacquered high-back bar chairs, seven black-lacquered booths along the wall opposite the bar. A sense of verticality about it all; including the person of the sharp-profiled, rail-thin, straight-backed Jim Glennon standing there with his very white shirt and very white apron behind the black-lacquered bar -- and the lone customer in the whole place with his shoulders all but glued square to the high-back bar chair, just facing his face to the mirror.

There's no juke at Glennon's. But if there were, the only song playing, and in continuous play at that, would just have to be the classic round, "Saloon": "Saloon, saloon, saloon ... it runs through my head like a tune ... Saloon, saloon, saloon ... "

We settle into the last booth, the booth farthest from the cold draft of the door. Barbara and I sit facing Jayne -- and the door. Ten minutes in, two dumpy women with pasty Silly Putty faces and one dumpy guy with a pasty Silly Putty face settle into the booth in front of us.

"Know who *that* is?!" whispers Barbara.

"Which?"

"The guy. It's Brendan Behan! The Irish writer drunk. You know, *Borstal Boy.*"

We knew of this boyo. His escapades preceded him acoss the Atlantic -- not the least of which, his knockabout tantrum on BBC. Boy English major Bobby, you are in for a *treat*! Too bad you don't have a tape recorder, or at least a pen and paper.

They stayed all of half an hour. Jim Glennon and the lone customer at the bar don't have much to say to each other -- they're like an old married couple. We're not saying anything to each other, either -- so we can eavesdrop. We're in a laboratory-ideal acoustic environment to hear the least pearl emanating from the Silly Putty lips of the The Wild Irish Rogue.

No need for tape recorder or pen and paper. They're totally inaudible. Aren't hardly muttering -- at most a low hum. Talk about colossally bad timing! Guess what the All-World Rummy Brendan Behan is imbibing?

*Fire*water, of course.

Negative. Water. *Water* water! Bow-ring.

You read his *Brendan Behan's New York* and you get the message. He would hit P.J. Clarke's up Third Avenue and Costello's across the way on Third Avenue when he was partying hearty. But it was Glennon's when he was "taking the cure." My feckin' luck.

But being Irish, it wasn't all bad luck for me that day. We cabbed Barbara to her place later that afternoon. Jayne and I continued on to Abingdon Square.

And it happened. We made love and made love and made love. And that's what it really was: making love. And again, the silly kid stuff. The playfulness. The warmth.

The letter from her when she got back to Cornell, saying she'd have to tough it out with the guy she was living with -- but not sleeping with now -- because to break the news about us would "totally devastate him." And she could never do that.

She went on to say, "I'm not behaving 'normally.' Normality being independent & self sufficient. I was impressed -- by the little things you did with and for me. I'm impressed by my own reaction and desire to receive more -- and my even greater desire to give."

Her next letter, in its entirety: "Dear Robert -- Ow are ya Sport? I would like to invite you to join me at the bottom of a gin and tonic. PS You have beautiful blue eyes and I have been watching them all day."

And she drove her veteran VW bug down and stayed at 16 Abingdon Square. ("home," as she called it) and stayed five days during Spring Break.

When she was ready to leave I had to ride shotgun with her to make sure she got to the West Side Drive on-ramp OK. When we got within range, she pulled over, I gave her a quick kiss and hopped out.

I ran the I-forget-how-many-blocks-it-was-but-it-must-have-been-at-least-a-mile back to Abingdon Square. But I didn't just run, man, I *RAN*! And I didn't just *RAN*, man, I *RAN AND HOPPED AND JUMPED LIKE A BLITHERING SILLY-GRINNING JACKRABBIT KID ON A POGO STICK!*

I'd never felt so insanely happy in my life. I couldn't have imagined it *possible* to feel so happy.

Her letter: "Everything we had said and done kept passing thru my mind. And I couldn't and still can't quite believe it. We're so natural. It honestly amazes me Bob altho I didn't want to, I admitted a rather horrible thought -- <u>never</u> before with <u>anyone</u> have I been <u>completely</u> myself. But with you, for the first time, I feel like Jayne and I think you feel like yourself. How wonderful."

Poetic License

There was a delectable Radcliffe intern I'd been eyeing since her arrival at Harvard University Press. I'd been seeking an opportunity to strike up a conversation -- dazzle her with my *Harper's* credentials and agile wit.

I glimpsed her alone in the coffee room one day. Sauntering in, I began pouring a coffee, thinking back to college days at UConn, and opening lines. I decided to play it safe. Not cute.

"I'm Bob Baker," I say, expecting that by "Bob" she'd have begun unbottoning her blouse.

"That's nice," she says, elevating her eyes to nowhere in particular on the ceiling.

This mightn't be so easy. "Who are you?" I venture.

"Cath."

"Nice name."

Silence. Not, silence-is-golden silence. Lead -- as-in-rhyming-with-dead -- silence.

"So ... what're you majoring in at Radcliffe?"

"Comp Lit," she says -- with disdain you could cut with a chain saw.

I'll show this vixen. "Oh, Comparative Literature," I said brightly. And with as knowing a smile as has ever been knowingly smiled, I added, "You mean, like ... *Yeets* (the poet Yeats, correctly pronounced

Yates) ... and *Kates* (the poet Keats, correctly pronounced Keets)?"

"Yeah," she said in monotone, "like ... *tits* (teats)."

She wheeled and split the room. I stared into my coffee.

Avalon

(Avalon: In Arthurian legend, an island paradise.)

There were relationships of the spicy sort with women in the years following my divorce. I also greatly enjoyed relationships of the platonic sort.

Susan Chandler was platonic/up a notch. Attractive, bright, spirited, artistic, unpretentious, blessed with honesty and goodness. I know that sounds like the Cliffs Notes edition of the Girl Scout Oath, but that's who she was. A gifted designer with a special flair, we'd worked on a number of projects together. She asked me once if I'd write copy for some ads she was working up for her brother who had a forge in Vermont -- crafting ornamentally decorated iron gates, plantholders, chandeliers, furniture and the like. I said I'd be more than happy to -- no charge, of course.

Months' later, as a thank you to me, she invited me to a weekend at her parents' place -- an island they owned on Lake Bomoseen in Vermont. I was doubly thrilled by the invitation: 1) I've always had a thing for islands; 2) Neshobe Island had once been owned by Alexander Woollcott, one of the knights of the legendary Algonquin Round Table, the clique of rapier wits from *The New Yorker* who marathon-partied the bar of the Algonquin Hotel in the '20s and '30s!

This would be literary-nostalgia Avalon, far as I was concerned.

We drove to Lake Bomoseen one Saturday in August. Zipped out to the heavily wooded island in a Boston Whaler, greeted at the pier by Susan's parents, Merritt and Midge, and headed up the path.

Viewed from outside, the sprawling, low-slung fieldstone home, the Algonquin Round Table 'clubhouse,' seemed to emanate from the earth, in perfect harmony with its surroundings, yet with an understated elegance about it, in the manner of Frank Lloyd Wright. But it was inside, where a gallery of black-and-white photos of giants of yesteryear adorning the walls of a corridor, on the shelves of bookcases, and in silver frames on the grand piano and side tables, proclaimed the place a shrine. Visitors to Alexander Woollcott's idyllic isle were an A List of Hollywood, Broadway and the New York literary establishment in the '20s and '30s: Laurence Olivier, Walt Disney, Ethel Barrymore, Vivien Leigh, Noel Coward, George S. Kaufman, Helen Hayes, Moss Hart, Irving Berlin, Harpo Marx, Edmund Wilson, Gerald and Sara Murphy, Robert Benchley, Dorothy Parker.

(Of all the great stories attributed to Dorothy Parker, this is my favorite, yet I've only seen it in print once. Goes like this: Dorothy overhears sweet-young-thing secretary at *The New Yorker* raving about a Halloween party she'd attended the night before. "And what was the best part of your delightful party, Darling?" viperous Dorothy asped ... *asked*. "Oh, that would have been when we all ducked for apples!," the secretary exclaimed. Without missing a beat, Dorothy observed, "There, but for a typographical error, is the story of my life."

Story has it too that Parker paraded Neshobe Island one summery summer's day wearing nothing but a straw hat. One version adds sunglasses.)

Susan gave me a tour of the eight-acre island. As we completed the circuit of the wooded path and arrived at the clearing near the main house, she pointed to two wooden structures. "That's a guest house, and that's a barn. The croquet gear's in the barn ... we'll all play a game before dinner. Funny story about Harpo Marx at croquet. He stroked the ball hard and it rolled down that steep slope ... one of the hazards of the game here. The wooden ball rolls into the water ... bob-bob-bobbing away. No problem. Harpo rips off all his clothes, swims out, retrieves the ball, pulls on his trousers, back in the game. The two guys fishing from the boat out there had themselves a good yarn to share at supper that night."

In 1989, there's a Boston Globe article, saying the Chandlers are selling Neshobe Island -- it gives me a gulp. The place was magic. I wonder if it's still there, if you know what I mean.

Singular Advantages

My first place after my divorce was a studio apartment at historic

Fort Sewall, with a panoramic postcard view of Marblehead Harbor. A year later, the owner wanted to skyrocket the rent. I couldn't afford that *plus* the rent for my office in Graves Yacht Yards upper yard building. I explained my problem to Donald Graves, saying I'd have to figure out a way to combine office and apartment -- somewhere elsewhere.

Donald came back to me a couple days later: "We were thinkin' ... how about it if we put a combined office and apartment in our lower yacht yard?"

And that's what happened. The Grave family reconfigured the front of the cavernous yacht yard building into a funky-studly four room apartment, which I moved into in 1979.

In 1981, for reasons known only to God -- or more likely, the Devil -- I found myself included in the list of "Boston's 100 Most Eligible Bachelors" which appeared on Sunday, September 13th in the Boston Herald American. At number 80, I was pretty far down the list; a fact which legions of jealous jerks pointed out to me. I squelched them by saying I had inside information that every one of the 79 guys ahead of me on the list was gay.

Being on the list doesn't get me free tickets to the Red Sox or a lifetime supply of dental floss, but it did have its perqs.

I had *the* greatest bachelor pad in Marblehead. Make that, *in the World*! Make that, *in the History of the World*! There I was for five sybaritic years, in that four room den of iniquity, picture window overlooking picturesque Little Harbor; I, the sole nighttime occupant, the Phantom of Graves vast lower yacht yard building, basking in my Eligibilityhoodedness.

Musique

She loved me back to life. "Women love men who love women," she told me. "And women *know* men who love women. You, Beggah, love women. So love me, Beggah, *love* me." Being the selfless sort that I am, I complied.

I officially met her at the Ad Club Christmas party at the Copley Plaza, December of '78. But I'd remembered her -- as in, who could forget? -- when she came to K&E in 1969 in the company of Dennis, the freelance artist she lived with. He'd drop off illustrations and prospect assignments from art directors at the agency. She'd leave a trail of guys walking into walls as she undulated the halls with Dennis. Word was she was 18 and from Montreal. Married as I was, I made no attempt to meet her; but neither did I disappoint my eyes.

This Ad Club party that year of my divorce was another story. More like, a new chapter in the oldest story, I suppose. I didn't spot her till midnight, and she was with a group of people. I sauntered up and tapped her on the shoulder.

She turned; I introduced myself. She looked me up and down and said, "Are you going to call me Saturday, or will I have to come get you?" She reached into a jacket pocket, handed me her card and laughed. The laugh was playful, her voice melodious.

She said, as if she'd known me forever, "Not before noon. Never call before noon, remember?" She turned her back to me and returned to the conversation.

Of course I called her Saturday. About 5 past noon -- I've always been pathetically uncool in the calling-for-dates department. Or just about any department, for that matter.

I picked her up at her apartment in Brighton that night. She suggested we hit a restaurant somewhere-I-don't-remember, which we did; and I had I-don't-remember-what to eat -- she was that intoxicating.

(If allowed just one word to describe her, "French" would do it. But my definition differs from the dictionary's -- i.e. a nationality, a language. For me to say she was French is to say saucy, vixenish, pouty, sensual, brooding, minx, sphinx, arty, mercurial, playful; bohemian in dress, kitten heels, underwear never, ever a tease of perfume; raven hair, mischief eyes, quizzical smile, sumptuous body; electric mind, etudes of Chopin on the piano, Camus and the somber side of literature -- meant to have been Picasso's mistress in Paris of the '20s, but inadvertently misfiled by the god of time and earning an up-level salary in commercial real estate in Boston in the '70s instead.)

We stopped somewhere-I-don't-remember after dinner for a couple of liqueurs. I drove her home, parked the car, walked her to the door of her apartment. To say I was hoping she'd invite me in is understatement. She put the key in the lock, turned, touched her fingers to my lips. "Not tonight," she said. "Call me tomorrow. Not before noon, remember?"

This has the smell of 'project' about it. Don't know if I have the patience for that. What the hell -- one more shot.

I call at uncool five past noon. She instructs me to pick her up for our date about 6. At uncool five past 6, I ring the doorbell. She invites me into the apartment, which is dark-lit and furnished in Grand Eclectic, though more towards Victorian Plush than anything.

She leads me to a couch resembling the one on which the Duchess of Alba reclined in Goya's scandalous painting, *The Naked Maja*. She bids me to sit, asks what I'd like to drink.

"Tall scotch and water, if you have it." She laughed. "I have oceans of tall scotch ... short of water." Mischievous. Love it.

She returns with the drink. Tells me to swivel about and extend my legs Albalike on the couch. As she hands me the drink, she remarks that my belt looks a bit tight – and is leisurely about remedying the situation.

When I finished the drink we went to another restaurant I-don't-remember-the-name-of. From then on, it was nothing but wild. *She* was wild. Because of her, *we* were wild. Lovemaking at whim, and in improbable places. Teenage stuff: letters mailed to me at my office: "Bob Baker, Lover, 85 Front Street"; "Bob Baker, Football Captain, 85 Front Street."

I'd told her 4's a favorite number -- I was born April 4th (4th day, 4th month). And it so happened my upcoming birthday was another set of 4s -- 44. (She was 27.) My birthday was on a Wednesday that year. The Sunday before, she said, "Beggah, I have something momentous to tell you." (Her speech was influenced by her father, who was English; her behavior by her mother, a Paris-born seductress, even in her advanced years. "Beggah," her pet name for me, was Britspeak for "Baker." I called her "Musique.") "Beggah," she said, "meet me at my place Tuesday at 3, and plan to spend the night. Dress nicely, Beggah, we'll go somewhere respectable for a change. Not your usual tattered football sweater."

I showed up as instructed. We drove to Boston in her Saab and pulled up in front of the Ritz. She left the car with the doorman. I followed her through the revolving door into the lobby. She marches her kitten heels purposefully up to the desk and registers for the suite reserved in her name.

A suite at the Ritz! For us to frolic some in the afternoon, and all through the night. For a bartender and waitress to set up bar and elaborate food spread at 6:30. For a surprise birthday party in my honor, beginning at 7.

In the course of the night, 30 or so friends from all aspects of my life. Boston ad people, publishing people, Cambridge people, an old college roommate -- where and how she dug some of them up, I'll never know. The best part was when the phone rang around 8. The voice snipped, "Three gentlemen from Marblehead, by the names of Berrigan, Donellan and Kane, are here in the lobby, *claiming* they've been invited to the party ... is it all right to send them up?"

Billy Berrigan, quickwit bartender from Maddie's saloon; Kevin Donellan, wry commentator on all things Marblehead; the inimitable rogue genius Killer Kane. "*Of course*, send them up!" I barked. "Why couldn't they have just *come* up?!"

When Berrigan, Kevin and Killer arrived, it was apparent that, though they were each dressed according to the *letter* of the Ritz dress code -- i.e. jacket and tie -- it wasn't quite the *style* the Ritz had in mind. Inasmuch as un-fashionable was equal to bad person in the Ritz's eyes, the Ritz was doing the civilized thing to embarrass three good people by detaining them. As it turned out, my three buckos from Marblehead mixed easily with the rest of the gang, and a rousing good time was had by all -- most especially me.

After the last of our guests departed, going on 100 o'clock, Musique gave me her gift -- a large silver-framed picture of Herbert peering inquisitively around a rock at the beach.

Herbert was an elongated goofy-faced stuffed hippo, given me as a thank-you by a couple I'd helped out some years back. As we lunched at The Landing before their return to Minnesota, I let slip that in my next life I intended to come back as a hippo, lolling about in muddy warm water all day, soaking up the sun. Wife Kris excused herself, returned a half hour later with the creature we christened Herbert.

A week before the party, Musique, unbeknownst to me, had hippo-napped Herbert -- to immortalize him on film. (The picture, which I still have, never ceases to break me up.)

•

It wasn't all suites at the Ritz by any means. It was more like riding a Black Diamond roller coaster in The Tunnel of Love. (Dumb metaphor be damned, that's what it was.)

On one of the numerous occasions it appeared to be 'over', I'm forlorning away a gray Saturday afternoon at The Landing Pub, lost in my loss, unavailable to the banter of the other denizens -- all male. The bartender pierces the gloom -- phone call: "Beggah, I'm coming out to Marblehead to see you. Don't leave. I want you to make love to me on the bar."

An hour later, she erotics through the door -- a dozen guys' jaws ricochet the bar. First, because she's a stopper; second, because she's brandishing a little chartreuse-colored stuffed lobster. "He's my peace offering," she said, as I folded her in my arms. "I found him at the Green Spot novelty store in Revere on the way. I want to keep my claws on you, Beggah."

I ordered her a drink, and looked at my watch. 4:40. How appropriate. I went to the pay phone in the hall, called Osborne's Florists, asked how late they're open. Just till 5. I tell them I'll be *right* by. Return to bar, tell her I've gotta get something -- back in 20. The guys at the bar are very nice about it. One of them tells me to take my time, they'll take real good care of her. Other guys agree. "Yeah, *real* good," they say, almost in unison.

That's what friends are for.

Half hour later, I back my way through The Landing Pub doorway, backfoot my way to her perch at the bar, turn, set the bucket of 44 red roses and one white in front of her. "You are a *madman*, Beggah!" she squealed.

We took a Baker's dozen (12 red, and the white) with us when we left for my place a half hour later. We gave the rest to the guys at the bar to divvy up. (Consider the either/or of reactions as the rose-in-hand guy walks through the door that evening. It's either, "Oh, how *romantic*, Jed!" or "What you been *up to*, Jed?!")

·

It lasted less than a year. One day, her kitten heels up and decided to ease along. As tough as it was, I owed her nothing but gratitude. She restored me to life, gave me new life. She knew how to *play* The Game -- and me. Read one of her letters and see what I mean:

"

70 Chiswick Road, Brighton - May 15, 1979

Without warning
As a whirlwind
swoops on an oak
Love shakes my heart
        -- Sappho

Dear Beggah:
I have rated all my lovers and the following are the results of my survey:
1. Kevin White (Mayor of Boston) 70
2. Agha Khan 1000
3. Bob Baker 44
4. Kevin Donellan 200
5. Herbert 1070
I just wanted to tell you that I am entrapped by your charms, liquidated by your wit, torrential (sic) by your passions, and riveted to your heart.

Musique

"

Veiled in unattainability as she was, she might well have been the 'realization' of the Existential mystery girl in the Pickwick Theater in my teens or the girl in the kiltie skirt in the common room at Bennett Junior College when I was at UConn.

No matter what ... she was a "Thank you, God."

Peg Who Was Diana

According to the calendar, Peg enters the picture in my college years -- that's when we met and got to know each other. According to my heart, she defies categorization. She's a world apart, and timeless.

Even the beginning has an extra dimension to it.

August 1954. I get a call from Don Edwards, a guy from New Canaan, a preppy enclave ten miles up the Merritt Parkway from Greenwich. He has a date with a girl named Nat Leonard this coming Saturday -- would I be up for a date with her supposedly attractive friend, Peg?

Sure, what-the-hey.

I meet Don at the movie theater on the neon-deprived main drag of the un-teeming sleepopolis of greater downtown New (yawn) Canaan. I hop into his car and we head up Oenoke Ridge Road to pick up the supposedly attractive friend. Since I only knew Don from howdy-do at UConn, I try to learn more about him. At one point, I asked what his dad did.

"Oh, he ... he's Robert Frost's editor," Don tosses off. He could just as easily have said, "He's the assistant bookkeeper for the New Canaan Horticultural Society."

(I mean, you mean ... *huhhhh*? I mean, here I am, Boy English Major, literary wannabe extraordinaire ... this man Don, he say *ROBERT FROST*???!!!)

"Your dad ... *Robert Frost's* ... *editor?*"

"Yuh."

"You ... you ever *meet* Robert Frost?"

"Sure."

"Wow. Spend any time with him?"

"Yeah."

"Tell me, tell me, *tell* me!" I keep pumping him. But Robert Frost doesn't seem to be a topic of interest to Don. Or, understandably, maybe Don wants to be known for something other than being Robert Frost's editor's son. (How's that for a job description mouthful on your resume: "Robert Frost's Editor's Son"?)

After concussing the poor bastard with 83 questions in 92 seconds,

I finally get a murmur. "Yeah, went with my dad up to Frost's farm in Vermont couple times when I was younger. Stayed overnight. Took a walk with him sometimes."

"*You*? You walked around the farm with ... just you and *Robert Frost*? More. What happened? Anything? Did he say or do anything you can remember ... ?"

"Nah. Not much. We just walked around. You know. Through woods and stuff."

"C'mon, must be something you remember about it. Anything different? Anything, anything, Don. *Any*thing! C'mon, Don, gotta be *some*thing."

"Nah. Not much. Oh, yeah. One thing funny. He had this old jacket -- we'd be walking along: sometimes he gets this stubby pencil and little pad from a pocket and scribbles. Rips it off, sticks it in other pocket. On the way back, we stop at his cabin up the hill from the main house. Opens door -- grabs the scribbled papers and chucks 'em in a beat up old leather mailman's bag on table there."

•

That anecdote is ripe with possibilities, not one of which is that I imagined it or made it up.

This much I know for sure. Don Edwards who lived in New Canaan in 1954 told me the story. Though not pretending to exhaustive research, I established high likelihood of validity. In Lawrence Thompson and R.H. Winnick's *Robert Frost: The Later Years* and Stanley Burnshaw's *Robert Frost Himself*, I discovered that Al (Alfred C.) Edwards who was head of Henry Holt and Company publishers in New York in the appropriate years, and who commuted to his home in New Canaan, was also a close friend of Robert Frost -- to the degree that he was "Executor of the Estate of Robert Frost." And though Don misspoke in calling his father "Robert Frost's editor" (technically speaking, he was Frost's publisher), Al Edwards did often visit Frost and stay overnight in the main house on Frost's farm in Ripton, Vermont. Frost's cabin was just up the hill from the main house on the property.

•

I swear, pulling Don's teeth would've been easier -- but it is possible this bit of Frost lore is a find. A previously unnoted, unpublished account of a valuable tool/resource which Frost devised and applied to his craft. There for the tapping when the ink in his mind ran dry.

(A not-improbable Frost scenario: Empty the old leather mailbag onto the table. Paw and scan the scraps. Most go smack back in the bag. Some get tossed in the wastebasket -- "The *hell* was I thinking?" Six, seven, a dozen maybe get saved and spread on the tabletop. Mix and match: "This and this might work together ... a germ somewhere in these three ... but how about this with *this*?" These two *connect*!")

Whether or not it's news to the world now, it was an incredible epiphany to me at the time -- a device I've used ever since, whenever I'm trying to assemble ideas, plans, schedules, scenarios or writings of any kind. I call it my Connect-a-Dot system: with a salute to R. Frost.

•

The blacktop driveway off Oenoke Ridge Road eases between a stand of oak and a sprawl of lawn and settles into a gravel oval in front of an imposing English country manor.

Don Edwards rings the doorbell. A minute later, the door is opened by a roundfaced middle-aged colored man in black waistcoat, black trousers, white starched shirt and black tie.

"Good evening, gentle ... "

A smiling brunette in a blue skirt and white blouse appears at his side. "One of you must be Don, and the other, Bob. This is my friend Thomas," she says, nodding towards the colored man, "I'm Peg, Peg Dawson." She had a low voice for a girl. Not down in the pits, just solid. Honest.

We shook hands with Thomas, headed towards the car, and I checked out my supposedly attractive date en route.

Attractive is about right. I mean she's nobody you'd kidnap a lime-green shoe over, but pleasing to look at in a Plain Jane way. The physical characteristic which caught me wasn't her smile, not in the traditional sense. Her teeth were well paid for, that was obvious. She had the usual mouth, made up of two lips as it was; though if she had any lipstick on, it wasn't but a touch. Not slathered bright like popular girls. It wasn't the smile at her mouth, it was the one at her eyes. There was the least squint at the corners; but not a Clint Eastwood gunfighter squint or Joe Montana sudden-death-overtime squint.

"I know you, I like you," the smile said. Nothing suggestive of negligees or haylofts at all. Just straight-on: "I know you, I like you."

When we got in the front seat with Don I noticed she had a Band-Aid stuck to one of her sorta-pudgy knees. Not obese; just on the edge of pudgy. She noticed that I noticed the Band-Aid and laughed. "As you can see, I'm good at tripping," she said.

"Oh, does that mean you *fall* for a lot of guys?" (or something equally corny) I said.

She laughed and married me with those eyes.

When we arrived at Nat Leonard's house we hit the rec room downstairs and proceeded to have a mellow-good time over the course of several hours, several gin and tonics, cheek-to-cheek dancing, a bunch of laughs and some easygoing smooching.

Saying goodnight at the door, I asked if I could see her again. "Yes," she said. "Call me ... let me know what time you can come for lunch with my parents next Saturday. Better yet, I'll call you."

•

Saturday at one, I pulled into their parking oval in Dad's unpretentious-but-presentable black Ford station wagon. I parked next to two gleaming luxury vehicles -- one black, one silver. Daylight had force-grown the English country manor to twice its previous size.

The heavyset colored woman in black dress and white apron who answered the door had the same great smile as Thomas. With a smile, I told her she must be Thomas'es little sister. She sailed into the jolliest laugh you ever heard. "No, son," she said. "I'm Evelyn ... I'm Thomas's *wife*."

"Well!" snaps the voice behind Evelyn.

Evelyn's laugh hangs in the air. She gives a half wave and shrinks back.

Mrs. Dawson, front and center, extends her hand. "Well," she says, "you must be Bob. I'm Peg's mother. S'nice to see you, won't you come in." Proclaimed with all the warmth of Hitler's torture specialist, Heinrich Himmler, slicking an icicle up your butt.

I can't resist. It's the Irish in me. As I'm shaking Mrs. Dawson's frigid flipper, I carol out to the departing Evelyn, "Nice to meet you, Evelyn!" Only then do I add, and very much in the manner of an afterthought, "Nice to meet you too, Mrs. Dawson." I don't know why I did it like that -- but I did. Yeah, I do. I can't stand bullies. I never could stand bullies. Even at my weakest and corporate ass-kissing worst, I always have to let 'em know.

Mrs. D glares. She's maybe 50, tall, withered tan. A string of pearls graces the neck of her silk print dress, a diamond as big as The Ritz dominates the brown parchment of her ring finger. Her eyes are darts. Every hair of her jet black bouffant damn well knows its place. It could well be molded, it could well be wax. She's as foreign to Peg as Attila.

"Come meet Peg's father," Mrs. Attila ... er, Dawson ... instructs me. Her purposeful march through the glaringly bright "perfectly elegant" living room indicates this introduction thing is something she needs to, and therefore will -- for decorum's sake -- get the fuck over with.

The room we now enter is the one I'd pick if I were sentenced to solitary confinement for the rest of my life: Mr. Dawson's den.

A minimally adorned, spacious, masculine room. Dark-paneled walls, soft lighting, dark-hued Orientals on the floor, bookcases, easy chairs. Paul Bunyan's leather couch in front of Paul Bunyan's fireplace. Over the fireplace hangs a large gilt-framed antique painting of a weary looking man leading a weary looking horse through a glade in the forest. There's an eerie light about the glade.

Tweed-jacketed Mr. Dawson rises from the couch and ambles over to greet me. He has soft contours. He extends his hand and says, "Hi Bob, nice to meet you," at the same time Lady Attila is saying, "Northrop, this is ... "

His handshake is warm, expressive. He isn't as tall as Mrs. Dawson, and he's obviously a good deal older than Mrs. His face is soft, almost a baby's. His eyes are almost Peg's, but not quite. They're near the soft green of the lightweight plaid shirt he's wearing, and there's Peg's knowing smile about them. But not quite the glow.

He's why she's Peg -- not country-club Beryl or Whitney or Gladwyn or Taylor. Her father is why simple Peg is simply Peg. It's that obvious, that quick: from his den, from his hand, from his eyes. *He*'s why Plain Jane is just plain Peg.

As if on cue, she bounces into the room and hugs me -- with her eyes.

"Well now. Shall we all repair to the dining room," drone-intones Mrs. Dawson.

God bless Peg. She'd obviously filled her mother in on the basics of my background. Which spares me her mother's acid silence when I'd have to confess that though I may *live in* Greenwich, I'm merely a student at a university not-long-arisen from the muck of cow-collegedom, a graduate of Iona (Papist day school) Prep, a resident of Chateau Lafayette (an *apartment* house) and a card carrying member of the hardly-to-be-mistaken-for-exclusive Greenwich YMCA. Thanks to Peg, only generic pleasantries are being exchanged at table in the "perfectly elegant " dining room when Evelyn and Thomas serve the first course.

Evelyn sets in front of me a large plate rimmed with toast points, at the center of which rests a small silver goblet containing what is most assuredly a small dollop of blackberry jam (S.S. Pierce, most assuredly), resting on what is most assuredly a bed of strawberry Jell-O.

How quaint, these rich folks. Dessert first. Beyond vanilla or coffee ice cream, I'm not a major sweet tooth. But, when in Rome ...

Having been grounded by my mother in the school of etiquette which predated even Emily Post, I know it's fitting and proper to wait for the hostess to make the first move -- and only then to follow suit.

Mrs. Dawson acquires the small spoon farthest right, obtains the teensiest smidge of S.S. Pierce blackberry jam, then incorporates a teensy near-edge of strawberry Jell-O, dabs the contents on the tip of a toast point, takes an ever-so-refined nibble. Linen napkin from lap to lips -- pitty-pat pitty-pat.

Let the Games begin!

Farthest-right spoon to blackberry jam, then to near-edge of strawberry Jell-O. To toast point. To mouth. Roll in mouth, swallow. On way to gullet without allowing taste buds to announce their verdict -- from "Sweets for Your *First* Course" which Mrs. Dawson obviously scissored from the latest issue of *Good Mansionkeeping*.

Once my taste buds retroactively-and-finally kick in, they inform my hair-trigger projectile vomiting mechanism that it had best the fuck most immediately and volcanically expel the "sweet treat" which is in fact the 180-degree opposite of "sweet upon sweet" ... it is a putrescent assault of *salt* upon *salt* ... !

Not sweet blackberry jam on a bed of sweet strawberry Jell-O. Instead: caviar (salt) on a bed of jellied madrilene (salt). A Blueblood standard.

Sweet Peggy sitting directly across from me. Only a miracle contained Vesuvius. Only a miracle prevented her from wearing the not-jam/not-Jell-O. Somehow, I steeled my way through the remainder of the Caviar Surprise -- once my buds recovered from the initial shock. The rest of the meal, thank God, was true to its appearance: filet mignon, somekinda rice, asparagus spears. Her saintly mother's darts were on me all the way, though. She had to have caught -- and delighted in -- my gag on the caviar, for sure.

After lunch, Peg and I ambled along the wooded perimeter of the lake lapping the extent of the Dawson's back lawn. "It's not just *our* lake," she said. "It's for everyone. It's the New Canaan reservoir. Isn't it wonderful!"

I was beginning to see that this was her nature, not making much of supposedly big deal stuff. Or herself. Anything unpretentious or shy or the least bit runt of the litter was elevated and praised. "Wonderful!" she'd sing out. And suddenly, whoever or whatever she was talking about took on a whole new light in your eyes. It wasn't a Little Mary Sunshine knee-jerk thing, either. You knew there was thought behind it. It made you feel good, even if it wasn't about you. She owned "wonderful." I swear, she could have started a religion just based on the glow her "wonderful" gave off.

We talked about a number of things on the walk. But when we got back to the house she focused on me. Her first question did catch me off guard: "How do you feel about shelling peas, Sir Robert?"

She knew it would get me, because she giggled.

So I gave it back. "The way I feel about shelling peas, Miss Muffet, is the very same way I feel about sidestepping a rampaging bull elephant ... it's not the worst thing to do."

"I was just thinking that if you wouldn't mind, we could just sit here on the porch and save Evelyn some trouble -- by shelling the peas for dinner. And we could talk and get to know each other and just enjoy ourselves together."

(Here I am a contestant on "Survive the Parents," one of the very first reality shows. I've already dodged "Banishment by Projectile Vomiting" and now I'm about to be subjected to the oldest one in the book, the Shell Game -- in this case, "The Pea-Shelling Shell Game." What's next, "Hamster-Tossing"?)

Hey. Bring on the peas.

She went inside and came back a few minutes later with a large brown paper bag brimming with unshelled peas, a stainless steel collander, paper bags for the shards, a vegetable knife for each of us.

She asked me serious, personal questions as we went about shelling. What I thought about God, what I dreamt about, what books I liked, what radio programs I liked, what my boyhood was like, what made me really happy, what dad's like, what my mom was like -- a flood of Old Greenwich, back-when, resurrect-The-Imaginary-Boy boyhood stuff.

When I went on some about the tremendous effect Mom who'd passed away when I was sixteen just a couple years before had on me, she came over and sat next to me there on the white ironwork bench. She took both my hands in hers and examined them, stroking with her index finger now and again one of the small liver spots or incipient hairline wrinkles I had, even at that age. She looked into my eyes: "You do have wonderful *old* hands, Bob."

That brought tears to the rim of my eyes -- because I'd just been talking about Mom, I guess. She stroked the back of both my hands and went back to her seat.

It was risky of her to do that. Her mother might've seen it and come screaming out, raking the air with a flaming sword. But she never looked anything but as calm as Buddha the whole time.

Late afternoon she walked me to the car. "Listen, Sir Robert, I was wondering if you'd be willing to escort me to the dance at the New Canaan Country Club the Saturday after next. The bad news is it's formal and you'd need a tux, and there will be stuffy people there -- even *our age* stuffy people. But we can just go for a while and have some dances and come home here early. And then I can *finally* get to share my music with you!"

On the way to Greenwich it occurred to me that you could actually have an emotional experience just by talking with someone.

•

"The Saturday after next" I pulled into the parking oval in my 'new' used '41 Mercury, wearing a proud smile and my rented tux. The Merc was only two years younger than my recently collapsed rustbucket Studebaker, but was in beauty condition, with a shine you could almost shave by. Its one shortcoming was the leopardskin-covered sun visors the previous owner decided to panache it up with. The fake leopardskin was glued on, too. Glued on for good. Or bad. Either way, I didn't have the dough to replace them yet. Meantime, nobody will notice. Right?

She sprang from the doorway as I was getting out of the car. Beautiful white gown, beaming, giggling with glee. Bounding. Mid-bound, a stumble. Both hands and knee area of gown connect with the gravel. Springs back up, still laughing, now clapping, as she continues her rush towards me.

"This is *it*! Your car ... it's wonderful! You'll just have to sit in back and let me chauffeur you to the dance. I'll call in advance and have trumpeters at the door for your arrival! And *you*, just look at you! So elegant! Just let me touch you, to make sure you're not just a *vision*!" She patted my cheek.

Attila.

"Oh, Mom, look at Bob's new car! Isn't it beautiful!"

Mother, arms-crossed mother. Arms-crossed mother approaches the Merc. Cases the back seat area. Cases the front seat area. Rilly

rilly cases the front seat area. What she rilly rilly is casing is the leopardskin visor area.

Arms-crossedly, turns. "Peg, dear. It's rather ... different. But wouldn't it be better for your friend Bob to take you in the *Chrysler* to the club?"

"No, Mum ... Bob's car will be just fine." She said that calmly, slowly. The expression on her face wasn't mean, just definite. My-strength-is-as-the-strength-of-ten definite.

She headed towards the house with her mother to have Evelyn de-smudge her gown. Mommy Dearest turned and said I could come in if I'd like. I said thanks anyway, but I'd as soon stay outside and count God's blessings. She looked funny at me when I said that. Good.

When Peg came back out, the smudge was disappeared. Evelyn could do anything, and do it well, Peg said. And *Thomas* could do anything, and do it well, she added.

The New Canaan Country Club was a stately white structure which, to my eyes, resembled a Congregational church more than a country club. It hadn't the sprawling elegance of the Greenwich Country Club. Its lines were vertical. Refined. Repressed.

Peg was right about "stuffy" people, too. There weren't but a few our age. Many were thirty, forty or even as licking the lip of the grave as fifty. Even worse, everybody was sober. Mope-sober. Apparently, pre-parties didn't exist in New Canaan. What we have here is one serious quilting bee.

To the moan-drone of the em-balmed band, Peg and I replicated other couples from the un-bombed crowd in rhythmic perambulations of the parquet. Which is to say, we had a few dances.

We held off till 9:45 before heading back to the house. Peg said that would be sufficient showing of the flag to satisfy her mother. *And* her parents would be in bed by then, which meant we could have the den and "our music" to ourselves.

Soon as we enter the house, she takes me by the hand. Through the vast raftered living room she pulls me, like a mother yanking a kid through a department store as the elevator door's starting to close. She's giggling to herself and not paying attention: I'm afraid she'll stumble. The thud will bring Attila downstairs, for sure. I have to admit, it felt good while she was doing it, though. Silly good, but good. So I just went along with it. I even made a brat face when she turned around to look at me once. She tossed her head and owned me with her eyes.

When we got to the den, she led me to the Paul Bunyan couch. With pats of the leather seat, she settled me there. She asked what I'd like to drink. I told her scotch, champagne and gin, if that'd be all right. She laughed. "OK, how about just scotch and soda, instead?" I said. She said my wish was her command, and left the room, laughing -- and without tripping.

Upon returning with our drinks, she went to a cabinet beside the Paul Bunyan fireplace, picked out some albums and set them on the table next to the record player in the corner. She turned on the record player, placed record on spindle, pressed a button, scooted to the couch, nestled next to me and took my left hand in both of hers. From the record player begins to sound the race and thrill of my boyhood anthem to adventure. My right hand is a fist in the air: "The Lone Ranger!" I exclaim.

"I remember you saying that's your favorite," she said. "It's wonderful ... stirring, isn't it? 'The William Tell Overture,' it's called." She caressed my hand with both of hers. I felt like a puppy.

Now comes "Sleeping Beauty." Then "Swan Lake." Rachmaninoff, Mozart, Bizet. My introduction to classical music. She prefaced the next album with, "This is Beethoven's Sixth Symphony, the 'Pastoral.' The music of nature. My favorite. See what you think."

When it finished, I agreed it was my favorite, too.

"More than 'William Tell'?" she asked.

"More than Bill Tell," I said.

•

A week later she headed off to her first year at college, and two weeks after that I started my sophomore year at UConn. A letter in October, on prim Vassar College letterhead:

"

I was home last weekend and some of us got together and played paddle tennis for an hour. I think it's a wonderful game, but it seems every time I play I end up falling down in typical uncoordinated fashion, and my knees look like they did in fifth grade when they were always covered with scrapes and band aids. I remember I never used to like band aids because they hurt coming off, but now they have so many colors and shapes that kids must look forward to skinning their knees and elbows.

That's a funny way to start a letter, I know, but I hadn't talked to you in a while and I didn't quite know how to start this. That's what was in my head, so it came out of my pen that way.

As you can see, I'm here at Vassar, and thus far I'm loving it. I've traveled some with my parents, to Bermuda and Jamaica, and even to Europe the summer before last. But here I can travel everywhere. In my mind. Door after door after door is opening and I just wish I was a hundred people at once. I've always been such a moth, it's fun to be among butterflies.

I've missed your wonderful old hands and your lively mind and I was thinking of you when I was home, so I summoned up the nerve and called you at home. You weren't there of course, but luckily your father was. I see where you get your sense of humor, he had me laughing so. And he's a gentle man, I felt I'd known him for years.

So now that eagle-eye Dawson has finally tracked down the ever elusive Sir Bob of the Bakers, she wonders if he might be willing to mount his noble steed and come be my escort for our Vassar Houseparties Weekend in November.

Wouldst?

,,

The letter went on to furnish details. She even signed it "Love, Peg." That was a first in itself, and a coup. A girl I scarcely knew, who I'd only listened to music with and shelled a couple of peas with, and she signs it "Love."

Better frame this one. Too bad it's not from Vicki De Castro.

I wrote her "wouldst" very much like to take her up on her invite to Houseparties Weekend.

Without going into the details, Vassar Houseparties Weekend --

with the glowing exception of Peg -- was cut from the same bolt of haircloth as the New Canaan Country Club dance. It was significantly *un*alive, and Peg and I had very little time to ourselves.

I only mention the Vassar Houseparties Weekend at all because it will come back to haunt me ...

Peg and I didn't connect at Christmastime or have any dates that winter, but we stayed in correspondence throughout the balance of the school year.

Come summer, I'm really looking forward to seeing her.

Saturday night, mid-July. We caught the early flick at the New Canaan movie house, then went back and settled into that den of dreams. At one point, she said, "I have to share my great news!" The great news for her was bad news for me. She's been awarded a Ford Foundation fellowship to the Salzburg Music Festival in Austria -- she'll be gone four weeks.

Damn.

We had two more dates before she left, both at the house. The last began with another stroll along the reservoir. After the walk -- would you believe? -- we sat on the porch and shelled peas again.

That evening, as we're sitting there in the den, I don't know what came over me. It could have been the scotch. My third of the night, after all. It's getting near time to bid bon voyage.

The record player's shut itself off. We're holding hands. She said something about what-I-can't-remember, and then I do the first stupid thing. I blurt out from somewhere in left field that she reminds me of my mother.

Instead of splitting my skull with a fire poker as might be expected of a coquette who's been equated with a quite-deceased elder woman, she leans over and gives me a sweet sweet kiss. Tears brim her eyes.

Never being one to quit while I'm ahead, I reload and re-blurt. I tell her I love her.

This is her first letter from Austria:

"

I can't help but think of this time the other night. By most people's standards that wouldn't have been a really big date, and yet the other night it was. And just about every time we get together, it's a big date. Do you know what I mean? I feel very lucky to know someone I can have a wonderful time with all the time -- even when we're shelling peas.

Last night when you left I walked up to my room and sat down on my bed and said to myself "he loves me." I went to brush my teeth and saw myself in the mirror and I looked and looked and I couldn't believe it. And I felt so good that I wanted to go and tell my Mum and Dad. I had the devil of a time trying to get to sleep.

I started thinking about how clean and pure it was. I was reminded of the brook we watched last Saturday night. And I remembered how you looked sitting there -- you were all sunburned.

,,

I received one more letter from her that summer -- also from Austria:

" "

I've finally met someone who's almost as nice as you are. He doesn't look like you or talk like you, but he's good natured and easy to talk to and get to know. He hadn't talked to an American girl in quite a while, so he started talking about his family and about home and pretty soon I found myself telling him all about you. He said he wished he could be more like you, but I know he could never be as wonderful as you are.

Can anyone be as wonderful as you are?

,,

By the time she got back from Austria, it was only two weeks till the start of the fall semester at UConn. So when she called, even as breathless as she sounded about wanting to see me, I fished up a whopper about not being able to get together because I was crazy busy getting ready to get back to campus early -- to help show the incoming freshmen around during Orientation Week.

The truth is that over the summer I've fallen in with and sampled the lips of girls with bright lipstick and am not about to downshift to someone who reminds me of my mother.

Her gulp was audible. She tried to sound chin-up about it, but I could tell she was disappointed. I called her later and asked about Europe and all -- but I didn't retract the lie. It bothered me some. But I let the lie stand.

I didn't hear from her again until October. She called me at UConn. I was totally unprepared when she asked if I'd be her date for Houseparties Weekend at Vassar in November. She'd caught me by surprise and she sounded so excited I couldn't think of anything other than "Yes, I'd love to."

Uh uh. Not another dreary weekend at Vassar. I thought about calling right back with a lame excuse that I had a mammoth paper due that weekend, even though Houseparties was a whole month away.

But I knew I'd probably screw it up on the phone. So I thought about it and wrote her the same cheesy lying excuse in a letter instead. The letter was puke-ripe with contrived sincerity and regret.

For two whole days my non-stop Catholic conscience Monsignor Ganley-ed carbolic acid into every pore of my brain. Finally I sat down and wrote a long letter telling the truth: that I'd lied. And that I was sorry I'd lied. This time I was honest at least.

A week later came her reply. It's the second most powerful letter I've ever received. Her writing gets smaller and slants downward as the letter goes on:

" "

I know that I want to write you, but I don't know what I want to say. I guess it's always like this when you feel you're saying goodbye -- you don't want everything to be left unsaid, but you don't really know where to begin.

Strange as it may seem, I want to thank you for your letter. Your honesty was something wonderful. I've often found myself lying, and I know how hard it is to tell somebody about it, especially when they want to believe the lie. I know how awful it is to lie, how tense you get for fear you'll be found out, and how dirty you feel inside. I somehow feel responsible for your having to go through the after effects of not telling the truth. I'm sorry I made you lie, Bob, I really am, and I hope you'll feel better after writing me.

It's funny, Bob, but I can't really believe that you're gone. I guess I felt it coming, but I didn't want to pay any attention to it, and I still hoped that if I could see you and be good to you, I could get you back. Now I realize you can never get anybody back unless they want to come. I wonder why I didn't always know that -- it seems so obvious. But I still don't feel your friendship is entirely gone because your letter was so sincere and it didn't sound cold at all. Your friendship is all that I ask for, Bob -- just the knowledge that you don't regret having known me and that you still believe in me a little bit.

And now that you've told me it's all over, there's something I want to tell you, something I couldn't have said before. You see I think I've learned something from both of us. Looking back on it, it seems we were both afraid of love, afraid to give too much for fear we'd get hurt. I needed you, but I was afraid of needing you too much and letting myself get too involved. There were so many things I wanted to give to you that I never could because I was afraid. I think you were afraid, too, Bob, afraid of letting yourself be open and vulnerable. It made me want to cry sometimes when I felt we both had something to give but just couldn't do it. I think we'll both have to learn how not to hold back, realizing that whether we get hurt or not isn't important, but how much we can give of ourselves to those we love is what matters.

Well, Bob, the rest is up to you. If you ever feel like coming to see me, please do, and if you ever feel blue, it might help to know that there's someone who will always believe in you.

,,

Whuh.

I went numb. I was collapsed -- not a breath of air in my entire body. Even Mom's death hadn't hit me like that -- at least there were signs that was coming. This was from nowhere. Arrows straight to my black heart. From all directions straight to my black heart.

I didn't know, I didn't know, I didn't know.

I didn't know she loved me. She never said those words, did she?

Did she even say that here?

She speaks English doesn't she? Would it've killed her to have said those three words, "I ... love ... you"?

Make it four, " ... Bob"?

Would I have acted differently if she'd ever spelled it out?

Damn Protestants, damn Wasps. Why the hell don't they just come out and say what they mean? What they *feel*! Why isn't everybody Irish?

I felt rotten about having hurt her like that and I felt rotten about losing her. I swear, if I knew how to punch myself silly, I would've. I hurt plenty as it was, but I knew I deserved more.

Suddenly I want her something fierce. But how to ... ? I thought and thought and thought about what to do, but I couldn't figure out what to do.

So I didn't.

•

More than a year later I summoned up the courage and a couple rolls of nickels and hit the pay phone to give Peg a call at Vassar. Not only did she accept my call, we had a good long conversation -- but nothing related to "I ... love ... you" of course.

I did ask her to our big SAE spring weekend, and surprisingly enough she said yes.

She came from Poughkeepsie by bus and I met her at the terminal in Hartford. She was the first to come tripping off the bus. With arms wide, and trilling my name, she came tripping off the bus. And tripping on the last step and landing on the pavement and skinning her knee, trippingly she came tripping off the bus.

You knew that was going to happen -- why didn't I?

We Band-Aided her up, and headed for UConn.

Comes Saturday and the Big Cocktail Party at SAE and we're all too beautiful to be true -- and don't we all know it, too. The room fair glistens with the sheen and preen of perfect teeth, shiny hair, chiseled features and radiantly plumed princesses.

The banter, fueled by firewater, is at fever pitch.

Full of myself, stepping on others' cleverness, near raging to be heard above the storm of gaiety, I fail to notice Peggy's no longer there beside me. But for an empty glass, I might never have noticed.

Where the hell is she?

There. Over there. In a sullen corner of the SAE lounge. Sitting there beside -- you've gotta be *kidding* -- Joe Grummel.

Joe *Grummel*? The biggest geek in the house? If not the *world*? Who's only a member because he's a 'legacy' -- his dad was an SAE? Who's twelve-feet tall, with a two-foot nose and moose eyes? Who, when he laughs, sounds like a cross between a jackass and a rooster? Who dresses like a used car salesman, but not as well?

That Joe Grummel?

That Joe Grummel. That's who she's with. Not only that, they're talking. Not just her: Joe Grummel is actually having a real live conversation with someone. Not only that, Peggy is laughing at things Joe Grummel is saying.

Now comes the worst part. In the midst of a momentary settling of the frenzy, the jackass-rooster laugh of Joe Grummel resounds the walls of the SAE lounge.

All eyes are *yanked* to the corner -- *my* girl and the ever-lovely Joe Grummel. Shamed, I've been publicly shamed. Is this how she gets even with me?

Minutes later, when she returns to my side, I ask ... "*Why?*"

Those eyes on mine. "Oh Bob, I had to. I looked over and saw him sitting there all by himself in the corner. He just looked so sad. So very very sad. And we were all having such fun. And then I noticed his eyes ... so sincere. And then I really looked at his face. That wonderful face of his.

"Can't you *see*, Bob? He's so homely, Bob, he's ... *beautiful*. And he's just as nice, Bob. Just as nice."

I'm on this planet, she's on hers. This incident did nothing to close the gap I'd created a year or so ago, a gap I'd done nothing but expand as I'd become more and more aware of what a totally terrific guy I am. And yet, in a far-flung pore of me, there's still a nagging need for her. Somehow she just won't quit me.

In an eleventh-hour attempt to perhaps rekindle the flame, on Sunday I took her to Diana's Pool before driving her to the bus station in Hartford.

Diana's Pool is tucked away about 10 miles from campus. This raw April afternoon overcast in gloom, the scene is overpowering in its serenity. Ice water glides between the evergreen-lined banks and down the steep of iron-gray rock to fall the gorge without a sound. No rush, no hiss, no ricochet. Reflected light can only be read into the still black pool down there.

We sit on a rock and gaze at the pool. And listen. To nothing.

She takes my hand in hers and presses it to her cheek. "This is the most wonderful place. And the most wonderful name ... Diana. Can that be my name with you from now on? Diana?" "Absolutely," I said, and then attempted to give her a serious kiss. She gently averted her head and said it was probably time to be heading for the bus.

•

We did stay in touch, and now she signed her letters, "Diana"; though I hadn't the foggiest idea what it was supposed to mean in the cosmic scheme of life. I guess you could say we were in a Romantic/ Platonic relationship. Or how about Platonic/Romantic relationship?

Neo Platonic/Romantic. Yeah, that's got it.

The last time I saw her in my college years was when she called me at Andover Lake and said the Vassar chorus was going to be singing Somebody-or-Other's "Te Deum" at Wesleyan College Saturday afternoon and if I wanted I could pick her up and show her my Gatsby digs and then return her to Middleton Sunday morning to board the bus back to Poughkeepsie.

The timing was perfect: as it turned out, my new love, Joan -- Miss University, remember? -- had to be in New Milford with her parents for a family whoopee that weekend.

When I picked Peg up at 4 in Middleton, the sun was shining. On the ride back to Andover Lake, rain danced the roof and hood of my '51 Lincoln.

When we entered the cottage, she went on about my stick-furniture joint as if it were Versailles. And then the view of the lake: "Wonderful," she sang.

I fixed a fire and we sat on the couch and talked about everything and held hands and then talked about everything else and played album after album on the hi-fi.

The rain kept on. Time kept on. It got late. Then early.

She said, "The rain's stopped, Bob. It's daylight almost. Soon you'll have to take me back to Middleton in your Chariot of the Sun. Can we go sit on your dock and watch the lake wake up? And we'll listen, too. Put on the Sixth, we both love that. It's so right for this."

I put the second side of Beethoven's "Pastoral Symphony" on the Webcor and jacked up the volume.

It was dank and cool on the dock. Mist covered the lake; there was nothing to see. The rhapsodies of 'our song' play from the cottage; build in majesty; now settle; waltz, lighten. Gain thunder and pace. Ease, to play on reed and horn and string.

A loon in silhouette ghosts the mist.

The strings regain, ascend, build-build, strive. Dampen, rise again. Regain, gain; begin to overpower, overtake. Achieve shimmering climax.

As if on cue, tint of gold plays the mist. Within a minute, the blanket of mist has risen a foot above the surface of the lake. By music's end, lakeside and sky and world beyond are awash in light, a postcard before our eyes.

We sit there in awe, holding hands. Just holding hands.

•

Nobody held hands like Peggy did. Or ever will.

• • •

•

3

Moves

You haven't followed patterns made by others.
At every crossroad you've thought outside the box,
and made your life your way.

Roland Merullo

•••

•

One Very Cold Night

This story's proof that some moves aren't as brave and clever as they are instinctive and smack-dab lucky.

Although I was living off-campus (illegally) at my Gatsby cottage on Andover Lake thanks to an inheritance from Aunt Edith my last semester at UConn, I still retained 'required' campus residence at my fraternity, SAE.

On-campus residence comes in real handy sometimes -- as on this blizzard-busting night. I dropped my date off at South Campus and headed straight for nearby Room 315 at SAE.

Bad decision. It's Hell Week. As I enter the lounge, pledgemaster Hackle is putting four pledges through pushups; he's holding *The Phoenix* pledge manual in one hand, a can of Schlitz in the other. Hackle's a former Marine.

The pledges, McKain, Fritz, Gilson and D'Amato, all jocks, are bright, upbeat, likable guys. Usually. Tonight, four days into Hell Week, they're zombies.

Hackle sways, glugs a headback of Schlitz, much of which trails his USMC T shirt. "Awrigh ya friggin' slimeball pledges, ya gah tha wrong. Gimme a fas ten pushu*ppp*s. I said '*Fas*,' goddam ih! Gimme 'nother ten. Hic. This time *fas*!"

"Whyn't you give em a break, Hackle?"

"Befuckingcau*huhu*s, they're just fucking ple*hehe*dges, Bay*hayhay*ker, and I'm a fucking bro*huho*ther ... which you'd know what I mean, Bay*hayhay*ker, if you weren't such a hic fucking trai*hayhay*tor!"

I headed for 315, hit the rack. Out like a light.

How much later it is that I hear, feel and smell the explosion, I cannot say. KABLAM. Hands wresting me from under the covers.

Stench of Schlitz. Blinding light overhead. The pledges, all four of them wrestling me into my clothes.

"McKain, D'Amato ... whuh the hell?"

"Chuck ... g'down, geh the car. We'll bring'm down."

They lash my wrists together, roughly strap tape over my mouth and around the back of my head. My scarf becomes a blindfold.

"Grab 'is duffle coat, Fritz, he's gonna wan' id up there. "

They rough-stumble me down the stairs, through the dining room, through the kitchen, out the back door. I'm shoved into the back seat of the car, a huge body compresses each side of me, my duffle coat plops on my lap.

Tires squeal, churchkey to beer cans: splush splush splush splush. If only I could talk to them. Good guys. I even sponsored McKain. Where they taking me? Don't get it.

Yeah I do. Hell Week. They're bone-tired, numb-crazy. *And*, drunk. On a mission for Hackle. Standard Hell Week scenario: kidnap renegade brother, leave him in the wilds of Somewhere Painful. Let him figure his chicken-assed way back to campus if he can. They better not fail. They're scared shit to fail.

I'm scared, they're scared. Not a good combination.

Words are spoken. Nothing memorable. Shitfaced zombies on missions don't get scripts abundant with quotes for the ages.

Car slows, crinkles on gravel, stops. They get out, get me out. Razor cold. Blindfold undone. Tape (ouch) ripped off. Hands untied.

We stand in a driveway between two farmhouse-style houses. There's a veteran but well maintained Jeep in front of our car, and a veteran well maintained barn beyond. I'm walked to the back door of the house, into the warmth of a kitchen. Seated at the table, a couple straight out of Norman Rockwell and "American Gothic" combined. Gilson's parents.

She, grayish hair in a bun, round face, apple cheeks, cupid lips. He, coal-black hair parted in the middle, weatherbeaten face.

"So this is your li'l traitor boy?" she whines. "Good thing ya called when ya did, we'z just about ta get on our nightshirts. Wouldn'a wanted ta miss this fer the world, though. Care fer a snort, fellers? You too, li'l boy? Gun' be cold up there on Wachusetts Mountain.

– 96 –

Gun' want anti-freeze in your boiler up there, li'l boy. Heh heh." She had a cute little laugh.

"Yes, thank you very much, Mrs. Gilson," I say in my *Book of Etiquette for the Newly Kidnapped* best, hoping to simultaneously buy time, calm the situation and maybe engage the 'mother' in Mrs. G -- if such there be.

Mrs. G fetches a brown quart bottle with no label on it, pours stiff belts into seven jelly glasses.

When we've all been served, Mrs. G hoists her glass, pricks my eyes with hers. "Y'know, li'l boy, you really oughtn't a be causin' my Chuckie and his nice li'l friends all this trouble like y'are. Whyn't you just keep your baby trap shut more in the future, y'know? Heh heh." Not so cute this time.

The pledges gape at me, their faces masks.

It was meant to be appleberry wine or such I suppose, but it tasted more like vinegar. I slugged it anyway. It might help "up there on Wachusetts."

"Gotta get goin', Ma ... keys to your Jeep, Pop?"

"In it."

"Thank you very much, Mr. and Mrs. Gilson," I say, as we make to leave. One last shot, worth a try.

"Enjoy it up there, li'l boy," she says -- with honey all over.

Even colder out now. Which reminds me of my duffle coat. Which is still on the back seat of the car. Right?

Yep.

As the four of them move towards the Jeep, I mosey/sidle towards the car. As not to alarm them, I casually sing out, "Be right there. Get my duffle."

Lah-dee-dah, out-for-a-stroll amble towards the car. Open back door, reach in back. But eyes are *glued* to the inside front of the car -- in particular, the ignition.

Wow ... adangle from the ignition ... keys. Like father, like son.

I reach across, click the lock on the opposite back door. Ease back out, duffle in hand, click the lock on my-side back door. Open driver door, lazy as a yawn.

Spotted!

Two, three, all four, running. Jumping, yowling in pain.

In. Hit front door locks: click, click. Bodies all over vehicle, fists pounding. Fright masks at windows. Howls of wounded animals.

Ignition. Reverse.

Gilson splayed on hood, beating on hood. D'Amato on trunk, *POUNDING* back window.

What if D'Amato falls off and I back over him? Maybe if I just stop, roll down window a crack, reason with them ...

Get real. *GUN THE FUCKER!!!*

D'Amato skids off trunk, to the side.

Car is on the street.

Free. To go. But where? Where the shit am I? Blindfolded the whole way up. How the hell would I even know where 'here' is?

End of this road, I hook a left -- good as a right when you don't know.

I'm on a serious road now at least. Headlights in rearview.

Faster, Bob.

Headlights farther back. But there. Still there.

Scream a sharp right. Smalltown shopping area. Left onto main drag. Another quick left. No headlights in rearview. But they will be.

Driveway between two stores. *Deadend* driveway between two stores: hope that's not an omen.

Kill the lights. They saw me turn in here, I'm bear bait up the mountain. Seconds later, my eyes *glued* to the rearview -- the Jeep bl*aaa*sts by.

Exhale.

Wait about 15 minutes. *Ever* so tentatively *pretend* the car back out the driveway and onto the main drag.

I finally figured out how to work the heater. It was a very good heater. Shivered all the way back, nonetheless.

Onward

After a wasted, party-hearty college career, and early release from the Navy to help care for my partially paralyzed dad in the daytime, and a part-time night job, I'm age 25, and can't let myself drift with the tide any longer.

Time to get moving. Forward, ahead. Can't look back. Onward, upward. *Excelsior*.

Resume? Let's see: "English major, Art/Philosophy minor; scholastic scholarships to Regis and Iona Prep; US Navy, Public Information Office; Fawcett Publications, office supervisor; lifeguard; quasi-physical therapist; deliverer of groceries."

Feeble.

"Former small-g Gatsby type ... ?"

"Former fiance of former Miss University ... ?"

Differentiation, that's what I need! Separation from the pack.

I went on a reading binge. Read anything and everything even remotely connected with publishing and/or advertising, the fields I was interested in. 37 books in a little over five months -- most related to publishing or advertising. I attached the list to my resume, as evidence of my passion, my interest, my drive -- my uniqueness.

Early August I send my resume package to top guns of companies I deem worthy of my talents. (That's Dad's idea: "Always send it to Number 1. He'll pass it on to the appropriate department head, of course. But you'll get special attention ... it 's coming down from ... Number 1!" Dad is savvy.)

I attached a short, punchy note, target-specific to each company. Example: Time, Inc., addressed to Editor-in-Chief, Henry R. Luce: "Dear Mr. Luce: *Time* is of the essence. Sincerely, Robert F. Baker"

Week later, letter from *Time*'s Promotion Manager offering an interview. I didn't follow up, though. I didn't have to. Dad's brother, Uncle Tom, set me up with his friend from Fordham days, Ed Lincoln. Ed's a big gun at McGraw-Hill, the business magazine publishers.

The launch of my Invasion of New York coincides with hurricane-force wind and Noah's ark-inspiring downpour. I head for the train in Greenwich, suit pressed, cordovans agleam, my spandy new raincoat a smart blue-black. My cheap leather carry case, though crafted of the hindquarters of small rodents, has a certain propriety about it, in that it is black.

Inasmuch as I am in famine of cash, I will walk the good walk to McGraw Hill, which Ed Lincoln told me is "just blocks from Grand Central."

No matter the storm, I'm plenty early. Fill the lungs and ... charge ahead! The Atlantic Ocean waterfalls from above; the frail are airborne. My spandy new blue-black raincoat is not water-repellent. It is, in fact, a blue-black sponge. I manage to get lost. I arrive late.

Ed Lincoln is reservedly tolerant of the slime seated across from him. He hardly winces at all when the slime hands its resume across the desk, causing blue-black drippings to mottle important papers in the process.

High-side estimate of the duration of the 'interview' is 3.2 minutes -- at the end of which, Ed Lincoln is wringing (p.i.) the slime's hand, telling the slime its resume will be referred to Mister Personnel, and the slime should be hearing from Mr. P. "in the darn near future," *and* how "darn good it was"of the slime "to come in on such a darn terrible day," *and* to "be darn sure to give" his "*darn*-darn best to" Uncle Tom.

Other interviews went better. Two weeks later I got a job offer: training to become managing editor of Alfred M. Best's insurance-trade magazines. It isn't *publishing*-publishing, but it is publishing. My foot's in the door.

I began commuting from Greenwich to Best's on Wall Street. On my arrival home one evening, Dad told me Ellen wants me to call her at Harper's "Something about jobs there." (Ellen Bond, my stepmother Agnes' niece, who was bright and witty, was an editorial assistant at *Harper's* magazine.)

Harper's, the oldest intellectual magazine in the country. Wow. As not to appear too hard-uply anxiously cravenly overeager, I held off calling *Harper's* till 9:01 the next morning. Ellen said "(Editor-in-Chief) Jack Fischer has three jobs in mind to talk to you about. One is Assistant to the Publisher of *Harper's* magazine. The others are with book publishers ... "

•

My meeting with Fischer was a blitz and a blur. No portly, wreathed-in-pipe-smoke, slow-talk enouncer of arcane wisdoms, Jack Fischer. Instead, a lean cowpoke; collar open, tie at halfmast, cigarette adangle, jitterbug tic of mind and speech.

Another three-minute interview. Yet another flunk, I figure.

Not so. Three days later, a call from Jack Hughes, the Publisher of *Harper's*. Jack Fischer spoke highly of me -- can we meet?

We lunched at elegant Two Park and ... we clicked. I mean clicked. "I'm ready to offer you the job here and now," Jack said. "All you have to do is pass muster with Mac, Frank MacGregor ... Chairman of the Board of Harper Brother's (the book publishers, parent company of the magazine), and a close friend. If he doesn't like you, no job ... but you'll at least get another free lunch out of it. I'll call you in a few days and we'll all three of us lunch at the Biltmore."

"Few days" pass. Few more.

Couple *weeks*. Gone. Dead. Forget it, Bob.

At Best's one morning, my phone rings. The voice is hesitant, tentative, almost a sadness to it. "Bob ... Jack Hughes ... where have you? ... where you? ... *been?*"

My "*H-huh?*" apparently didn't answer the question.

"*Twice* now I called you, *twice* you agreed to meet Mac and me beneath the clock at the Biltmore ... *twice* we waited almost an hour for you ... twice you never showed, or even bothered to call. What's the story? What the hell's the story!?"

After some plenty quick, plenty frantic detective work on my part, I solve the mystery. Come to find out there's a guy by the name of Bob *Becker* who's a fast-talking ad salesman -- a Bob *Becker* who picks this time in his fast-talking life to also be working at Alfred M. Best.

As a newcomer at Best's, I'm virtually nonexistent to the gum-chewer receptionist at the switchboard. One can only assume Jack Hughes had twice before called and caught the gum-chewer mid-gum click and she steered the call to Bob *Becker*.

The fact that Jack Hughes isn't attuned to my voice, combined with the fact that Becker's a hale-fellow-well-met, dictate that the scenario played out somewhat as follows -- as confirmed when I later spoke with Becker.

First time --

Jack Hughes: "Bob, hi, Jack Hughes."

Bob Becker: "Oh, hy*eee*, Jacker! How be ya!"

Jack: "Great. Listen can you meet Mac and I under the clock at the Biltmore, Thursday at 1?"

Becker: "Count me there, ol' Bud."

Becker shows Thursday at 1, doesn't recognize any backs he's previously slapped, leaves a half hour later. Jack and Frank MacGregor show, rock on their heels for an hour, have lunch.

The call the following Monday again catches the gum-chewer mid-click.

Second time --

Jack: "Bob, I guess Thursday didn't work out for you. Can we make it the Biltmore at 1 *this* Thursday?"

Becker: "Count me there, ol' Bud."

Ditto outcome.

I'm not 100% sure that's how it went, but it's a good bet. I do know this: Becker did show up at the Biltmore those two Thursdays, didn't see anybody he knew, and left. Jack Hughes, Publisher of *Harper's* magazine and Frank MacGregor, Chairman of the Board of Harper & Brothers, did show up those two Thursdays and were, for all they knew, stood up.

The great news is that Jack Hughes and Mac hung in and gave me the benefit of the doubt -- and a third shot. The greatest great news is, I got the job.

This 24-year-old loser *extraordinaire* -- delivered by catapult to the position of Assistant to the Publisher of the rather estimable *Harper's* magazine. I am *in*!

Mornin', World.

Wings Spread

My York. *New* York. Not the *Old* York of my grandparents and parents and aunts and uncles. I'm here to put *my* stamp on it.

. Eagle.

Cocksure cock of the walk; king of the hill; bull by the horns; tiger by the balls. Anointed by God. Blessed among men, women and all the ships at sea. "My strength is as the strength of ten, because ... yes ... because I am ... *me* !"

•

The confident six-story, red brick edifice at 49 East 33rd Street was the Harper & Brothers building. Harper & Brothers, the book publishers, owned *Harper's* magazine, the oldest monthly magazine in continuous publication in the country.

The editorial offices of the magazine were on the top floor, keeping company with the dark-paneled executive suites of Harper & Brothers' pin-striped, double-breasted lords almighty. My *someday* goal is that sixth floor -- the editorial department of *Harper's* magazine.

When I started at Harper's, I continued commuting by train from Greenwich, as I had at Alfred M. Best.

I'll never forget my maiden voyage to Best's, which was located in the Wall Street area.

When I boarded the subway at Grand Central, I got a seat; there were plenty to be had. At the first stop, a maddened hive of humanity infuriates aboard -- every seat is confiscated with a vengeance, every strap strangled in death grip. A lady of sizable size occupies the strap in front of me. Beaming my Boy Scoutiest smile, I make to stand and offer the lady of sizable size my seat. The "No!" she barks at me is accompanied by a look that says a helluva lot more. The look *blisters*: "You, *Buster*, are one serious *PRE-VERT*! Y'ain't foolin' me, *Ace*! Siddown, ya scabby dirtbag *PRE-VERT* in your fancy-ass suit! Ya piece a shit from Weschestuh or Connedicuck or whereveh it is ya pieces a shit inhabitate. Lee me a fuck alone, OK!? OK, *fucknose*!?" I take the sizable lady's hint and sit back down.

I scarce ever take the subway again. Or bus. First time I'm on a bus, it's jammed assholes- to-elbows and gets stuck in traffic in front of the New York Public Library. The almost ten minutes we're anchored there, I'm transfixed in horror watching people circumnavigate, and even *step over*, some poor wretch lying on the sidewalk there, as likely dead as passed out! Nobody seems to care which.

That's when I decide that crowds, especially of the captive-witness variety, are no longer on my dance card. So I cab it or hoof it most everywhere thereafter.

Prior to getting an apartment, I'd exit *Harper's* around 4:30 to cab to Grand Central to snag a seat in the bar car on the 5:29 express to Greenwich. You'd best arrive early because 'regulars' take turns getting there early, to commandeer and face-to-face a pair of seats, creating a booth of sorts -- so the jolly four of them can whack back enough Johnny Walker Black to cop a buzz *just* above the horizon and drop fifty/hundred at poker by the time they hit Westport for a quick snap or three of Johnny W at Mario's across from the depot till the Mrs. shows up with a station wagon of screaming meemies and they head home for more octane and a shout fight before hitting the hay for no sex and she throws a raincoat over a nightie to give him a sodden, sullen ride to the station at suddenly-it's-six the next a.m.

My boss Jack Hughes has an easygoing sense of humor. I'd been filling him in on my search for an apartment and he's reminded of a story from his own apartment-hunting days.

Mirror, Mirror

When Jack first arrived in New York, he found a job real quick, but not an apartment real quick. So, for about a month, he stayed in a hotel, while he continued his search.

In the course of his ablutions one morning he became aware of a soreness in an innermore aspect of the region of his situpon. Being the inquisitive sort, he decided to see what he could see about the problem. But this would be difficult, because Jack neither had eyes in the netherward vicinity of the problem, nor was he quadruple-jointed.

Jack, though, was an ingenious man. Aha!, he thought, I shall make inquiry to see what I can see -- with the aid of a mirror. Easy as that. There were, however, only two mirrors in his quarters: one over the bathroom sink and one on the wall just above the bureau.

The bathroom sink mirror was in-ass-essible, if you catch my drift. Only the mirror above the bureau made sense.

He stands on a chair, ups his naked self to the bureau top. Scrunches around to face (if that can be the word) the wounded situpon region in the direction of the mirror.

Now in semi-squat mode, he elevates the view-impeding maleness with his hand. He now lowers and bends his head inward, wall-ward, to peer between his legs and see what he can see reflected from the mirror ...

The movement of his head creates a pendulum effect ... tilting him forward, tumbling him from the bureau, *crashing* him to the floor, breaking his collarbone.

•

"So what's with the sling, Jack? Broke your collarbone, you say? How'd that happ ... ?

Whaddya mean, I wouldn't believe?"

Rent-controlled Apartment

Dan Brooks, a very cool guy I knew from UConn who was working at Dancer Fitzgerald ad agency, made the apartment connection for me. Seems he'd made the find of all finds in Lucia (pronounced "loo-CHEE-a") Welling, a real estate lady who knew where the rent-controlled apartments were buried. Lucia'd lined up Dan's apartment on Jane Street for him, and Dan was able to suave her into finding me one. A real gem.

More like an oversized jewelry case -- with a Swiss-watch kitchen and cameo bathroom. But a terrific location: 16 Abingdon Square, in the West Village. *And* ... the icing on the gravy, only 65 rent-controlled bucks a month!

Wow! $65 a month. Hell, the Smith, Radcliffe, Wellesley girl-graduate secretaries and editorial assistants working at Harper's so they could rub elbows with "literature" and maybe marry a guy in a tweed suit were only making 65 a week. I'm making 105 a week, which is a near-princely sum then, especially for publishing. That same dinky apartment *un*-rent-controlled was 300 a month, easy. As Hal Young from UConn days not only would say, but did say, "That is like a sore dick ... ya can't beat it."

The furnishings in my studio apartment were few. A daybed doubled as a couch. Two waist-high bookcases along the wall facing the daybed held maybe 100 books. A table with a lamp on it. One folding chair. No rug on the floor. Nothing gracing the walls. Nothing. At first.

Off the Wall

I caught enough grief from female visitors about the "barrenness" of my digs' walls that I finally did something about it.

On a day to be indelibly inscribed in the long and storied history of Apartment 2A, 16 Abingdon Square, I scissored the zipper area from an old pair of khakis and Scotch-taped it onto the wall facing the daybed/ couch.

From that moment on, an expression of horror commingled with shock would suddenly consume the face of any new lady fair sitting next to me on the daybed/couch. She'll point to the khakis' zipper on the wall there, and exclaim: "What ... whatever is *that*?"

And I'll simply suggest she go to the wall, and see firsthand what it is.

She checks it out. "I have *no* idea," she says.

"It is what it appears to be," I say. "Your basic fly on the wall."

Old York

Pete Hamill says nostalgia is the dominant emotion in New York.

Not that I had a social life of any dimension the first month or so. I hit artsy/literary saloons in the Village, like the nearby White Horse Tavern and Chumley's. And I flicked out a lot. One weekend, I hit *two* double features, *back-to-back* movies, both Saturday and Sunday.

Familiar New York lore resurfaced -- things I'd come to know from excursions as recent in memory as shoots to 52nd Street jazz joints, all the way back to when I was a kid and aunts Grace and Edith traipsed me to every known museum and tourist attraction in the city. Dad's sisters were *spectacularly* selfless people. Spinster ladies, they lived together and taught in the New York public schools. I'd stay with them and they'd shower me with attention and show me the city during Easter vacation week in my grammar school years. Grace and Edith had a number of great expressions, but my favorite was, "a caution." A "caution" was anything funny in an impish way. I can still hear it: "Oh Edith, look at that face little Bobby's making! Isn't he just the *caution*, though?!" And the two of them would rear back their lovely homely heads and roar with laughter. Such glorious human beings.

It was good to see they still hadn't replaced the extinct light bulbs in the first two letters of the ESSEX HOUSE hotel sign on Central Park South, either -- it had the same risque entertainment value as the Hotel Hooker in Willimantic, near the UConn campus. The Hooker was named after a Union general in the Civil War, but whoever named a *hotel* the Hooker weren't too intelly-gent, doncha know. (Can't you just hear some salesman on the phone with his wife: "Yeah, Alice, had a good day in Jersey today. Couple calls to make in New York tomorrow, then up to Connecticut. Depending how it goes, I'll spend the night at the SEX HOUSE in Manhattan tomorrow night. Either that, or I'll be in the Hooker up in Connecticut. Kiss the kids g'night for me. Love ya, hon.")

•

There's a bunch of New York in my blood. I was born in the Bronx. Both my parents were thoroughbred New Yorkers. My Dad's father was a New York City cop who died when Dad was fifteen. Dad went immediately to work to put his brothers and sisters through college. Youngest brother, Buddy, died in his freshman year at Fordham; another Fordham brother, Don, went on to a career in public relations at Con Ed. Dad's favorite brother, Tom, married Fordham classmate Malcom Wilson's sister, Irene. Malcolm was Governor Nelson Rockefeller's Lieutenant Governor for fifteen years, and became New York's 50th Governor in 1973 when Rockefeller vacated his third term, having been appointed Vice-President of the United States by President Gerald Ford.

One of the time-honored Fordham-Irish Baker family traditions was membership in the New York Athletic Club -- housed in a palatial 24-story building on Central Park South. Uncle Don suggested I join the AC. He and Uncle Tom will sponsor me, it'll be cheap money -- $75 annual dues in my age bracket.

I more than got my money's worth out of the AC. Many the pilgrimage after work to the dark haven of the sprawling second-floor men's bar. A 50-cent pilsener glass of Budweiser; then to the vast free spread on the buffet table: cold cuts, cheeses, breads, soups, stews.

The best times were Sundays. I'd rise whenever the afterbuzz of Saturday night allowed, cab to the AC, grab a *Times* in the lobby, elevate to the solarium-white of the 14th floor dining room; brunch on Bloodys, steak, sausage and hash browns. Then to the 10th floor, and poolside sybaritic bliss: machine-gun massage in the Hydra-headed shower; then, wrapped in 5-foot terrycloth towel, stretched out on chaise; white-uniformed Irish waiters bring Heinekens and sliced chicken sandwiches as I graze the *Times* and maybe doze or add to my collection of Famous Naked People swimming the pool there: the writer Gore Vidal, comedians George Gobel and Red Buttons -- even Joe Dimaggio once.

Marilyn Monroe wasn't ever bob-bob-bobbing the pool with Joe, though, sorry to say.

Upward?

Publisher Jack Hughes went along with most everything I suggested or asked for. He treated me as an equal right from the start. As if I'd come to the job a seasoned publishing executive.

He put it this way: "I want you to know my job well enough to take it away from me. To have the attitude you *can* take it away from me. I have ulcers, real bad. Probably have to have part of my gut cut out ... maybe next summer. I need *you* to be *me* while I'm out. And if I go, you're the man. I'll mentor you. Talk about starting at the top.

One of the major perqs of the job: attendance at Monday morning editorial meetings. The publisher needs be aware of the editorial content of upcoming issues to promote it to the media, advertisers and the public. Jack Hughes and Jack Fischer, the Editor-in-Chief, were natural-born enemies from the getgo. My arrival made me the ideal candidate to represent the Publisher -- both Jacks liked me. That's not a brag, it's a fact.

That elevator opening onto the editorial floor every Monday morning was the doorway to Heaven. Think about it, Bob. Just seven weeks ago you're ducking out of your supervisor job in the basement of Fawcett Publications so you can shoot upstairs and cruise the editorial files of *True* magazine just to get the *feel* of editorial. And here you are now a sanctioned impostor "whose presence is *required*" in the company of the *editors* of one of the country's leading intellectual journals.

Even more preposterous, this sanctioned impostor is frequently asked to make observations on the editorial content of upcoming issues of the magazine. Editorial-type observations -- as-if-I'm-an-editor-type observations.? And occasionally an editor or three laughs/laugh at a wry observation I make? Or agrees/agree with an idea I suggest.

The meetings are a font of first names. Make that, First Names. Make that *known personally to the editor who's speaking* First Names: Joe, Jack, Bobby (Kennedy), Adlai (Stevenson), Norman (Mailer), Bill (Schlesinger), John (Lindsay), Adam (Clayton Powell),

Henry (Luce) ... and on and on.

The editors themselves are giants in their own right, as well as characters in their own right. The clipped speech, stub-stub-stub-stubbity-stubbed-out butts and childlike fascination with any subject under the sun of Jack Fischer. Russell Lynes with his cigarette holder and Eustace Tilley manner*ed*isms; commentator on the arts and popular culture. Gauloise-smoking Bob Silvers who reminds me of Orson Welles in his puffy dark looks and genius; a former editor of *The Paris Review* and, later, co-founder and editor-in-chief of *The New York Review of Books*. The acerb, on-the-money socio-political perceptions of the other cigarette-holder holder, Marion Sanders who espouses any cause the least hair Left of Right. The sit-up-straight, snow-crowned Katherine Jackson, the fiction editor who succeeds in getting Reynolds Price's first novel, *A Long and Happy Life* published in its entirety in a single issue of *Harper's*. And, the Secret Weapon: quiet-spoken Catherine Myer, who is titularly the bottom-of-the-totem-pole poetry editor and who is maybe fiftyish and looks and dresses the Emily Dickinson part of the spinster lady she is -- but is, in truth, the Duchess. Only when something is impossibly wrong, or seemingly irresolvable, does she volunteer. But when she does, she is to the quick: the wrong is righted, the problem is solved. She is the Collective Mind of the editorial department. The glue. We come to enjoy each other's minds and wit, the shy Catherine and I.

I go extra out of my way to get on an elevator-conversation and pop-by-the-office-say-hi basis with the other Titans who stride the sixth floor. The regal, pipe-smoking, Brit-tailored Cass Canfield, Chairman of the Executive Committee of Harper & Brothers; amiable, solidly built Ray Harwood, who's President; tall, aquiline-handsome Evan Thomas, son of Norman Thomas, the six-time Socialist Party candidate for president -- Evan's Executive VP and, oh by the way, *very* close to the Kennedys.

Frank MacGregor (Mac), the silver-haired, equally Brit-tailored, Lionel Barrymore lookalike; the Chairman of the Board greases my path, introduces me to The Bigs; makes me feel one of the gang -- even an *important* one of the gang.

Only in the movies.

Fast-Track Roller Coaster

In May, Jack Hughes tells me I'm going to be Acting Publisher of *Harper's* this summer. In early July, he's having that ulcer surgery he'd mentioned and he'll be out at least 8 weeks.

"You'll be running the show. Everyone will answer to you. "Oh, and I'm putting you in for a $10 a week raise," Jack said. "It'll just about cover the antacids you'll be needing while you're in charge."

Not a week later, right after the Monday morning editorial meeting, Jack *Fischer* invites me into his office and closes the door. "Bob, how would you like to be my Thurber ... my Front Desk?"

Wow.

James Thurber, the legendary creative genius! I asked Fischer what "Front Desk" meant. "Harold Ross concocted an administrative editor position at *The New Yorker*, which Thurber held for a while. (Thurber's title there was Central Desk.) We'll call it Administrative Editor here. Someone to keep the idiots from my door. Get to know the whole editorial side, maybe be Managing Editor someday. But to start, keep the damn-fool idiots from my door. I think you're the man. Interested?"

What's next ... *God* ?!

Small problem. Make that, *major* small problem. A major small problem called 'Monsignor Ganley' -- a.k.a. a Catholic conscience. I'm already committed to Jack Hughes, to act as Publisher, and cover for him till he returns -- two, three, who-knows-how-many months from now. As great as the greatest opportunity that may ever cross my path is, I have to reward Jack Hughes' investment in me and honor my commitment to him -- at the very least until he recovers from his surgery and returns to the office.

I told Jack Fischer how flattered I was, because I'd do *anything* to get into editorial -- but I'd have to fill in for Jack Hughes till he got back, however long it took. He said he hadn't heard the Jack Hughes' surgery news yet. Fischer said he respected me for standing by Jack Hughes, and he'd seek out someone else to be his Thurber. Then he said, "Maybe you can do some first readings on the side, in the meantime. Just in case I don't find the right person."

(Chance of a lifetime done in by Conscience. And, truth be told, Fischer had the inclination and the power to install me in the job on the spot -- there was no love lost between the two Jacks. And while Fischer was a liberal, he was nails-tough-*opposite* the super-sensitive variety. He rarely met an adjective he ever liked.)

Everyone agreed I'd done the right thing. But losing that 'oner' ate at me the whole summer long. For sure Fischer would find the right person for the job among the army of seasoned editorial types who'd *kill* to set foot on the editorial ladder of *Harper's*.

I did first readings on my own at night, nonetheless. I jumped at and welcomed that opportunity; it gave me yet another form of connection with editorial. *Harper's* received 3,000-plus unsolicited manuscripts a year. Editorial assistants did 'first readings' to screen (i.e. *throw* out) the 99% dross and send writers the pre-printed rejection letter which had all the sincerity of a yawn.

Throughout that summer, I lugged libraries' of manuscripts home to Abingdon Square: articles, short stories, essays, poetry. I raced through that evening's mound, delivered my verdicts to editorial the next morning.

Every two-hundred or so, I'd come across a piece that grabbed me by the brain or the heart -- or both. I'd jot down comments, and put the manuscript on the 'slush pile' desk in Managing Editor Russell

Lynes' office, for consideration higher up the editorial chain.

But it might well chill the hearts of aspiring Pete Hamills or Doris Kearns Goodwins at the time to know their hard-sweat manuscripts were, in many cases, being eyeballed in 97 seconds give-or-take, by a guy whose editorial experience was limited to perusing the manuscript files of *True* magazine, and whose editorial acumen was further diffused by refills of Clan McGregor scotch and imaginings of lush maidens in diaphanous attire. Or less.

A bonus opportunity came my way in late July when Buzz Wyeth, Managing Editor of the Trade Book Department, asked if I'd do first readings for the "Harper Prize Novel Contest." He'd pay me $2 for each manuscript I considered.

The scary truth of the matter is that either the quality of American prose being what it *wasn't* at the time or the quick hook I gave manuscripts which didn't show promise straight out of the chute pocketed me 52 whole dollars one week! (Do the math -- scary.)

The 8 weeks Jack Hughes was out of commission went by quickly. Jack, God bless him, had put the operation on cruise control, and my duties as 'Acting' Publisher called for 'acting' (showing up) more than 'doing.'

The very *morning* of the Monday in early September that Jack Hughes returned to work, I got a call from Jack Fischer. "Bob ... seen a bunch of people ... they're not right ... you're still my Thurber. Don't know if you're still interested or not ... "

High Over New York

My storied reign as Administrative Editor of *Harper's* magazine began Monday, October 2nd, 1961. The only celebration consisted of the brass band parading my heart. I'd arrived at my field of dreams ... Editorial.

It took Editor-in-Chief Jack Fischer three typewritten pages just to *outline* the job. Truth be told, 97% had to do with stuff a guy at Burger King could do with his left hand while flipping hockey pucks with his right. Scheduling, assigning, double-checking. Minutia, minutia, minutia. For those who hold that God is in the details, the job of Administrative Editor had the makings of a world-class religion. Only a small percent had to do with anything remotely creative or editorial: "7-b. Do first readings"; "7-d. Take over part of JF's (Jack Fischer's) correspondence" -- and the one that still breaks me at the very thought of it, good old everlovin' "2-e. Interview unheralded job applicants, *un*promising authors, crackpots and miscellaneous visitors."

Freeing of Speech

Jack Fischer didn't come by my office often, but when he did it usually signaled a surprise of the upbeat sort. Like the time he enters, followed by a burly, pipe-smoking older man in a three-piece tweed suit. With a nod in the direction of the amiable-looking gent, Jack says, "Bob, this is Morris Ernst, he's ... "

I finished Jack's sentence: "... the famous attorney who overturned the ban on publication of *Ulysses*! *That* Morris Ernst?"

"Well, I don't know about famous, Bob, but that was my case."

(James Joyce's *Ulysses*, one of the enduring classics of world literature, was first published in Europe in 1922, but was banned in the US, because it allegedly violated obscenity laws. In a landmark case, a brilliant presentation by Morris Ernst to Judge John M. Woolsey in 1933 won the day, opening the door to publication of *Ulysses* in the United States.)

"I'm honored to meet you, Mr. Ernst," I said. *"Pornography,* they claimed. How *ever* did you pull it off, Mr. Ernst?"

He gestured with his pipe. "Simple as this, Bob. Basically, all I had to do was prove that fuck isn't a dirty word."

That immediate and straight on, and coming from this tweedy eminence, "fuck" was an attention-getter. This is the Victorian-prim *early* '60s, mind you. Never was heard the magic word around the offices, nay never. I smiled to myself. Jack Fischer's eyes got big and he grimaced – there was still a degree of the ingenuous Oklahoma fundamentalist country boy about Jack.

Descent

One of the "unpromising authors" shunted my way was Michael Sienawski. As Jack Fischer said, "He knows Evan Thomas and has an in with the Kennedys through his Jet Set connections. Wealthy

Russian emigre, wants to do a piece on Brazil, his home base now. Humor him. But discourage him. Diplomatically."

My first meeting with the well threaded, well buffed Sienawski is for a quick drink at the Oak Room bar at the Plaza; we then head over to the Kennedy suite atop the Carlyle for a cocktail whoopie celebrating an international purpose or person I never discover. A gorge of worthy hors d'oeuvres, an abundance of preening people.

Everyone's speaking French, save moi. My francais is pretty much stuck at "La plume de ma tante." So I mostly stand there looking pretty and drinking pretty much, while Sienawski gads the room.

Our next meeting place is the Brook Club, the extremely exclusive men's club on 54th, off Park. (The Brook was the *only* social club Jack Kennedy listed membership in.) Our dining room is out of Ingmar Bergman: a sullen-lit, elongated, high-ceilinged baronial hall. Four men are seated across from each other at the distant end of the table, a table which easily accomodates 40 people. Our footsteps echo our advance of the somber, musty chamber.

Sienawski introduces me. The only two of the four whose names I recall now are Serge Obolensky, a Russian playboy who'd once been married to Czar Alexander II's daughter, and Ghighi ("Giggy") Cassini, a.k.a. society gossip columnist Cholly Knickerbocker who coined the term 'Jet Set.' Giggy also happens to be brother of Jackie Kennedy's-couturier-in-waiting, Oleg Cassini. This tomb at first would seem an unlikely hangout for these Jet Set butterflies, but as conversation slogs along, it's befitting. If this can be called 'conversation.' I'm trapped there for two hours wondering if they'll ever have anything to say. These Continentals who peacock the globe at the pop of a cork, who own every toy known to Croesus. What memorable repartee is exchanged, what wit gets aired, what insights imparted?

Nada. Bores. Gossip and grousing. Valley Girls trying to out-ditz each other at a sleepover: "And Antoine says to me ... and, would you *believe* ... !" The single statement of memory, and only because of its patheticness: "Do you recall the time ... not so long ago, at that ... when one could afford to maintain *500* polo ponies in Argentina? And now ... now ... a mere ... *300*!?"

My final get-together with Sienawski takes place over lunch at La Cote Basque, having already communicated to him the notion that his proposed Brazil piece is not an *immediate* prospect for *Harper's*. (That "immediate" dangle buys him hope, and me another free lunch.)

I'm at the bar when he shows up with the satinous, voluptuously contoured Celestia. Mid-lunch, when Celestia heads off to the ladies', Michael leans over and offers, "She's yours, Bob, if you wish. 7 o'clock. Here is her number."

As we bid goodbye in the doorway of Cote Basque, Sienawski hands me his card, "Please come visit, Bob ... my guest, anytime. Sao Paulo, or Brasilia. Both ... if you choose."

Some unpromising authors are less unpromising than other unpromising authors.

•

As I burst from Cote Basque, frantically flagging down a cab, I damn near stumble over some stupid guy sprawled out on the sidewalk. But being quick-footed, thanks to basketball days, I'm able to vault the guy -- *just* as the cab screeches to a stop. Lucky timing. Great footwork. Close-assed call.

On the ride downtown it ... WHONK ... hits me -- like a sledgehammer. "You *jumped over* that poor guy, Bob! Remember how *disgusted* you were when you saw them walking around the guy on the sidewalk in front of the Public Library when you first got here, *Bob*!? And now it's *you* doing it, and like it's *natural* for you to be doing it! Even *praiseworthy*! Man, I mean if you hadn't a sprung over that sucker ... if you'd, God forbid, stopped and tried to *help* the guy, that fucking cab woulda been outasight. Right?

Are you a *New Yorker* now, Bob?! Another faceless suit-in-the-cold-blooded-crowd?! Or are you 'yourself' -- the Bob Jayne resurrected.

I looked at an ugly face in my mirror. I did not call Celestia at 7.

Flight

(This following, shown for its relevance to my thinking, is the core of a letter from Jayne, my love of the moment, awaiting me at my New York apartment -- which gave me the juice to consider a lifestyle move.)

" "

Dear Rob, I'm driving myself nuts with fluctuating indecision. Friend Allen told me the best way to solve problems is to run like hell from them. I've put in for a European charter flight leaving June 29, from Boston. Altho I can't say definitely I strongly suspect I am not coming back -- for an indefinite period of time. Probably a couple to three years. All depends if I like it and if I can get a job. What this means to and for us is quite obvious. (Etc, etc.) Jayne

" "

Jayne. The one who -- however fleetingly -- turned me into a me I could like. My real self, maybe. And here I am coming off an experience -- me 'vaulting' over the guy spreadeagled on the sidewalk -- my selfish, self-absorbed *worst* self. And I'm the one who was nauseated just a year ago seeing people lah-dee-dah parading around a guy passed out on the sidewalk in front of the New York Public Library lacking only musical accompaniment.

What have I become!?

Caught up in glitz and glamor. Titles and Cote Basques and phonies speaking French and cocktail parties. And how many *real* friends have you made? Other than Jayne, how much *real* anything has there been in your life here in the city -- including yourself? *Most of all*, including your pathetic phony-assed self?

And what's this terrific Me *doing*? Making schedules, making lists, writing reports, checking *details*. 99-and-9/10% of me wasn't *doing* or *creating* a godamn thing. Nothing new. At work, or in the world around me. Good ol' Bobby Baker, the kid with imagination and *ideas*, flipping details 'stead of burgers -- details paid better, at least.

Whoa! Ease off! Reverse engines, pal! Where you think you're going, Buster Baker Man?! Huh?! You gonna up and chuck it all, man?! I mean you're on the Express Elevator to Success, pal! In the Success Capital of the World, New York Citeee, man! In 19-and-62, man! In 19-and-62, man, New York Citeee is the Mecca of Success! And you be headed for the *Penthouse*, Bobby Boy. The *Pent*house of the *Mecca* of *Success*, Bobby Boy! Use your head, man! You cannot leave. That would be *crazy*, Bobby, *crazy!*... You *cannot* leave.

Oh yes I can.

•

From Heaven it came --

Less than a week after I'd experienced a combined Crisis of the Heart (Jayne's letter announcing her departure for Europe) and a Crisis of the Soul (the *un*human being New York was turning me into), Jack Fischer walked into my office. "Bob, I'd like you to go to Boston to visit our sister publication, the *Atlantic Monthly*. Emily Flint, she's the Managing Editor, said she'd be good enough to background you on their editorial procedures. How they process manuscripts, editorial assignments, schedule first readings, etcetera ... the nuts and bolts I covered in my job description memo to you when you started. And on the flip side, you'll fill her in on how we work. Emily's a fine, intelligent woman. You'll like her."

I took the train to Boston and cabbed to the Ritz. I looked out at the Public Garden from my room, and thought to myself: This is where you belong. People walking along the sidewalk across Arlington Street there -- they're even looking at each other. One man even said hello to another man, and they stopped and talked. A woman laughed and made a funny face and waved to someone across the street. This is it. If only there were a way to swap the lemmingstyle of New York for the lifestyle of Boston, *and* work in a stimulating environment, *and* make a decent dollar.

If only.

I'd arrived late afternoon and met with Emily Flint next morning. I could tell right away she was -- to use another great Hal Young term -- "good wood." We set to work and burned the daylight oil comparing editorial procedures. We took a lunch break at the Ritz at 2, courtesy of my *Harper's* expense account. In the course of my single martini, I ventured to test tricky waters with Emily. I opened up about my Crisis of the Soul; and, how, as much as I liked *Harper's* and how promising my future was, I had to escape ... New York.

"Your timing might be good, Bob," Emily said. "I got a call from Mark Carroll, managing director of Harvard University Press yesterday afternoon. He's looking for someone to take charge of book promotions. We'll call him when we get back. You never know."

Emily called, put me on the phone and we set up an appointment for the next day. The meeting went well: I filled Carroll in on what I'd been doing in the area of promotion for the magazine and said I'd Special Delivery samples when I got back to New York. The salary was $6000 -- excellent by both Boston and publishing industry standards, *and* $5 a week more than I was making in New York.

Carroll said to send him a resume and samples, and he'd get back to me quickly. On return to New York, I fire off resume and samples ... and hold my breath. Never gonna happen. Too good to be true: pull off a lifestyle-*and life*-enhancing career move in a measly two-hour interview in my one shot at Boston for who knows how long.

Less than a week later, Mark Carroll calls me at *Harper's* to say the job is mine. He adds to the good news by saying he has leads on apartments in Cambridge and they'll pay my expenses to come take a look. The primal scream I released when I got off the phone, must've convinced the secretaries outside my office I was in death-throes combat with a "crackpot author," so I stuck my head out the swinging door to reassure them I was just fine. I'm not sure they thought I was.

Now comes the hard part, telling Jack Fischer. Telling Jack Fischer that the kid he created a special 'Thurber' job for, the kid who made it onto the masthead of the February, 1962 issue of the magazine, this same ingrate kid is pulling up stakes to move to musty old Boston so he can put "Harvard" on his resume. What an ingrate kid. The Ingrate Gatsby all over again.

Not so. Jack Fischer not only took it well, he expressed his approval. "Bob," he said, "If I had my way, I'd move *Harper's* to Boston ... tomorrow." Not only that, when I landed in Cambridge, he sent me a nice note: "I don't need to tell you that we're missing you badly, and that everyone at Harper's was extremely sorry to see you go. From time to time I expect you'll run across an author or article idea in the Cambridge area; if so, I hope you'll let me know about them. As you know, we don't have formal scouting arrangements; but we always make a modest payment as token of appreciation." I not only hadn't burned a bridge, I had a first-class human being validating my efforts at *Harper's -- and* urging me forward.

If a Chinese restaurant named a dish after me, they'd call it Dum Phuk Luk.

Sequel

June, 1962, I'd made the lifestyle move to the job at Harvard University Press in Cambridge.

I get a call from Jayne at HUP. She's headed off to her European adventure Friday night; she'll be in the Boston area during the day and can meet me at my place in Cambridge, if I can leave work early. We can visit a couple hours before she links up with her charter group in Boston. The conversation -- more like, her *monologue* -- is. that. cut. and. that. dry. period.

She makes it abundantly clear the visit will *not* include the making of love. She does say she hopes we can get together one last time, because ... she hopes we can.

Despite the fact it's only my second week at HUP and the air about the place is decidedly uptight, nobody-exhale, everybody's-got-an-ivory tower-crammed-sideways-up-their-ass, I tell Cal Jonson, my boss, that I'm leaving early Friday to be with a lady love who's headed off to Europe ... for maybe forever. I can tell by the grimmer-than-usual expression on Jonson's standard-issue death mask that leaving work early costs me points, and that the use of an emotive word (lady *'love'*) on workplace premises, *and* on company time, adds significantly to the penalty.

Get used to Yankee Brahmindom, Bob.

Tough excrement, YB, get used to New Yorkitude.

My mode of transport when I first descended on Cambridge was a no-speed bike. I pedaled to 401 Broadway at the appointed hour -- Jayne was already there, sitting on the curb. She was wearing a green print-patterned skirt of some filmy material, and her knees were not primly together.

We descended to my cellar apartment and made love, and said hardly anything. I was crying when I phoned for the cab. And when I kissed her goodbye before she got into the cab.

She said she'd write.

New Yorkitude

Uncle Don and I are headed to a Friendly Sons of St. Patrick dinner at the Astor when I told him I was leaving New York. Uncle Don, the ultimate diehard New Yorker, asked why. To spare him psychobabble, I said I needed peace and quiet.

There we were, stranded in the middle of horn-blaring 42nd Street when I said that. "Y'know, Bobby," Uncle Don said, "that's funny. We New Yorkers, your Aunt Dixie and I, we think that right *here* -- he points to the macadam -- right *here*, would be a great place to have a farm. That's a New Yorker, you see."

Despite the incompatibility between me and New York lifestyle at the time, there was -- and is to this day -- an attachment of my Bronx-born *soul* to New York, as deliciously exemplified in the distant echo of my father, every now and then, from out of nowhere, belting out at the top of his kid-from-the-Bronnix lungs: "My gal's a corkah/She's a New Yorkah/I buy her everything to keep her in style/Hey boys, that's where my money goes ... "

There's what I call "New Yorkitude," confidence in the cocky range -- it's come to my aid more than once when I need a jumpstart. The word made flesh is the one about the tourist walking down Fifth Avenue who goes up to the New Yorker and says, "Excuse me, sir ... could you tell me how to get to the Empire State Building, or should I just go fuck myself?"

Charlie on the MTA

1964: I'm now assistant to the head of the trade books department at Little, Brown, in Boston. 11 o'clock, my phone at Little, Brown rings -- it's Jayne, my New York love, breathless. Calling from dockside, Boston Harbor: she and shiny new husband guy have oceancrossed the Atlantic as passengers on a Danish freighter which will be leaving at 3 for New York and I should quick come down to see her and meet the shiny new husband guy.

Dunno if I can deal with this. Dunno.

Ah well. Cab to ship, kiss the glowing Jayne, shake the hand of shiny new -- Benny -- who is the other side of shiny. In fact, Benny is a lank, bearded, somber Dane on loan from the brooding, mist-swirled moors of the Ingmar Bergman oeuvre.

Or so he seemed at first.

We descend to their cabin. An ice chest of Carlsberg beer appears -- from the ship's cargo of Carlsberg beer. Benny pops the caps with a neat trick. He circles the top of the bottle with his index finger and thumb, cap ridge just above the horizon, angles cap ridge almost flush to big bone at base of index finger, takes coin, levers it between ridge and bone -- pop. (For a while, I could replicate Benny's neat trick, but long since lost the knack.)

Appears next a bottle of Aqvavit. Benny pours us each a shot, purses his lips, and, to the accompaniment of an emphatic inspirated hiss of air, gulps the vile liquor. He cops a couple long glugs of Carlsberg. "This is how vee do it in Denmark," Benny says, with a radiant smile Ingmar Berman would've kicked him off the brooding, mist-swirled set for.

So this is how vee did it in Boston that day. And vee did it.

And dih it.

And dih ih.

Ten minutes of 3. I'm standing atop the gangway. Sorta-weave-standing atop the gangway. Fond farewells all 'round.

Now I'm on the pier and we're all waving and blowing kisses to each other -- I, waving as much with body as hands. Too drunk go back work. Too poor take cab all way Cambridge. Simpppppp-pull. Take sub-way. Find MTA stay-shun. Nice sub-way come. Ged on nice sub-way.

Ride nice sub-way. Id stopppppp. Ged off, go up stair. Light very too bright. Look aroun'. No Cambridge. Where this? "Jamaica Plain" sign say. 'maica Plain way far Cambridge. Down stair. Nice sub-way come. Ged on ... id stopppppp.

Off. Stair. Light. "Roxbury" sign. Far Cambridge.

Stair, nice sub-way; off, stair, light. "Braintree." Far.

I've no idea how I finally found my way to Harvard Square, or what exotic subterranean ports I'd visited en route.

I do remember noting it was 6 o'clock and my inside jacket pockets were stuffed with small Danish cigars; an outer pocket held an unopened bottle of Aqvavit; the other outer pocket a rolled up large-format paperback of Delacroix's paintings (*Delacroix's Paletter*), the text in Danish.

I smoked the cigars, gave the Aqvavit away. The Delacroix I still have.

Our Hearth Afire

Nancy Blake came by my office at Little, Brown a couple times a week to drop off reports filled with numbers. The fact that she was Scandinavian-pretty and outgoing moved me to ask for another number -- as in 'telephone.' Affirmative.

Not too many heartbeats later we were on a marriage track. We shared a love of the written word and children. In a short while we'd all but worn a path between my place in Cambridge and her apartment on Beacon Hill, just over the rise from Little, Brown.

•

It's a whiteout blizzard. Nancy and I leave work about 2, hop the T to Harvard Square, *fight* our way the 637 steps to my apartment at 8 Story Street.

We struggle through hang-ten drifts to the house. I manage the key in the lock, we enter to the solace of our cave. I force the door shut against the howler.

Off coats and boots. All the comforts of love in a blizzard: full larder, full liquor locker, fireplace.

Fireplace.

Yep, fireplace. One a them'n. There it are, right thar. But. No firewood.

Well now ... how about that?

Well.

What you could do, Bob, is simply put your boots and greatcoat back on, reopen the door and muscle-flop your way 519 steps to that itsy-poo provisioner to the elite, Sage's, on Brattle there, and pay the $157,000 plus tax for what is labeled "Firewood" but is really six toothpicks tied up with a red bow on top. That's what you could do, right?

Well.

Of course, on the *oth*er h*aaa*nd, there are the kitchen chairs. Which are wooden. And the table ... wooden. The rickety kitchen chairs and rickety kitchen table. Yep, them'n. The rickety kitchen chairs and rickety kitchen table landlady Mrs. Pratt probably got for 3 bucks at the Salvation Army. We never use the kitchen chairs, because we always eat in the living room.

Well.

That was a two-chair night. The next blizzard was a two-chair. The next, a table. The table couldn't be justified because of non-use. We did use the table to set things on. No, the table went up the chimney in answer to a Higher Calling: "When you're in love, table-shmable."

Fortunately, Spring arrived before we ran out of furniture.

When Nancy and I got married, we moved next door to the second-floor furnished apartment in Mrs. Pratt's house at 12 Story Street. 8 Story was the ultimate bachelor pad, but that's what it was -- a bachelor pad. 12 Story had a nicely furnished living room and sizable bedroom.

Mrs. Pratt needed to find new tenants for 8 Story. So she inspected 8 Story for damage. No damage in the living room. But when she crossed the threshhold into the kitchen ... "Where are the chairs and the ... *table?*"

I told her the truth. To Mrs. Pratt's credit, she took it pretty well. The replacement firewood (a.k.a. furniture) she obtained from the Salvation Army cost me $30. Still, it was a bargain compared to the toothpicks with a red bow at Sage's.

It is only myth that a grainy photo of me, accompanied by the legend "Deranged!," was posted in realty offices throughout Cambridge soon thereafter.

Administrate Out the Door

Trouble.

Randy's secretary, Sue, comes into my office: Randy would like to speak with me. I follow Sue down the hall, cross the great Oriental rug in Randy's office, sit in the chair across from Randy who's seated in the great leather chair behind his great wide desk.

Randy looks up from whatever he's writing. Zero expression on his face. Says not a word, puts down pen, rises from great leather chair, walks around great wide desk, crosses great Oriental rug, shuts the door with a quiet-as-he-can-make-it-quiet click.

Randy Williams is famous for his *open* door, Bob.

Randy recrosses the great Oriental rug, walks around the great wide desk, reseats himself in the great leather chair.

The expression on his face has plunged from zero to death mask.

I'm fired. I am not Outsized or Downsized, Redistributed, Released or Let Go. I am plain old All-American flat-assed fired. The thrust of Randy's Farewell Address: "You aren't cut out to be an administrator, Bob. You've got some creative in you, though. Maybe look into something like advertising, perhaps."

Not Ideal

This is the first week in August. Nancy and I are getting married next month. I'm awarded a bounteous two weeks severance ($270). Nancy earns a monumental $65 a week. Our rent is $110 a month.

Life will go on, Bob. You'll get married. After the wedding reception, you and your bride will spend your first night in your new apartment. You'll sit on the edge of your connubial-just-slightly-smaller-than-a-cruise-ship, older-than-God bed to untie your shoes, and the ship will not sink, because it will instead CRASH to the floor. And landlady Mrs. Pratt is not a thing of beauty in her nightgown at the door to see what the Mad Renter of Cambridge has wrought this time. And she will concede that it was the bed's fault, because it's so old, and she will get it fixed one day soon and she's sorry about it happening on our wedding night.

And you and your bride will pull apart the bedstead and set the pieces in a corner and get under the covers tucked into the mattress on top of the box spring, and in each other's arms you will laugh till you cry yourselves asleep.

'tween

All told, I was out of work three years. According to the 1964 calendar, it was only three months; but a month equals a year when your wife's the breadwinner at 65 a week and you don't know where to even start looking for a job. After Nancy headed off to work, I'd shave, shower, open the closet door and gaze vacantly at the five Brooks Brothers suits and 21 regimental-striped ties. No need for a suit, Bob. So I throw on khakis, button down and highly polished Weejuns and slouch my 29 year-old butt to Harvard Square to pick up the Globe. The only khakis I see in Harvard Square are on students -- some of the students are even wearing suits.

So I slink back to the apartment, settle into an armchair, read the paper, glom the classifieds, make some calls. Spend the rest of the day pacing the floor in my highly polished Weejuns, feeling sorry for myself that the phone doesn't ring. Then, when my wife comes home at 5:30, I feel worse for her -- then worse still about my useless self.

A 'Mother' of Public Relations

I did sort of have one sort of job in that three months, though. In truth, it was more like a guest appearance; a guest appearance lacking applause -- unless you count one hand not clapping.

George Hall, treasurer at Little, Brown, called a week or so after I'd been fired. He said Edward Bernays, the self-proclaimed 'Father of Public Relations,' was writing his autobiography and needed someone to send permission requests to sources quoted in the manuscript. "He lives up the street from you, on Brattle," George said. "I gave him your name and said you might call."

I call. Mrs. Bernays answers. She instructs me, with 911-urgency, to come right there. I throw on a suit, lace up my highly polished cordovans, hasten pronto-speed to the castle of PR, which would best be described as 'Charles Addams-Victorian' (a.k.a. 'The Munsters). Befittingly, a stern-faced, elderly female gnome with painted black hair opens the door, after my fourth ring -- and at discreet 45-second intervals. Big rush.

I smile, proclaim my name. She says not hello, gimlet-eyes me with great suspicion, instructs me to follow her. She marches me through darkened cavernous rooms to a small study at the side of the house. Sunlight shines on the Sire of Spin, a small man in his seventies who's wearing a light-gray, three-piece suit. His face is mouselike, the skin, mouse-gray. The look in his eyes, "All Business All the Time." He introduces me to Frau Bernays, who -- no surprise -- is one and the same with the gnome who opened the door and marched me all the way here to be introduced to her.

Huh?

Mr. Bernays takes me upstairs to a tiny sunbright room on the third floor, where a foot-high manuscript rests on a table, along with ballpoint pens and pads of paper. A monster copying machine which has to have been one of Thomas Alva Xerox's early prototypes consumes an adjacent table.

Mr. Bernays explains the job: I'm to photocopy pages which might require permissions. He will pay $2.50 an hour. I will work from 10 till noon. I'm to leave at noon; come back at 1, work till 3, three days a week. $30 a week. "If that will be satisfactory, you might as well start now, inasmuch as it is 10 minutes to 10."

It will be satisfactory. He leaves the room and I begin reading, to get the sense of what I'll be working with. Names of kings, presidents of countries, captains of industry and commerce, social leaders, labor leaders, Hollywood and High Society types, teem the pages:

I might as well be reading, *Who's Who in The Known World from 1920 to 1960.*

A half hour into my perusal, I sense a presence behind me. I turn my head to see the gnome in the doorway, not-smiling at me, then vanishing. I return to the manuscript, to happen on the fact that Mr. Bernays is, in fact, a nephew of the late (not that he was always late) Sigmund Freud.

A half-hour thence, the gnome of the nephew of the late Sigmund Freud again appears, again not-smiles, again vanishes. Then twice more, at half-hour intervals: until it becomes noon, and time for my until-1 intermission.

The phone's ringing as I enter our apartment. Good, maybe an interview, I think to myself. Instead, it's the gnome of the nephew of the late Sigmund Freud. "Do you have have anything with you?" she asks. That being a fairly open-to-interpretation question, I seek to narrow the scope. "Do I have any *what* with me?"

"... *thing?* From *here?*"

"Ahh, no I don't Mrs. Bernays. Nope, I actually do not."

"If you have anything with you, return it immediately. Otherwise, you cannot return here ever again. Do you understand?"

Obviously, through her husband, the nephew of the late Sigmund Freud, the gnome had klieg-lit my mind and channeled my hastily conceived plot to swipe the archaic Xerox machine, cop the tables and chair for firewood, and use the manuscript as fire starter.

Curses, foiled again!

Glory Daze

Of the several talents I've been blessed with throughout the years, high among them, in ascending order, were: 3) the ability to flip a coin in the air and catch it behind my back; 2) knowing all the words to the way-back version of "On Top of Old Smokey" -- able to bewail you with all 9 morosely interminable verses of that dirge at the drop of a bar bet, and; 1) a kind of luck I call "to the rescue" luck which has to-the-rescued my sorry-assed butt (double use of rear end metaphor) time and again.

To-the-rescue inspired me to call Ingalls Associates, a top Boston ad agency, early October, 1964; create a sample ad portfolio for Copy Director, Ray Welch; and on October 22nd, start at Ingalls as a cub copywriter at the peak of the storied Creative Revolution in American advertising.

For the next ten years I get to enjoy the 'postcard' version of my soon-to-be forever-after home town, Marblehead -- which is to say, at a glance, on weekends -- because weekdays I'm busily-dizzily commuting to Boston to overstuff my wallet, whilst simultaneously overstuffing my ego.

•

In *From Those Wonderful Folks Who Gave You Pearl Harbor*, Jerry Della Femina, one of the klieg lights on Madison Avenue during the *Mad Men* Creative Revolution party-hearty era of the '60s and early '70s, says, "Advertising is the most fun you can have with your clothes on."

Make that, "*was* the most ... "

But fun it was. Psychedelic fun. Creativity bursts its chains and runs amok. Driven by Flower Power, cannabis is the flower du jour. Far Out is Way In. Iron-jawed MBA 'suits' bow to mischief-minded creative coocoos. Creativity rules. And should you start amassing silver at awards shows, such as New England ad-dom's Oscars equivalent, the Hatch Awards, you are a star. And stars earn much money, and get to take three-hour lunches. Sometimes, more-hour lunches. And the work day is kindergarten, and there are merry bands of off-the-wall playmate coocoos and coocoo-ettes to joke with and brainstorm with and an endless rainbow of Magic Markers to make wacky doodles with. And copywriters start thinking with Magic Markers instead of Smith-Corona typewriters, and supposedly non-verbal art directors start coming up with nail-it headlines. And from this kindergarten comes some childlike advertising`... which is to say, "fresh." And the liquor often flows in the conference room at 5, because new accounts get celebrated, and promotions get celebrated, and people come and go, and it's surprising how many people, just like clockwork, will tend to have a birthday every year. And often the parties continue beyond the conference room and oft off into the Boston night. And some, into the early Boston next morn. Yes, it's the fabled Boutique Era in American advertising. The Creative Revolution. Before focus groups crash the party -- before *numbers* start writing the ads.

Torrential, madcap fun. A regular circus, in fact.

I was in the Boston troupe. My act -- my best trick, if you will -- was negotiating the Ladder of Success astride a pogo stick. And without a net.

Yup, for ten years I b'doyng-b'doyng my carefree way upward the Ladder, sometimes two rungs at a time. Only one-and-a-half times do I miss. But even then, to-the-rescue luck is there to catch me. Next thing I know, I'm back on the Ladder, and, miraculously, in one sense or another -- title and/or money -- I'm a rung *above* the one I'd slipped from or been knocked from.

Ta da!

Ingalls is the best of all possible places to launch my advertising career. My salary, $7500 a year, is a decent sum for 1964. For college graduates in that still-lingering shadow of the Depression era, the goal, the magic number, is FIVE FIGURES! $10,000 ... *maybe* by your late thirties. (*If* you play your cards right, make no waves, spitshine the right apples.)

I'm 29. My boss, the copy chief Ray Welch, is 25. He's making an unheard of 12K; he drives a Porsche (albeit used). He looks like Paul Newman; he shoots a hustler game of pool. He 'won' his tuition when he was at Dartmouth -- playing Five Card Stud. He smokes Camels, which he lights with *one* hand: flipping the matchbook cover open with his index finger, bending a match to the striker -- gaining ignition with a deft flick of thumbnail to matchhead. A stub No. 2 pencil balances in the cleft of his left ear. His shirtsleeves rolled up, Ray never ever wears a tie.

No guy never-ever-wears a tie to the office in 1964. Even the lowly office boy wears a tie to the office in 1964.

Ray Welch is way-cool way before 'cool' is cool.

But if Welch is cool, the agency's creative product is hot. The air's electric -- how different from the muffled halls of publishing. There's evidence of life here: a buzz. The current of human exchange. Laughter, conversation, argument. "*Ee*ehaw!"s of discovery resound the corridors.

Looking back on it now, I realize I couldn't have asked for a better boot camp than Ingalls. The education gained my first two years there provided me 90% of the who-what-how-why I'd need to advance my cause at other ad agencies over the next eight years. My education was both broad-based and intensive. In religious terminology, it would be 'Baptism by Total Immersion.' Actually, more like, 'Baptism by Avalanche.'

Just three writers and three art directors jackhammering away on 36 accounts. If not for the fact that we turned out highly effective -- and, award-winning -- advertising, we produced at such volume the term "sweat shop" might've seemed apt. (There was the week I processed 31 job orders -- 31 copy assignments. My average output was in the high teens. We're talking the likes of billboard and posters, brochures, print ads (headlines and text), radio scripts, TV scripts, slide shows, speeches, promotional ideas, product and corporate name ideas, etc., etc.)

The account list was a Chinese menu. Among the 36 accounts: three banks, furniture store, two shoe manufacturers, a ski resort, state department of tourism/economic development, a vintner, college, motel chain, six tech accounts, a meat packer, real estate developer, two clothing stores, canned goods manufacturer, employment agency, and ... the fortune cookie ... Volkswagen.

Anyone who's seen *Mad Men*, or is even the least hip to advertising lore will cite the Volkswagen campaign created by New York's Doyle Dane Bernbach in the early '60s as *the* breakthrough campaign of the century. Almost overnight that campaign consigned 'boilerplate' and 'formula' advertising to oblivion and lit the torch for the Creative Revolution to follow. By some happy quirk of fate, little old Ingalls in the sticks of Boston was one of the hens'teeth-few agencies other than Doyle Dane empowered to create ads for Volkswagen -- to be specific, for Volkwagen distributors. It only amounts to five or six ads a year for Northeastern region distributor, Hansen McPhee. But hey, it's Volkswagen, pal: any copywriter or art director in the world will sell Momma, Poppa and Fido up the river for a shot at a VW ad in his or her portfolio.

Unsurprisingly enough, neither of the other copywriters nor I get a whiff of crown jewel Volkswagen. Not only is Ray Welch way-cool, Welch is way-no-fool. Only Welch writes Volkswagen.

The thought of *ever* writing a VW ad consumes me, *and*, almost costs me my job. I'm not told that -- not in so many words. But I can feel its hot breath. I'm writing *every* assignment in Volkswagen-speak. It doesn't matter that it's a trade publication ad for Stowe-Woodward's humongous rubber-covered rolls for the paper processing industry. Instead of a headline like "2.3297% Faster!" as the briefing I'd been given would suggest, I show Ray something like "Ugly Is Only Skin Deep" -- as Volkswagen-speak would suggest.

The thing I can't seem to get into my thick mick noggin at the time is that the purchasing agents who read *Paper Processing Weekly* do not buy Volkswagens. They do not buy Volkswagens for the simple reason that they do buy Buicks. And they do not buy Volkswagen advertising for the simple reason that they do buy Buick advertising.

Sex. A Buick ad has sex appeal because it features a satin-gowned blonde possessed of a highly polished cantilevered bosom standing next to a highly polished Buick. And "2.3297% Faster!" is drop-dead sexy to a purchasing agent in the paper trade; while "Ugly Is Only Skin Deep" can only have been the product of a copywriter low on red corpuscles, who is lightweightedly asexual -- at best.

Or ... a copywriter who hasn't figured out that he has to get into the mind of the typical consumer of that product, and promise reward *in language the consumer can damn well RELATE TO!*

You have to be a Method Actor. You have to *be* whoever you're talking to, and speak in his or her voice. You're Mrs.Vandernoggen for diamonds; Joe Six-Pack for beer; Midas Pennywatcher for Certificates of Deposit.

It's the better part of of four months before this home truth finally grabs hold. Time after time I walk into Ray's office and hand him copy. He leans back in his chair, gives it a glance, snaps the No. 2 pencil from his ear, crosses out and scribbles. Hands it back, goes over it with me. Ray is patient. But wearing thin. I can see that. To some degree, he's rewriting everything I produce. I'm getting paid $7500 a year for Ray to write my stuff.

About four months in, a few pieces I produce get by relatively unscathed. Some even get presented to the client by the suits -- and then get shot down. The last time this happens, I'm destroyed. I was sure I finally had a winner this time. "Back to the drawing board," Ray says, as he hands me the reject -- with comments.

He sees my anguish. Resting his hand on my shoulder, and looking me dead-on, he says, "Bob, Bob ... the first thing you gotta learn in this business is to kill your children -- and move on. Kill your own children, Bob. And move on, Bob. C'mon now, give it another go. OK?"

I'll never forget that. Kill my own children: it shocks the hell out of me. But, lesson learned. It introduces me, thunderously, to something I'd had very little experience with in life, or, frankly, any interest in: Reality – with a capital R.

I hear the dread hoofbeats of the posse. It's time to get smart. Survival-smart. Lone Eagle-smart.

Ray buys the next version of the ad -- the No. 2 never leaves his ear. The client buys it, too. With enthusiasm, too. Pretty soon, all clients are buying my stuff. With enthusiasm. I'm getting the feel of every client on the Chinese menu: how to speak the language of each, the unique voice of each individual client.

What's more, I'm learning to adapt to each of the formats: print ads, flyers and brochures, radio, TV, promotional items, posters and billboards. Each form has its own psych, and stylistic parameters. At other agencies, a cub copywriter such as I would spend his first year specializing, working on just one or two accounts, and in one format. If, for instance, I started out at Batten, Barton, Durstine & Osborne (which comic Fred Allen said sounded like a trunk bouncing down a flight of stairs), my job description would've been such as: Bank of Boston/ brochures; Warren Paper/direct mail; Gillette/TV.

By the end of my first year at Ingalls, my job description reads: all accounts (except Volkswagen)/all formats. I'm working the room. Up, down, all around. Wow.

Unrequited Puppy Love

Soon after an honorable mention in New England advertising's Oscars, the Hatch Awards, I get a call from Jay Hill at Bresnick, one of Boston's biggest ad agencies at the time. Jay was quitting Bresnick to assume a comparable post at another top agency, BBDO. (About a year later, Jay and three other adventurers will form their own agency. Said agency, Hill, Holliday, Connors, Cosmopulos soon became one of the dominant agencies on the regional and national scene, and, as Hill Holliday, remains so to this day.)

Jay Hill said he'd seen some of my work and was recommending me for his job as Copy Group Supervisor, and the salary is $15,000.

Make that, an *enormous* $15,000! Just months ago I'd leapfrogged from $7500 to the magic-number $10,000 -- and here I have a shot at making *half-again as much*! In the blink of an eye, maybe. Talk about 'funny money,' huh? What the hell, take the interview. Nothing to lose, right?

The interview with Ray Clarke, Bresnick's Creative Director, goes well. In fact, Ray offers me the job. On the spot. So do I take the job?

Then? There? On the spot?

I do *not*. In fact, I go back to Ingalls and tell the owners, Joe Maynard and Joe Hoffman, about the offer of 15 -- and before they have a chance to respond, I blurt out that I love it here at Ingalls, and if they'll just raise me from 10 to *12*, I'd prefer to stay, I'll gladly stay!

Loyalty is one of my tragic flaws. In my next life, I'll probably come back as a puppy.

The double-Joes say they're sorry -- but no.

So off I bop to Bresnick, where in the course of the next year, I luck into a major ad campaign coup, my first silver bowl and another boost in salary.

Upstart Gigs Startup

One of Bresnick's biggest accounts was State Street Bank. State Street had been chosen to be the first bank east of the Mississippi to introduce this new-fangled contraption called a 'credit card': Bank of America's BankAmericard.

The BankAmericard project is mammoth. Only first team on this one. The Bresnick vets. All the secrecy of the atomic bomb's Manhattan Project. BankAmericard is to Ray Clarke at Bresnick as Volkswagen was to Ray Welch at Ingalls -- No Others Need Apply. Especially, it seems, B Baker, Boy New Kid.

Several campaigns were presented to Fred Davis, State Street's Marketing Director, who was a savvy guy from Marblehead I'd met and chatted with a *total* of maybe fifteen minutes on three different occasions.

Fred Davis didn't like any of the several campaign presentations shown him by the Bresnick A team. He disliked the followups even more.

The deadline to launch the big-budget BankAmericard campaign is fast approaching. I get called to Oscar Bresnick's office one day, and the diminutive, quite-Napoleonic Oscar informs me in less than Little Mary Sunshine fashion that client Fred Davis wants to meet with me *off* agency premises tomorrow for the purpose of creating the Bank Americard campaign.

An important client and a mid-level creative sitting down together to create a mega-dollar campaign introducing the first credit card to New England! Every rule in the *Agency Hierarchy & Agency/Client Relationship* manual -- out the window.

Fred Davis reserved a room for the day at the Preston Beach Motor Inn in Swampscott, just over the border from Marblehead. We talked and scribbled from 8 to 1, took an-hour-two-Bloody Marys-and-a-steak sandwich break for lunch in the dining room, and called it a day -- and a campaign -- at 4:30.

I asked Fred later what made him take this radical step. After all, we may have swapped a few quips, but he knew little about my work. What made him think I could deliver? "I like to break rules," he said. "I could tell right away you do too. This campaign called for rules to be broken."

The BankAmericard launch -- Shopping Card -- was a success. My reception back at the agency was ... mixed emotions. On the one hand, jealous anger. Why had *I* been singled out to conspire with the *client* to produce in 7 hours and two drinks, the campaign that saved the day -- *and*, the agency's ass. On the other hand, there's awe; begrudged awe, but awe nonetheless. I *had* been singled out; Fred and I *had* saved the day -- and, the agency's ass.

Heartfelt

The State Mutual Insurance Company ad for disability income insurance which won me my first first-place bowl at the Hatch Awards came easy -- in a mixed-up manner of speaking.

It came easy, because it came from the heart. It came hard, because it came from the heart -- by way of my Dad: something he said when he was partially paralyzed and confined to bed and I was helping take care of him after I'd been discharged from the Navy.

As I sat in the chair across from his bed in our apartment one day, he rolled his eyes upward and heaved a deep deep sigh. "I have nothing to do all day but stare at the ceiling," he said.

Consuming 80% of the ad for disability income insurance is a black-and-white photo of the drab-gray ceiling of an ill-lit room. The format established for the campaign dictated a two-part (1. - 2.)

headline formula. My headline:

1. Stare at this ceiling.

2. Now figure out how you'd support your family doing this for a year.

The Puppy, He's Baaack!

The first place in Hatch wins me another 3 grand a year in salary at Bresnick ... and not long after, a phone call from the two Joes at Ingalls: they want me back, as Copy Director. Ray Welch is stepping down, to go out on his own, to take a shot at 'freelance.' (In those days, a creative person 'went freelance.' He did not 'become an entrepreneur.' 'Creative person' and 'business' *never* to be found in the same sentence.) I told the Joes I'd like to return to Ingalls. But my salary's jumped from 15 to 18, and it'll take a nice round 20 to make it happen. Couple days later they call to say 20 will be fine. Only fourteen months' previous I told Joe and Joe I'd much-much prefer to stay at Ingalls if they'd just pay me 12!

The movie wouldn't be titled *Revenge of the Puppy* -- there was nothing to be avenged. On the other hand, *The Puppy Wakes Up* would work.

Values

I'd been Copy Director at Ingalls about a year when I got a call from a guy I knew at Kenyon & Eckhardt, asking if I'd be interested in talking with them about becoming Creative Director of their Boston office. K&E was a national/international agency. The Boston branch, one of the five biggest agencies in New England in its own right, handled some sizable accounts, including the largest single account in New England at the time, Underwood Deviled Ham and the B&M beans and associated products line.

Speaking of large, the Creative Director salary is $30,000. (Equivalent to about $200,000 nowadays, according to a recent *New York Times* piece.) I take the interview. And with the roll I'm on at the time -- Vegas refused to book it -- I'm offered the job. *But*, I'm told, I must first obtain the blessing of Chairman of the Board of

K&E International, Stanley Tannenbaum. Stanley is to be found at the top of the Pan Am Building which is in Manhattan which is in the City of New York, which is a place I not long ago chose to escape because it was turning me into a me I didn't like.

Tannenbaum and I are seated at the end of an enormous conference table in the cavernous conference room. Stanley has expressed a liking of my ad portfolio, and he leans forward: "Bob, let me ask you. If you work out well in Boston ... maybe we'll bring you down to New York in a few years?" As swollen of head, besotted with numbers and dizzied with notoriety as I was at the time, my response was back to basics. I couldn't believe I was saying it, but this is exactly what I did say: "Can't happen, Stan."

Tannenbaum is stunned. And though "Who is this punk?" prints out on his forehead, he calmly asks, "How come?"

I hadn't rehearsed it, because there was no way I could've anticipated Tannenbaum's proposal. It just came out: "In the first place, Stanley, because ... I left New York because I didn't like New York. For me. It wasn't right for me. But the real reason is ... here are my priorities in life, Stanley. First comes my family. That's Number One. Then comes *where* I live ... Marblehead, which is where I want to live forever. Then, and *only* then, comes my career."

He squints. A knowing grin slides his mouth. He says, "C'mon now, Bob, I'm talking serious money here. Let me blue-sky you. We're talking maybe ... 75 thousand here."

I know this sounds all too Jimmy Stewart to be true, but this is verbatim-honest-to-God what I really did say: "Uh uh. Stanley, you can buy my talent; you cannot buy me. You cannot *invent* the number to get me to New York. It just does not *exist*, Stanley. The number honestly does not exist."

Amazingly, despite that abrupt rebuff, I got Tannenbaum's approval, and the job. They must've figured they could convert me. Wrong-o.

Show Biz

Just to give you an idea of what a hyper-bizarre happy-go-kindergarten Silly Season the late-'60s Creative Revolution era in advertising was, when I left as Copy Director at Ingalls to become Creative Director at Kenyon & Eckhardt, K&E ran a full-page ad in a September, 1969, issue of *Boston Magazine* and *New England Advertising Week* announcing my move, with my picture and headlined, "We've Just Hired an Award-Winning Baker."

Not to be out-kindergartened, Ingalls ran a full-page ad in *Ad East*, with a photo of the upper torso of a guy in a suit and tie -- with head airbrushed out, and a headline reading, "We Just Lost Our Award-Winning Copy Head." The text went on to say that despite my move, Ingalls would somehow not only survive, it would prosper -- as truly and well it did.

Them was show biz days, and fun in their upbeat outrageous ways, while they lasted.

A Moving Experience

Downstairs at Rosalies's was the where-to-be-seen scene for Marblehead's Beautiful Singles in the early '80s. It's Saturday night and I'm standing near the bar in conversation with Victoria who is beautiful.

So what is *this*? A tassel loafer-shod foot sidles itself ever so slightly in front of my cordovan-shod right foot. The tassel loafer belongs to the guy who even in kindest terms is to be described as an Arrogant Punk.

The AP has not only angled his foot in front of mine, he is now leaning his wonderful head into conversation with Victoria. Said head and upper torso have now all but eliminated me from Victoria's view -- poor thing.

AP's conversation-hijacking head is bobbing up and down and he's pitching his woo to Victoria at 100 miles an hour which *s-o-m-e-h-o-w* inspires the tip of my cordovan to rise and come gently to rest upon the tip of his tassel loafer.

AP angles his wonderful face at me. "Do you reaize you're standing on my *foot*, Baker?"

"Well if that's the case, then why don't you maybe think about moving your foot?"

He tassel-slithered away.

Independence Day

The Wilson, Haight & Welch ad agency was a study in extremes. The doddering case- hardened account executives, most of them transported by gurney, as I envisioned it, from the long-ago lofty Bresnick agency, in clash with the award-winning live wire whiz kids creative team I was brought in to assemble -- hopefully to staunch the exodus of clients which had been taking place over the past year-and-a-half.

Wilder Baker, who headed up the agency, was a savvy marketing guy, but not an alchemist. There was no way he was going to effect a productive marriage between the account executive and creative teams. The exodus continued.

It finally reached a point that one of the accounts of interest was a pleasure palace/night spot which could have only been more kitschily imagined by Liberace.

In order to protect the innocent I'll disguise the name of the pleasure dome and the client. We'll call it The Fontainebleau, and the client, Silvio Fonzelli -- both names are in the ballpark.

Having been a creative practitioner all these years, I'd never made any new business presentations, but for some reason Wilder wanted me to accompany him on the initial pitch. Maybe he figured a couple of Brooks Brothers slickers would wow the hell out of old Silvio.

So we show up at The Fontainebleau and make our way to Silvio's office, which when Wilder knocks on a door large and imposing enough to have come from the Vatican, triggers a muffled shout from inside to come in.

So we do.

Inside reminds me of J.P. Morgan's library from the Morgan Library in New York. High-ceilinged, vast, dark-paneled, somber -- in direct contrast to the rhinestone fury of the rest of the Fontainebleau.

Silvio does not bother to rise from behind the enormous some-expensive-kind-of-wood desk to greet us. He's a guy with a face like Danny de Vito, who if he did rise, would probably be in a degree of tallness in the NQM (i.e. Not Quite Much) range.

We take our seats in the chairs across the desk from Silvio. Wilder grabs his attache case, sets it on his lap, pops it open, withdraws a manilla folder, leans forward: "Mr. Fonzelli ... Silvio, if I may. I'm Wilder Baker and this is Bob B ... "

"You know what you *mayyyyyy*! You *mayyyyyy* keep callin me *Mistah* Fonzelli. Cuz dat's who I am to da two a youse. Mistah Fonzelli. OK, boys? Ya got that, fellas? OK?"

(A word about Mr. Fonzelli's diction as presented here. I promise it's not an attempt at parody, or caricature. It's the way the man spoke, and was perhaps exaggerated by a clogged sinus, which made his enunciation even more swallowed and leaden.)

"Da firs ting yuz gotta know boud me is you don wanna fuck wit me. What I say goes, ya see. I mean it goes my way, ya see.

"Give ya n'example a what I mean. We wuz a couple days away from open'n dis place. Da gran open'n's nex week. It's a fuckin Friday an the fuckin sidewalk out front ain't there yet. There's no fuckin sidewalk, ya see what I fuckin mean? That ain't no fuckin good, right? Right fellas?"

Wilder and I give Silvio ... er, Mister Fonzelli, simpering smiles, and in unison, we say "Right."

"So I go to da guy who's in charge a da udion, and I tells him ya gotta put that fuckin sidewalk in over da fuckin weeken, and he has the fuckin balls to say ta me, 'Mistah Fonzelli, we're udion workers. It's udion rules. We don' work weekens.' "

"I looks ad the fuckin udion guy an I sez, 'I god some fuckin news for ya, fella. If that fuckin sidewalk ain't in by Monday, youse personally are gonna fuckin be in it ... ya fuckin get what I fuckin mean?'

"An guess what, fellas? Guess fuckin what?"

Without questioning the logic of how the union supervisor was going to be embedded Jimmy Hoffa style in a sidewalk which hadn't been built, Wilder yes-manned for both of us this time: "The sidewalk was in on Monday."

"Youse fellas are priddy smart. I tink I like youse guys. So long as youse fuckin know what I fuckin mean, ya fuckin know what I fuckin mean?"

Wilder and I both nodded. Wilder said, "Sure do."

"Dat's 'Sure do, Mistah Fonzelli', right?"

"That's right, Mr. Fonzelli," we bleated in unison.

My head was starting to spin. I couldn't wait to get out of there. The guy was scary.

The upshot of the meeting was that Wilder told Fonzelli we'd put together a budget recommendation and a media plan and work up some ad concepts to show him, and get back to him.

On the way back to the agency, I asked Wilder how the hell he could get any further involved with this head case. He said, "Hartford (the agency's headquarters office) wants us to chase every bit of new business we can. We're on shaky ground with a couple of our big clients ... I can't go into it with you. The bottom line is, this isn't a showcase account, but it could help keep us alive."

That was it. The Irish in me surged. A fury rages within me ... at what I'd become. e.e. cummings' line, "there is some shit i will not eat" nails it. *No mas.* Out, time to bust out ... of this corporate so-called culture where I have to swallow my pride and my values in pursuit of the almighty dollar, *and* ... question mark, question mark ... *security*??

I drafted a three-page letter to the powers-that-be in Hartford. In the letter I reviewed the track record of the Boston office: the loss of business, Wilder's allusion to other imminent losses, the humiliation of prospecting accounts like the Fontainebleau. I said the best thing to do would be for the agency to gradually retrench, take what accounts it could and handle them from the Hartford office. Eventually close the Boston office, giving everybody good severance pay. My main concern was for my creative team. If they got out early, with good severance, it would buy them time to relocate. (I already had three months' severance assured me, per a letter of agreement.)

The powers-that-be in Hartford didn't take kindly to my letter. They kindly took and fired me.

A year-and-change later, they closed the Boston office.

July 4th, 1776 was Independence Day for the United States of America. July 27th, 1974 was Independence Day for the united state of me.

My Move ...

At the end of that summer of '74 I'd arrived at another crossroads. I was living on the three months' severance from my job as Creative Director of a major Boston ad agency, and I needed to figure out 'What next?'

Two factors were givens, the third was the big question. The givens related to the title of Creative Director: 1) Relative to the 'Creative' aspect, I was a top-flight, award-winning creative talent; 2) Relative to the 'Director' aspect, I was a for-shit administrator who despised meetings, memo-writing and firing people.

The question was an either/or: Should I return to the ad agency corporate box scene as the hotshot creative (no 'director' thanks) I'd made a healthy-wealthy living at the past ten years? Or, should I take the risk of all risks, and go out on my own as my own boss, offering my hotshot creative services to a hardly-waiting-with-bated-breath world at large?

The either/or decision would have to wait. Short term, I needed to grab some freelance creative projects to support my wife and chillun. Phone calls were made *muy pronto*. I'm in luck, three appointments next week; one at Ingalls, the birthplace of my advertising career. The fellow I'll be seeing, the new Creative Director there, needs no introduction.

David Herzbrun had been a top creative honcho at Doyle Dane Bernbach, the New York agency which singlehandedly launched the Creative Revolution in American advertising in the 1960s with its breakthrough minimalist campaigns for Volkswagen -- beginning in the late 1950s (the likes of "Think Small" and then "Lemon," the VW ad sparking vigorous argument between Don and Roger in episode 3 of the first season of *Mad Men*).

And of all the memorable commercials for Volkswagen in that era, David Herzbrun's 'Snowplow' is arguably the standout. I'll let David tell you about 'Snowplow' -- in this excerpt from his memoir, *Playing in Traffic on Madison Avenue -- Tales of Advertising's Glory Years*, published in 1990:

In the early spring of 1963 we finally got approval to shoot the one commercial we most wanted produced. It was a spot that answered the question: "Did you ever wonder how the man who drives the snowplow gets to the snowplow?"

We hired Leon Clore's Film Contracts to shoot the commercial. They set about finding some place in Europe where there was still snow. They finally located an area of high meadows near St. Cergue, straight up from Geneva. At St. Cergue, we finally achieved the effect of the overhead shots of the car steadily making its way over snow-covered roads on its way to the snowplow.

'Snowplow' took top honors at the Cannes Film Festival, the American Film Festival, and the Museum of Modern Art in New York selected it to be the first TV commercial to be included in its permanent film collection.

, ,

Dukakis for Governor

David Herzbrun had been wooed to Boston by Ingalls president Joe Hoffman, a man who could sell snake oil to a snake oil salesman. David had only recently come aboard when I interviewed with him. He said he really liked my portfolio, had nothing to offer at the moment, but would definitely keep me in mind. He even sounded like he meant it.

Days' later, Dave did call. He said the agency had just taken on the Dukakis for Governor campaign, and he'd pay me $5000 just to come in and freelance the creative on it -- Election Day was November 5th, about six weeks away.

A no-brainer. Absolutely. Make a few bucks, buy myself more What Next?-time, work with good people.

I teamed up with talented art director Paul Regan, and we burn-baby-burned. In the course of a month we turned out four TV spots, two full-page ads ("It's Time" and "We Need a Governor"), half-dozen long copy flyers handed out at MBTA subway stations ("What Mike Dukakis Can Do to Make a Long, Hard Day a Little Bit Easier for

You") and three radio commercials.

As always, stories along the way:

Missed Point

Somewhere in the course of the campaign, it came out that Frank Sargent's wife Jessie might've made an inappropriate contribution to Sargent's war chest. Something minor. Nothing illegal. Just enough to earn small mention in the Boston papers.

That night, we're at Channel 2, taping a commercial. On a break between takes, standing there with Dukakis ... it hit me. "Mike," I said, "you could have some fun with this with the press. Give them a Gee whiz, golly shuckins look, scratch your head, and say, 'Y'know, it just occurs to me: Can you think of another famous pair in American history named ... Frank ... and ... *Jesse?*' "

Dukakis looked at me as if I'd just farted.

●

The month sped by. Suddenly, it's Thursday, October 31st, and I'm typing the signoff to "Tomorrow Is a New Day," the last ad, the full-page ad signed by Dukakis which will run the day before the election next Tuesday, November 5th.

Dukakis won.

David Herzbrun generously overstated the case in his memoir, "I hired a wonderful writer named Bob Baker, left him pretty much alone, and got unearned credit for a winning campaign."

Dukakis won, I won.

"It's Time," as one of my Dukakis headlines said. Time to stop flipping coins, Bob. Time to bust free of The Box. Bite the bullet, go into business on your own; get a life -- *have* a life.

Time, at long last, to *play* The Game.

Rookie Jitters

"Lifestyle entrepreneurship means creating a business around the kind of lifestyle you want." -- *Lifestyle Business Magazine* (2017)

I'd made the gutsy decision to go out on my own a couple weeks before Election Day.

Talk about questionable decisions! 1974's a recession year. Wife and two kids -- all of $2000 in the bank. Nobody, but *nobody*, in *any* profession, even *thought* about venturing beyond the protective security of the corporate womb in those years. And setting up shop in a *suburb*? A creative *coocoo* who knows *nothing-nil-nada* about running a business! Out of the *mainstream*? All by your single, solitary self? "You gotta be *crazy*, Baker, crazy." That was the kindest word all but the uninformed few used, crazy.

No computer, no fax, no email, no Internet, no web site -- they don't exist. No "How to Cut the Mustard on Your Own" guides. Other 'lifestyle entrepreneurs' to network with? Network? *Lifestyle entrepreneurs*? *Huh*!?

Nevertheless ... I paid ten bucks, filled out a dba (doing business as) form at the town hall in Marblehead November 4th, 1974. To make a statement, to make it official. To the world; but also to myself. Sort of a contract with myself, a promise to myself ... a *gamble* to myself.

Next to "Name" on the form, I wrote "Baker Advertising." I'd thought of other -- more 'creative' names. "All Creation" was one. David Herzbrun steered me clear of that approach. "Don't get cute," he said. "You're a name in Boston. Use your good name."

Location, Location, Location

One thing for sure, I couldn't work at home. Our house is 'tight quarters.' Need place where I can meet in privacy with clients or vendors. Another major consideration: wife and kids' routines.

Talk about luck. It was as if the script had been written at breakfast Saturday morning and it's flickering away on the silver screen just hours later -- because from what-if to done-deal, that's about how it happened.

The handwriting on the surface of my morning coffee said: "Waterfront, down by the landing at the harbor. Start there."

I drove down to the town landing about 9:00. Only minutes' later, a fait accompli ...

2nd floor Graves Yacht Yard building, $100 a month.

Prime location: at the heart and soul of Marblehead -- the harbor. Close to home, 25 steps to The Landing Pub, about 125 steps to

Maddie's, home of great chow and thunderous drinks.

I signed a lease. It was all of 9:30. Talk about wow.

•

Baker Advertising officially opened its 'door' on Wednesday, November 6th, the day after the election. Inasmuch as the winner of the election was the *un*-riproaring Michael Dukakis, the celebration in the ballroom of the Sheraton Cambridge the night before had been significantly *un*-riproaring. Had a couple drinks, home around midnight -- fired up to get to my office in the morning.

The furnishings were few and functional. My conference table was home grown: a circular six-foot-diameter wooden spool rim resting on a large wooden packing case. Around the table, five sturdy straight chairs, courtesy the Ellis's attic. My executive chair: an old oak rocker in the Stickley mode purchased from Sachs Antiques, across the street from Graves. It needed a seat cover, which wife Nancy made happen with a bolt of fabric. The chair cost $12: I love it. The monumental metal file cabinet was excavated from the basement of Ray Ellis's law firm in Boston.

The walls were 'wall-to-wall' with favorites -- pushpinned ads, photos, sayings, posters (W.C. Fields, Humphrey Bogart), framed awards, medals dangling from ribbons, cartoons, souvenirs, curiosities.

I told everyone the office was my Our Gang Clubhouse. I absolutely loved the place.

There was one piece of furniture missing, though. Not a necessity, but still ...

What Price?

In the beginning, I had no money and all kinds of time. Time to sit glued to the phone waiting for an answer to dozens of prospecting calls I'd placed. Hadn't gotten one of those newfangled phone answering machines yet ... damn well should.

Meantime, can't afford time away from the office. Better stay glued to the phone. For sure, the instant I hit the john down the hall to comb my furrowed eyebrows will be the very instant the phone chirps, and the guy at Polaroid I've been hard-wooing will let it ring 967 times. Then, at #967, relent, pass the crash project which would have reduced our mortgage by three years onto some lesser -- but alas, reachable -- talent.

More than once, I'd return from the john, hear the phone promising away, race the hall, bust through the doorway on the 967th and -- but of course -- last ... ring.

A week of this imprisonment is too much. Once again I take my cue from Dad: "Every now and then you've gotta get out and blow the stink off." And its corollary, "Bob, when you're flat broke, that's the time to go out and buy yourself a new suit."

In this case, the new suit would be a new couch -- sort of. And "out" would be four miles to the Morgan Memorial used furniture store in Salem.

Allowing myself no more than an hour, I rocket to Morgie. Right there in the center aisle ... *Voila!* My prize: a dark brown obscenely Naugahyde, seven-foot obscenely Naugahyde couch.

Did I mention it's Naugahyde?

Ugly, but functional. Made a bip less ugly, and all the more functional by the attractive $20 price. What the hell, ugly is only Naugahyde deep, and it'll do the job. I pay the Morgie lady, tell her I'll come back to get it.

Zip back to our house, swap my car for Nancy's Squareback, NASCAR-return to Morgie. Morgie lady points: "That's your couch ... and there's another just like it. Lady in Swampscott bought it just after you. Thing is, she needs it delivered ... willing to pay $10 just to have it delivered ... nice lady."

The Joker comes to life. Yo! Swampscott's minutes away, the couch is a feather. Drop it off, back at the office in no time. Have that ten spot as first earned income. Frame the sucker, show it to the grandkids. What a hoot! First money old Baker Advertising International captured ... *dee*livering a couch. What a hoot.

I get directions, lower back seat of Squareback, open hatch, slide couches in -- perfect fit. Off to nice Swampscott lady's. Takes a while to find nice Swampscott lady's, though. Precious minutes away from phone. Never mind, this is a symbolic mission. First dollars for Baker

Advertising -- made all the better for the *hi*-larious circumstance.

That's the house. Great. Climb the worn steps, ring the worn bell. Time goes by.

tick tick tick

Precious ticks tick away. Finally, nice little old round lady opens el door-o. "Hi, Mrs. Nicelittleoldroundlady, I've brought you your couch from Morgan Memorial."

She looks surprised at first. Here's this shapeless, sweating man, his shiny Upwardly Mobile automobile in the driveway stuffed with couches.

Her expression settles as the gears of logic engage: "Isn't he the enterprising young man, though. Nicely dressed, and a nice car for his delivery service. He'll go far, he will," reads her expression.

"You can bring it right through this door, it's going in this room," she says.

I *careen* the steps, grab the damn Naugie from the car, bip back up, through the doorway, ask Mrs. N where Naugie goes. "Oh, eventually it'll go right there ... where that couch is. But first you have to take that couch out and set it in the back yard. They told you about that at Morgan Memorial ... didn't they?"

Let me tell you about "that" couch. It wasn't a couch at all. It was a mammoth boulder carved in the shape of a couch, around which the house had been built. It was the Rock of Gibraltar with a sorta-gray-brown cover.

"No, Ma'am, they said nothing about moving that couch. I thought I was just delivering this one," I gulped. "There is no way I could move that couch ... even an inch, Ma'am. I'm sorry, Ma'am."

"Well, you see my husband is recovering from an entire body transplant (or something equally extreme) and he's upstairs and I wanted him able to be downstairs here where it's comfy and he could look at the TV and ... " Tears came to Mrs. Nicelittleoldroundlady's eyes, and I felt bad for her.

"I understand," I said, "I really do. It's just that it's physically impossible for me to move that couch. I really am sorry." Here I am, a tangle of emotions. Pity for the poor woman's plight, pity for her husband. Panic for the time I've been absent from the probably-ringing-its-receiver-off 'Horn of Plenty' back at the office. Wounded pride, because she's failed to realize she's dealing with the One and Only Presidente-Supremo of the soon-to-be-worldwide cartel, Baker Advertising.

I shrugged, turned to leave.

Mrs. Nicelitttleoldroundlady taps me on the shoulder, reaches to hand me a dollar bill: "For your trouble ... thank you."

"Thank you, Ma'am, hope it all works out for you," I said, declining her offering.

My race back to the office was fueled by more mixed emotions. Maybe I should've taken the dollar; I'd have something to frame, something to show for it at least.

My mission did produce a form of reward. The phone was *not* ringing as I started down the hallway to my office.

Mass Impolitics

In commerce, as in politics, you've gotta "work the room." With the acquisition of an answering machine, I started calling marketing directors of clients I'd worked for, seeking project assignments. I also sought out written endorsements from as many upper-echelon previous clients as possible, to include in presentations of my creative portfolio as evidence of 'satisfied customers.'

The most recent upper-echelon client who, on several occasions, had praised my work was -- drum roll, please -- no less than the brand spandy new darn-well Governor of the whole darn-well State/ Commonwealth of Massachusetts, one darn-well *Michael* darn-well *Dukakis*, that's darn-well who!

No phone call here. Letter, typed on fresh-from-the-print shop Baker Advertising letterhead. Essence of the message, "Congrats, Michael, on your well deserved victory ... oh, and by the way, as you can see by my stationery here, I too am setting forth on an epic new venture ... so we're both setting forth on epic new ventures ... we're both new kids who need all the help we can get ... and another 'by the way': remember how you said some nice things about my work to me in person; could you maybe say things about my work to me in a ... like ... *letter*? ... it could be very helpful."

I sent the letter to him at the State House. A week later arrives in the mail an envelope from the Office of the Governor. Oh-boy, oh-boy.

Nice stationery, with the seal and all -- but a *form* letter. The same letter Joe Derf who contributed $1.98 got: "Kitty and I wish to thank the shit out of you for your help ... "

Hey, that's OK. Honest mistake. The man is obviously swamped.

Better idea. Do another letter, with much the same message. *But,* enclose a copy of the letter of praise Michael Harrington *voluntarily* sent me after his successful run for Congress in the late '60s -- and subtly *suggest*: "This is more like what I'd hoped to get from you. And if you'd care to appropriate, or even exceed, some of Harrington's superlatives, that'd be just mighty OK by me" -- *and* send this letter to Dukakis at his *home* on Perry Street in Brookline. The same home where we'd shot a commercial with him and his nice wife Kitty and son John. The same home where Dukakis made several favorable comments about my work.

So a week later, another envelope from the Office of the Governor. Oh boy, this is it ...

Nope. "Kitty and I wish to thank the shit out of you for your help ... "

Dollars-and-Yankee- Sense

It was getting to be nervous time around Baker Advertising. I'd started early November; weeks had passed; Thanksgiving came and went. Christmas fast approaching; no business coming in; our checking account heading south.

The Man Upstairs came to my rescue. Not the guy in the office above mine. The capital-G MU had Don Blodgett call me. Though Don was a Yankee Brahmin blueblood, he lacked the flinty iceblood manner of the breed. There's a warmth and gentleness about him.

Don had recently purchased the chain of Eaton the Druggist drug stores and wanted to talk about a new look for their newspaper ads. He came by the office and I showed him my work. In the course of conversation, I asked if he'd heard the locals' longstanding joke about Eaton the Druggist. He hadn't. So I told him: A guy calls the store -- when the man at the store answers, the guy asks, "Are you Eaton the Druggist?," the man at the store says, "Nope, just ballin' the counter girl." Don looked embarrassed -- I kicked myself for being a wise guy. Don made nothing of it ... he asked me what I'd charge for the project.

My first business challenge. I had no experience in What to charge?. Whenever I'd done freelance work, the amount was specified by the client up front, for me to accept or negotiate. This was the first time I'd been asked to come up with the price.

I'm Alice in Wonderland. What to charge? Want to do it right. We need the money. Can't be greedy, but not give it away. But he's a Yankee. A Yankee and his money are never soon, or easily, parted.

A guess -- in this case, an *un*educated guess: "$1200, Don," I said. "I think $1200 would be about right." His face contorted as if he were trying to swallow a cannonball wrapped in barbed wire. "Well, let me think about that, Bob," he said.

An old-time Yankee thinking about money is never a good thing. A week goes by; haven't heard -- probably never. Christmas just 10 days away. Gotta do something. I call. "Don, here's a thought. How about you pay me $600 cash and give me a *credit* for $600 in items from your stores, at their *retail* price? Barter. That way you're only out of pocket whatever you pay wholesale for the items -- it's a giant discount." Don says, "Sounds like a good way to do it."

That Christmas, a number of adult presents came from Eaton the Druggist: two Polaroid cameras, bottles of perfume, stationery, fine soaps, chocolates. We used a chunk of the cash on Richard and Kate's presents.

It wasn't exactly a moonshot, but Baker Advertising had attained liftoff. Best of all, it had been attained by a *creative cuckoo* coming up with, of all things, a *business* idea ... barter!

Wonders will never cease. Yay, wow, yay.

•••

·

4

Ideas

Thunder is mighty, thunder is impressive;
but it is lightning that does the work.

Mark Twain

· · ·

•

An Idea Was Bugging Him

I drove my fiancee Joan Weatherley to Cambridge for the Radcliffe Publishing Procedures course mid-July. On the way, we stayed on Cape Cod with her grandfather and his wife. Forris W. Norris was the sly old bird's name.

Forris Norris took us to lunch at Oyster Harbors, a posh club at Osterville on Nantucket Sound. From the instant we crossed the threshhold and throughout lunch the help and members alike went out of their way to fawn over Forris. When I asked about the fuss, he allowed, "Oh, I founded this place. I'm the one who opened Cape Cod to real estate development in the late twenties, actually."

That's a tall claim: "You *opened the Cape to real estate development*? How'd you do that, Forris?"

"Simple as mosquito control. When I first came here from Nova Scotia in 1920, I got into real estate. Moving property then was like pulling teeth. Prettiest spot on God's earth -- but nobody wanted to be here. Especially in summer. Damn mosquitos. Whole Cape was riddled with 'em. Tidal marshes and bogs bred 'em like crazy. When I headed up the Cape Real Estate Board in 1926, first thing I do is introduce mosquito control. Opened the whole Cape to development! Made a killing. Later, in Florida -- same thing. Nobody knows me for that, except here at Oyster Harbors; but I don't care. Got the money to show for it."

Herman the Gem

Herman Gollob was the bright-star hotshot editor at Little, Brown in 1963. When I came aboard he was in the process of chainsawing/ scalpeling James Clavell's 3-kajillion word manuscript of *King Rat*. Herman was *enslaved* by the manuscript. He needed a break, relief; a little comic relief, which I was able to provide in some small fashion. Many and long and wet and filled with cackles of laughter the lunches Herman and I had at faux-marbled-and-columned 10 Beacon, just down the hill from Little, Brown.

Herman had stories: The time he went to see the actor Anthony Quinn about a script and wound up sparring with him -- literally. Quinn was into boxing.

The time he went to the hospital to visit one of his authors, genius-storyteller and fellow Texan, Donald Barthelme. Barthelme had had a growth removed from his upper lip. In his Texas twang, Herman recalled, "I go in the room. There's old Don sittin' up in the bed, his lip all sewn up. I look at Don -- and I cannot resist: 'Don,' I said, 'I gotta tell you. You're the first person I ever knew who went to the hospital to *get* his-self a harelip!' Killed him to keep from poppin' those stitches."

Herm and I schemed schemes galore over lunch, and there was one we actually pursued.

Boys, boys!

My idea: a university press specializing in publishing first fiction, instead of typical university press fare -- *Manipulative Instincts of the Female Slug; Contrivances of Counter-Iambic Pentameter in Hanscom's Poetry* and the like.

What more natural function for a university press than publishing first fiction? A university now also serving as a launching pad for writing talent -- attracting a 'writing' faculty and 'writing' students -- thus becoming known as a 'writers' school.

Herman liked it: "But where would you go with it?" I thought the ideal would be a small-to-mid-sized college, with an excellent academic reputation. "Like Middlebury, in Vermont, they already have the Bread Loaf writers' program in the summer. Or, in this area, Brandeis."

"Actually, I know someone who has an in with the prez of Brandeis, Abram Sachar," Herman said. "I'll see if he can get us in to see old Honest Abe."

Couple weeks later, we walk into Abram Sachar's office, our

carefully prepared proposal in hand. The word for Abe Sachar is ... skeptical. The expression on his face when he greeted us was probably the same he wore even when he fluffed the mildly aromatic shaving cream on his face every morning. It said, "Something don't smell too good." His handshake was tentative, and quickly withdrawn. "*Sooo* ... what's your idea, bo*yyys*?" he asked, hardly had we sat.

Not two minutes into our presentation ... this look of chopped liver consumes Honest Abe's face ... he leans foward in his chair, shakes his head side to side: "Boys, *boys*! You just cannot do that, *boys* ! It won't *work*, boys! It just won't work. OK, boys? Huh? You see what I mean, *boys*? Huh?"

That was it. He didn't say *why* it wouldn't work. He didn't say, "Thanks for coming in." He gave us each a limp hand across the desk and "Bye, boys," accompanied by a flaccid wave as we turned to leave -- headed for the turnip truck he obviously assumed we'd arrived by.

Nowadays, two guys *leaping* forth from the admin building intermingling "Boys! *Boys*!" with maniacal cackles would summon SWAT teams.

•

Herman was also teaching a course Wednesday nights at Cambridge Center for Adult Education, just around the corner from my apartment. Since it didn't start till 8, I suggested he come by 8 Story after work and have a scotch and a nibble before class each week. He liked the idea and came by the cave Wednesday nights and we laughed it up till he'd meander over to the Adult Education Center on Brattle at 7:55.

At Little, Brown one day, Herman said he had big news, and a good idea. The news: he was heading off to become Editor-in-Chief at Athenaeum, a top-flight publishing house in New York. The idea: he'd recommended me to teach Writing & Publishing next semester.

One definition of 'mixed emotions' in those days was, "Watching your mother-in-law drive off a cliff in your brand new Cadillac." My emotions weren't equally mixed. It was 90% downer. I was losing a best buddy to the city I'd rejected, the city I'd fled. It was comparable to losing Jayne to Europe, the continent which was magnet to all my flames. On the plus side, I was flattered Herman recommended me as his fill-in.

(In addition to top positions at Little, Brown and Athenaeum, Herman went on to become Editor-in-Chief of Harper's Magazine Press and closed out his career as Editor-at-Large at Doubleday.)

Whuh?

I agreed to teach the course. Though it was hard to figure out exactly what I was teaching, and where to start. Have you ever heard a course description more all-promising than this?

"

WRITING AND PUBLISHING
Robert Baker
Formerly Editor, Harper's Magazine

In this workshop offered to those who write for pleasure and profit, you will gain valuable advice, experience and constructive criticism. Critical discussion of your own work and that of others will stimulate aspiring writers and develop wider knowledge of the writing craft. Styles of writing, the procedures and practices in the publishing world, the author-editor relationship, rewriting and revision will be considered. It is hoped that publishable work will result from these informal meetings. It is assumed that members will write.

"

I referred to it as "All Knowledge 101." I'm not sure how much anybody learned in the course. But then again, nobody died from it either.

Far as I know.

Helluva Great Idea

It's fun to look back at things which were more than just words/ headlines; things which were 'ideas.'

Early September, '65. The job order says Medomak Canning Company in Waldoboro, Maine will hold a sales contest for their New England food brokers, running from October 1 through December 15.

Now, while the Medomak people are very nice client people indeed, they are also very Yankee client people. Pursed lips, pursed purse. As evidence of their Pursedness, they're willing to spend as much as 300-whole-dollars ... to announce the contest, and -- oh, heh heh, by the way -- to include the cost of the prize!

The important thing to realize, Baker, is that food brokers drive Cadillacs. Food brokers wear pinky rings. Food brokers torch the tips of expensive Cuban cigars with $300 bills. There isn't an object in the world costing $300 which will move these broker loads off their air-cushioned dead asses to push *three* extra cases of One-Pie pie fillings to the stores, never mind the three or four *hundred* extra cases the Medomak folks wish to hope might capture the $300 gonfalon.

I morph into Method Actor mode, in the course of which it occurs to me that guys who wear diamonds on their pinkies also have hamfisted egos to match. Working the 'ego' notion, a sizable thought shoots the chute: a banner towed by an airplane to my wondering mind's eye does appear.

But first -- how much? How much would it cost to get a plane to tow a banner with a message on it somewhere in New England? Probably the moon. But ... can't hurt to check.

Miracle of miracles, *not* the moon. Joe Maynard, agency principal and the account executive on Medomak scouts around, and -- believe it or not -- finds a guy (in Middleton, Massachusetts, I think it was) who specialized in the high art of banner-towing, a guy who would banner-tow anywhere in New England, and for the paltry sum of $250! And, not only that, *that $250 includes the cost of the message on the banner*!

This is the letter the food brokers received:

" "

Dear (Addressee's Name):

You are eligible to win one of the great contests of all time. The One-Pie pie fillings "HELLUVA GREAT GUY!" contest.

If you should be the winner, on January 1st, 1966 (New Year's Day), an airplane will fly over your home -- at a time convenient to you. The plane will be towing a banner which says "(YOUR NAME)

IS A HELLUVA GREAT GUY!"

The plane will pass over your home several times, as your neighbors, fellow townspeople and assembled guests gathered there on your lawn applaud wildly. You, of course, are surprised -- your usual humble and unassuming, suave and charming self.

, ,

The winning broker, a pinky ring from Worcester, sold-in an astounding 442 extra cases by the December 15th deadline. The runners-up weren't far behind.

•

Oddly enough, I take as much satisfaction today from that small triumph as many of the big-budget campaigns which would later win me awards, ink in the trade press, money and titles. In solving that $300 puzzle, it's the embattled Lone Eagle loner: me against the seemingly Impossible Problem. Untying the Gordian Knot with a simple twist of insight. This is the mindset which will come to my rescue in the future -- in business and the Game of Life.

Awards/Rewards

Spring of my sophomore year at Ingalls, I win a Hatch Award. It's just an Honorable Mention, but it signifies a beginning ... of ascent.

The Hatch Awards loom large on the New England advertising scene -- the equivalent of the Oscars to Hollywood. Agencies submit only their best work because the entry fees are steep. Despite that, Hatch draws a couple thousand entries every year. Entries are judged by A-list creatives from around the country.

Hatch presentation night is gala, the tickets expensive. Only the certifiably 'beautiful' get to attend: top agency executives, top creatives, babe-caliber secretaries.

An hour-and-a-half before the presentation, The Thousand Beautiful, spiffed to the nines, armed with cocktails, stroll the entries mounted on display panels in the outer hall. They gaze vacantly at an ad now and then. Mostly, they cast about for familiar faces -- and, perhaps, the wink of a new job.

The grand finale is the presentation of Best of Show. The Oscar of Oscars, the best of the best: the best of 2000 ads. If you win a Best of Show at Hatch, you are galactic. To apply them-days-Oscar male-female references, you are Paul Newman or Katherine Hepburn.

Even a third-place Hatch bowl makes you a star. A small star, but a star, nonetheless. Instantly. *First*-place winners get heaped with cash, garlands, lissome secretaries and lunches off the clock.

Even I, with but two years' experience, but now with a Hatch honorable mention to my name , benefit from Star System Lunacy. My salary rocketed from $7500 to ... THE BIG FIVE-FIGURES -- $10,000! ... overnight. Wow-wow-wow.

So much for sanity. Not that I complained ... perhaps you can understand.

Heady Stuff

On return to Ingalls as Copy Director, I am, as Hal Young would say, "a Great Dane ... one tall dog." I have a corner office, four excellent copywriters in my charge; I get to hire a copy department secretary who, unfortunately, is afflicted with the look and lines of Sophia Loren, but who, in her *favor*, does know how to type.

My heady income now affords me the luxury of long moist lunches at the bar of elegant Joseph's Restaurant, which is about 20 paces from our offices at 137 on Boston's *tres chic* Newbury Street.

And on Fridays, I and a gaggle of laughing fellow rovers venture so far as to cross the street and descend the steps to the welcoming dungeon of the Darbury Room -- where you almost have to light a match to identify the person next to you at the bar. (Rumor had it that the booths in the dark recesses of the Darbury Room were Mafia hangout by day, and hooker playpen by night -- inspiring Whitey Hamilton to christen it, "The home of the pros and cons.") Emerging in liquefied state from the air conditioned Darb at 3:30 on a halogenic August afternoon is lobotomy effect. But a small price to pay for 2 1/2 hours of unconfined rollick and roll.

On the work side of the ledger, I put my mark on some ads.

Cooking!

• I finally get to work on VW: One ad plays to the Beetle's engine-in-back feature. The headline says, "Much of what it is, it owes to backward thinking." First line of copy: "We put the horse behind the Wagen."

Another for the Beetle. Headline: "Runabout." Copy: The Volkswagen sedan will runabout 27 miles to the gallon. Runabout 40,000 miles on a set of tires. Runabout serving you faithfully for years. Runabout $1639 new." (Check that price in 1969!)

• For Curtis Farms supermarkets: I jump-start this one -- come up with the *idea* for the ad first. Account exec presents it to client, client likes it, ad runs, wins first-place Hatch award. This is my first complete package: idea, media, timing, execution.

The idea: full-page ad in Boston papers the first shopping day after New Year's, 1969 -- all items featured in the ad would be priced at either 19 cents (¢) or 69 cents (¢). The twenty items in the ad were priced at 19¢ or 69¢. The headline simply said: Happy 19¢69¢

(A pun fun headline for a Curtis Farms special on chicken: Cheep Cheap.)

• A Fenway Motor Inns billboard on the Mass Pike. This is the first ad I both wrote and art directed. The copy, as I initially typed it, said, "You are sleepy. Very sleepy." When the art director showed me the layout, it came to me. "Hey! It should be all lower case -- no punctuation. It's sleepytime thinking, right? Ready-to-drift-off time." He fought me on it, but I prevailed. And so -- with "Fenway Motor Inn" and the exit number below -- it read:

you are sleepy very sleepy

Two Hatch award firsts this time: one for copy, one for art direction as well. (Fenway had to pull the billboard, though.The concern -- that it might be hypnotically suggestive, and cause accidents -- a stretch perhaps, but a valid consideration.)

• The fall of '68, Ingalls handled Michael Harrington's run for Congress. Michael was a liberal not afraid to take risks. The trick was to capture his rebel nature in a theme line. Harrington's handlers were looking for something in "truth-motherhood-apple pie" mode. I wrote some in that vein, but informed the account executive *my* favorite was a line not in that vein: "He has the guts to do what's right." With great reluctance, the account executive agreed to show it, assuring me in the same breath it'd get shot down, and he was right about that. Make that, he was right about that ... to start with. Everyone in the meeting hated "guts." *Until*, Michael arrived ... and loved it. Months later he wrote me on Congressional stationery singling it out as "the benchmark event in the campaign."

Surpri(z)e!

My first 'mega' award is a mystery wrapped in an enigma. One fine February day, Bob Corriveau tells art directors Milt (Willy) Wuilleumier and Paul Regan and me to show up at Commonwealth Photography at 9 tomorrow for a picturetaking. We show up at the studio all suited up and first thing the photographer does is tell us to exchange our cool ties for these clunky plain-white *canvas* ties which span six inches at the wide point near the bottom. The photographer marches us across the street to the Boston Common and shoots the three of us side by side -- he's kneeling, framing us against the sky.

Afterward, we press Corriveau for an explanation. He gives a coy wink and a singsong, "You'll s*ee*e ... you'll s*ee*e." We keep pestering. He keeps coywinking. So we fuggeddaboudit. At the big-deal Boston Art Directors Show in March, we are reminded of it. Demonstrably.

End of show, the emcee summons Willy, Paul and me to the stage for the ... Best of Show presentation ... for our full-page *New York Times* ad for economic development in New Hampshire. A begowned female presenter now proceeds to loose-tie about each of our necks one of the aforedescribed clunkburger ties. But each clunkburger is now magically transformed. Three different ties, no longer plain-wrapper-white. Each brought to *Wow!* life at the hand of illustrator-artist Jerry Pinkney -- each with its distinctive Art Nouveau rendering of the Goddess of Art in the upper half, and, bursting from a lush floral bouquet at the base, a medallion proclaiming BEST OF SHOW. (Pinkney was awarded the Caldecott Medal in 2010, the nation's top award for children's book illustration.)

The mystery is completely unraveled when the awards books are handed out at the end of the show. There, at center of the white cover, a black-and-white photo of the three of us silly-grinning the camera, each of us sporting a segment of the ad's headline now superimposed vertically on the clunkburgerer white ties: "Clean air" (Willy's tie) "for sale in" (my tie) "New Hampshire." (Paul's).

Show Biz.

Eventually, I had the tie framed. The colors have faded some -- it's still a glory.

Brain Tissue -- A Casual Case Study

1970. The Vermont tourism competition had all the ingredients, everything required to whet my appetite:

1) Long-shot odds: *50* ad agencies in New England and New York had been invited to compete.

2) Pocket-change budget: the total advertising budget was a ludicrous $150,000 -- *down* 25 thousand from the previous year's budget. By comparison, our biggie, Underwood -- the largest ad budget in New England at the time -- tipped the scales at 5 million.

3) Knotty creative problem: Vermont's previous ad campaigns had been designed to attract "quantities of tourists" -- raw numbers, of *any* demographic (economic) or psychographic (attitudinal) description ... body count. Coupon ads offering Vermont travel information ran in mass market publications like the *New York Daily News* and the *Cleveland Plain Dealer*.

The assignment can only be described as multiphrenic -- or whatever the word for schizophrenic-*plus* would be. The briefing strategy went like this: "We invite all you hippie and trailer dirtbags to be sure to stay the hell *away* from Vermont. On the other hand, we invite all you filthy-rich dudes to be sure to show up in your Beemers in teeming hordes ... *BUT*, on the *other*-other hand, don't think about sticking around and ... *developing*."

As conflicted as the strategy was, it was grounded in logic: 1) 1970 was the height of the Hippie Revolution. The Woodstock Music and Art Fair took place just across the border in New York State only months' previous. After Woodstock, hippies marauded Vermont in graffitied VW buses (IF THIS VAN'S A'ROCKIN' DON'T BOTHER KNOCKIN'), spending nothing, trashing rest stops, campgrounds, and countryside, even as they worshipped Vermont's beauty -- and thought about locating (i.e. squatting) there. 2) The trailer and RV tribes who obtained campground info from Vermont ads in the *Daily News* and *Plain Dealer*, spent as little and trashed with as much abandon as the hippies. 3) The State wanted to attract upscale tourists who'd respect the environment, *and* manifest that respect in the form of lavish spending in resorts, inns, restaurants, antiqueries and shoppes. The banana peel on this come-hither to the upscale was, "After you've come thee hither for a spell, get thee speedily the hell thither." Vermont wanted to keep it "Vermont for Vermonters." Come spend a week ... or two: accent on *spend*. But we're not up for a land rush or real estate development. No matter how much money you've got, we like things the way they are -- environmentally and real-estatedly.

The Vermont assignment was analagous to that HELLUVA GREAT GUY! brokers' contest: pinchpenny budget, complex creative puzzle. But for the 50 agencies competing, it's "Budget be damned!" this is a showcase account. The chance to do advertising for a mini-Switzerland whets the appetite of agency creatives to a slather, advertising which wins awards, advertising which elicits a "Do that for me!" from prospective clients in a new business presentation.

I particularly liked the low-budget aspect of the challenge. Find a way to not only make do, but do much with not much. Our media people came up with a plan which went against the grain: instead of chasing mega response from The Great Unwanted via affordable mass market publications, we'll go with fewer ads, in pricey publications with upscale readership -- those with significant expendable income who will respect the environment.

We recommended going after "Quality Dollars" -- full-page ads in *The New Yorker*, the *New York Times Magazine* and *National Geographic*. Which meant Vermont (its ad agency, actually) would be betting that fewer ads than ran in mass market publications in previous years, running this year in elite publications, could still pull a respectable coupon response -- and from an affluent audience.

Needless to say, given fewer ads, *and* the "I must wash my hands, Muffy, I've just filled out a ... *yuk!* ... *coupon!*" mindset of the upscale audience, the ads themselves better be damn good to achieve even a 'decent' coupon response.

Now that we've determined who we're talking to, who we're trying to woo, it's time to figure out what to show and tell these fine people. What to show and tell these fine people, what to show and tell ... uh, let's see ... uh ... uh ...

Almost Blew It

It wasn't going at all well. Truth be told, it wasn't even going.

Sitting in my office, staring at the blank sheet of paper poking its head *just* above the carriage of my Olivetti. "Hi there, Mr. Blank Sheet of Paper," I say to it. It, being blank, it don't say squat-nada-zilch back.

In an *Advertising Age* interview once, the brilliant Doyle Dane copywriter Phyllis Robinson said, "If you're up against it, stuck for what to say, just sitting there in front of the page in your typewriter, you have to override that blankness. Just type anything. Anything to get you started."

OK, Phyllis, here we go. I try "The quick brown fox jumped over the lazy blue dog" -- but I'm never sure I've got that right anyway, so that's a no-go. So I bappity-bap some free association.

Such as: "Vermont is green ... Green Mountains of Vermont ... Vermont cheese ... cows ... hordes of cows in Vermont ... no, *herds* of cows in Vermont ... more cows than people ... Vermont is like Switzerland ... Swiss cheese, Vermont cheese ... cows ... Swiss cows ... *switch* cows ... The capital of Switzerland is Montpelier ... heaven on earth ... The capital of heaven is Montpelier ... green hills, blue mountains, azure sky, verdant woods ... *azure? verdant?*, you gotta be kidding ... woods... wood ... how much wood could a woodchuck chuck if a woodchuck could chuck wood? ... wood ... could ... good ... Let the good times roll ... nah, that's New Orleans ... rolling hills ... merrily we roll along ... along ... a long ... 'It's *a Long* Way to Tipperary' ... that's an Irish song ... Irish whiskey ... Irish martini ... time for lunch"

Lunch.

Wet lunch = dry martinis.

Wake the hell up! Presentation a week from tomorrow! Need at least four comps (ads in finished form) with headline *and* complete text. Get together with art director Bill Clark, and kick around "the look." Bill needs couple days, *at least*, to get illustrations done, or find "swipes" (photos from client's files or stock catalogs).

13th hour, up against the gun. My damned fault.

I never-ever take work home with me. The last night of "a week from tomorrow," Vermont is home with me. There in bed, in the tossing-turning dark, I wrestle the entire State of Vermont and I am not winning. Can't get a grip on it. When, finally -- metaphorically speaking -- The Light Bulb goes on.

When -- realistically speaking --. the light bulb can*not!* go on. To be more specific: the light bulb in the lamp on the bedside table cannot go on. Because of my wife's unfortunate affliction. My wife Nancy, who was normal in every other way, had this one slight flaw. She really, really, really did like to *sleep* at night. I, being normal, hold to the creed that sleep is a waste of time.

Nonetheless, I allowed Nancy her malady. Which meant I could not turn on the lamp on my bedside table and jot down ideas. Never ever. Rather, I must formulate them, commit them

-- in the dark -- to memory. And, by morning, forget them.

The 'Night of Vermont' is different. Aurora Borealis explodes my head. Ideas are shooting stars. A killer idea zangs my brain ... pen from drawer. *Worst* idea ever imagined occurs to me ... turn on the light. Trash that sucker. Too young to die. What to write on?

Kleenex box, bedside table. White -- mostly white. Take pen. Scribble-scribble in the dark on mostly white Kleenex box. Scribble-scribble ... toss and turn ... scribble ... scrib ... couple blinks of sleep ... morning. Off to work. Oops. Forgot nice Kleenex box.

No prob, call nice wife. Ask nice her to get nice Kleenex box from bedside table, read my gems over phone. Minute later: "Bob ... sorry. Can't read it ... all I can make out is one 'the.' "

Shoot home, back to K&E with my cardboard Rosetta Stone, solve my scribbled rune. There were just two scratchings from the briary on the Kleenex box with merit. Both were game-breakers. They essentially 'solved' the campaign, established the tone and delivered the message.

I showed Bill Clark the two lines and his eyes got big. He sat there with a pen and layout pad and -- I'm not kidding -- in a matter of 15 minutes of Bill talking aloud to himself ... "Vermont is such a clean place ... need clean look ... white space ... need coupon doesn't look like coupon ... " he came up with the look. In his mind's eye -- because his pen never touched the layout pad. That's how Bill worked. He saw it in his head; he worked it in his head. And, seven times out of ten, when he finally put it down on paper, it was close to the finished product. And it was Tiffany. Always it was Tiffany.

The next day he showed me the 'look' he'd come up with: Page awash in white space. No border. Cameo-ed color photo, offset on page, set down from the top of the page, the copy in text size just below the lefthand corner of the photo. Diagonally offset from the photo on the page, below the word Vermont in elegant script typeface, merest wisp of a coupon. The elements seem to float on the page.

I'd have to say that of the two copy lines from the Kleenex box, "Come home and visit." solved the marketing problem best. The photo: a country road wending its way towards a pristine farmstead worthy of the cover of *Yankee Magazine*. "Come home and visit." positions Vermont as "home" -- a welcoming, comfortable place. You are invited here, Mr. and Mrs. Upscale ... but only for a "*visit*."

A "wow" escapes me at the sight of Bill's design of my other idea. My single word of copy -- Listen. -- barely whispers beneath a photo of blue sky, mountains in the distance, greenery in the foreground. The effect is a palpable hush.

We show the layouts to the account exec Suits, and even they register what verges on a damn-near-might-even-be-mistaken-for-a smile of approval."*But*." (An italicized "but" is the first word a Suit is ever taught.) "We need two more ads. One for winter, for skiing. And another summer ad." I already had the summer ad 'in the can.' I'd written a 'cow' ad for the *New Hampshire* Department of Tourism back when I was at Ingalls, but they'd shot it down. Nothing goes to waste.

Photo of a cow resting in a grassy glade at the side of a stream: "Cows really like it here. / They seem to like a lot of green grass./They have a thing about sunshine and blue skies./ They find living near gentle mountains and clear lakes very pleasant./Cows like clean air./ Living near old farm houses and red barns is a cow's idea of a good idea./Cows enjoy it here in Vermont, a good, clean, easygoing place./ Frankly, they'd probably be flattered if you came by to see them./ They're only human."

The winter ad photo; a deep-powder slope, totally devoid of people (no people in *any* of the ads in the campaign, per my hard-argued *insistence* -- the easier to allow me-the-reader to envision *myself* in the picture): "This is a picture of pretty girls, and ski lifts, and Olympic types slashing the powder, and the apres-glow at the lodge./ This is a picture of Vermont, where no two snowflakes are alike."

Long story short, we won the account. The campaign ran in upscale publications, and *significantly* outpulled the number of coupon responses to the previous year's bigger-budget mass market campaign.

To top it off, the Vermont campaign won Best of Show over 2,100-plus other entries in the Hatch Awards competition that year. *Which*, I remind my mirror whenever I get down in the dumps, is New England's top advertising award.

The success of the campaign, the Hatch Best of Show, numerous national awards -- thanks to Bill Clark, *and* Kimberly-Clark, makers of epiphany-inspiring Kleenex boxes as well.

Measured Response

Another fun puzzle: an ad in a candy retailers' convention program which would attract attendees to our client Schrafft's Candies' booth. I asked the Schrafft's people if they had any new candy products. Well, actually ... no. No new candy products. No new candy products. Anything else? New packaging, maybe? Nope. Actually, no. No new packaging. Anything? Don't you have *anything* new to attract people to your booth? Uh ... well. Yeah. Actually, yes. We actually do have a new candy display rack for stores. A candy display rack, huh? Boy. Wow. That (yawn) sure (yawn) is (yawn) exciting. What does this (yawn) display rack look (yawn) like? Well ... actually, it's made of white plastic-coated wire.

What's the size? It's good sized, actually. Five-feet wide. How high? Good-sized. Sixty-six inches high. Sixty-six inches, eh? This was the ad. The top 4 lines are headline-sized type:

5'6"

and

really

stacked.

Come see me at the Schrafft's booth.

Original Concept

The beauty of the 'star system' in advertising's Creative Revolution was that if you'd won a few awards and gotten some ink in the trade press, you were a desirable commodity. Another plus: people moving from one agency to another, getting promoted, getting fired, no biggie -- nature of the beast. Advertising is a *notoriously* volatile business -- accounts come and go, people come and go.

Only days after I'd been ousted in bully fashion from K&E by a redneck-equivalent boss (more on that later), I get a call from Ed Chase, head of Harold Cabot, a major Boston agency, inviting me to dine with him and his Creative Director Court Crandall at the Union Club.

After dinner, I presented my portfolio -- they made me an offer on the spot: $32,000. I said that'd be fine; so they asked what title I wanted. "Creative Director," I said. "That's what I've been, that's the title I'd like."

Ed Chase said, "Well Court here's already our Creative Director ... how about Associate Creative Director?"

"No, but thanks," I said. "I really don't want to be *Associate* anything."

They said to think about it and give them my recommendation.

And so I became the first-ever *Concept* Director in the ad biz, and possibly The Then-Known World ... I've never heard it since, either. (From the front page of the March 17th, 1971 issue of *New*

England Advertising Week -- with picture. Headline: "Bob Baker New Concept Director at Harold Cabot." Further in the article: "As Concept Director (probably a first of its kind in the advertising agency business) Baker's function will be to advise on all areas of the Cabot creative product.")

One of my 'concepts' from Cabot days:

Ideal Poster

The Ad Club offered a six-week course for people seeking to enter advertising on the creative side. Each two-hour session was taught by top creatives from ad agencies, a different duo each week. The current week's instructors would critique students' solutions to the previous week's assignment, and then discuss this week's topic and outline an assignment.

The week Ray Welch and I were the instructors, we were to critique poster ideas for the Red Cross blood drive. Since this was the Vietnam era, many of the ideas had to do with battlefield situations -- "Visual of a soldier with an IV in his arm. Headline: 'Please give. I need it more than you.' " -- and the like.

The ideal just popped into my head, and straight to my lips: "Y'know the ideal poster doesn't need any words. For instance ... " I took a black Magic Marker and drew the outline of the Red Cross on a large layout pad " ... what if the Red Cross didn't have a lot of red in it?" I filled in just a bar of red Magic Marker at the bottom of the white interior of the Red Cross outline.

Back at the agency, abetted by the elegant eye and hand of art director Russ Veduccio, we created a stunning poster which the agency produced and donated to the Red Cross for blood drives. It won Best of Show in the Boston Art Directors Show, and national awards as well.

Use It or Lose It

A call from a guy named Wilder Baker (his real name), head of the Boston office of Wilson Haight & Welch, headquartered in Hartford -- at the time the largest ad agency in New England. Would I have dinner at the Harvard Club with him and Jim Wagner to discuss the possibility of becoming Creative Director of their Boston office.

After dinner and showing of portfolio, I'm offered the job. I then proceeded to tell them something which for-sure registered on the Richter Scale. I, a *creative cuckoo*, told a couple of suits that I wanted a ... *letter of agreement*! Nobody in the advertising world (or hardly any other world for that matter) knew about letters of agreement back in 1973. Most especially, creative cuckoos.

So they humor me. Give us a draft agreement and we'll see, they said. This was my draft:

" "

This is to confirm our conversations regarding employment with Wilson Haight & Welch. It is agreed that you, are to be paid an annual salary of $35,000 and you will be paid an additional $2500 the morning of your starting day. It is agreed that in the event of termination (by us) you will be kept on payroll at your present rate for at least 3 months. It is understood that you do not fly and therefore will not be expected to do so.

, ,

When we met again, they (surprisingly enough) said they agreed with my draft -- with one exception. That starting bonus of $2500. Hell, they weren't the only ones who hadn't heard of a starting bonus back then. Other than the occasional 'signing bonus' in professional sports, the category hardly existed in 1973!

Jim Wagner said, "Bob, we can go along with the rest of your proposal, but ... what is *this* ... this $2500 *starting* bonus thing?! We've never heard of *that*!"

I leaned forward. "Jim, let me ask you this: Have you ever heard of such a thing as a ... *Concept* Director before?"

"No, Bob. Not really. No, Bob, I haven't."

"Well, Jim, I am one, Jim ... and that's one of my concepts."

I got the w-h-o-l-e

d-a-m-n

p-a-c-k-a-g-e.

The only picture I have of Peg who
was Diana -- her Vassar yearbook.

UConn yearbook caption: Miss University /
Joan Weatherley / Kappa Kappa Gamma.

Joan's engagement picture.

Wow! Time

The Creative Revolution in the Mad Men era sparked by Doyle Dane Bernbach's breakthrough Volkswagen advertising in the '60s ignited a blaze of glory for creative coocoos that raged into the mid-'70s.

Those were wild and crazy days. Happy crazy, but over the top crazy. Advertising gone show biz, Hollywood make-believe -- Oscar-caliber award shows, glamour, glitz, publicity, booze, hype, buzz ... buzz-booze-buzz.

Every creative with a few good ideas and that je ne sais quois quality better known as "shit luck" had his or her turn as a rock star it seemed. My starburst began in '68 when an ad for economic development in New Hampshire won Best of Show in the Boston Art Directors Show. A 'Best of Show' tie hand-painted by now-famous artist Jerry Pinckney was draped about our necks as we three who created the ad arrived on the stage. (1)

In 1969, when I ascended from copy director at Ingalls to creative director at K&E, K&E ran an ad in Ad Week ballyhooing my arrival. Not to be outsillied, Ingalls ran an ad in Ad East a week later with a photo of a headless guy in a suit: "We just lost our copy head" ... "but we'll survive just fine, thanks." They were right. (2)

1970: The March issue of Ad East anointed me one of "Top 10 Creatives in New England" based on their poll of leading ad agency creative people throughout the region.

Also in 1970: Elected a director of the Advertising Club of Boston, along with advertising legend Jack Connors, who was also proclaimed "King of Boston" in a Boston Magazine cover story just a few years later. Jack, better known to me as a prince among men, is the gent at far right in the photo -- I'm standing next to him. (3)

In 1971, Best of Show in Hatch Awards, New England advertising's top creative award, for the state of Vermont tourism campaign, created with fabulous art director Bill Clark. (image on back cover)

1972, Ad Week feature article on my origination of title of "concept director" in move to Harold Cabot agency -- "probably a first in the advertising business." (image on front cover)

1973, Best of Show, Boston Art Directors Show, for my Red Cross blood drive poster. (image on back cover) The contingent standing behind me in the photo is a Who's Who of Boston advertising creative luminaries in the Mad Men era. Notable among the notables: way-cool Ray Welch, farthest left; blinking-eyed Jay Hill, co-founder Hill Holliday, second row, farthest right. (4)

1

2

3

4

The one and only Killer Kane.

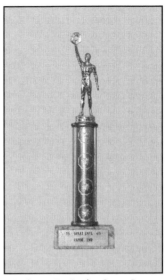

2nd was 1st in the Great Race.

Linc Hawkes and Humpy -- the only bull Linc would tolerate.

Blow Me No Smoke

9:15 of a Tuesday morning. I stroll into the Suzuki dealership on the Lynnway smoking my pipe. I'm here to check out the Samurai, the new Jeep-like vehicle I've seen zipping around lately. I scan the showroom, spot the vehicle, walk its perimeter, open driver's side door, eyeball the interior, shut door, scan sticker, step back ... look around for salesman.

No salesmen in view. The first evidence of salesmen is the sound of salesmen. I look around and see way back in the showroom a half-dozen desks with feet resting on them. The feet are attached to guys in suits who are leaning back in chairs, smoking, drinking coffee and laughing. I move into open space where they can see me. I stand there puffing my pipe, and see that a couple of the guys do in fact see me.

I feel stupid just standing there. So I amble among the cars, occasionally reemerge -- casting forlorn gaze in the direction of the smoking-coffeeing-laughing boys in the outback.

This continues for 10 minutes, and couple times when I reappear, their laughter builds in volume. Like I'm punchline to a joke. Which I probably am.

Finally, one of the laughing boys deigns to remove his feet from desk, rise from chair, and s-a-u-n-t-e-r towards me lazylike, as if this is high noon on the main drag of Dodge and we're about to slap leather. "Yessir, how can I help you?" he says when he's about four feet away and seeking to get the handle on an elusive speck of lint on the lapel of his well pressed jacket.

Despite the firestorm inside me, I grab a puff on my pipe and calmly ask -- very, very calmly ask -- "That Samurai, I want to check it out ... so what took you so long?"

"What?"

"I said, 'What took you so long?' I've been here 10 minutes and you guys saw me, and you just ignored me."

He looked at me the way you look at a child when you're about to teach them to look both ways before crossing the street. "Sir," he said. "We have a saying in this business. You never sell a car to a pipe smoker. They can never make up their minds."

I knew where the guy was coming from. Pipe smokers are slow movers. Procedural. Weighing alternatives. A million what-if's. Puff, puff, puff -- let me think about that, I'll get back to you. Maybe. Next year. If not next year, then next -- puff, puff -- reincarnation. Or so.

Thing is, though, as with some other generalities, there's pipe smokers ... and then there's Bob Baker pipe smokers. I said to the guy, "Pipe smokers, huh? Can't make up their minds, huh? Well let me tell you a story. A God's-truth story." --

"

Summer of 1973, with that hiring bonus of $2500 in pocket, I figure it's time to maybe look into a somewhat more substantial vehicle for our Norman Rockwellian 4.0 family: 1.0 husband, 1.0 wife; 2.0 children (1.0 boy, 1.0 girl).

I head over to the Porsche-Audi dealership in Lynnfield one Saturday morning. As I pull into a parking place front of the showroom, a smart looking vehicle slides into the parking spot next to me. As I got out of my car and the driver was exiting the smart looking vehicle, I said, "Hey, what's that? It looks pretty sharp."

He said, "New Audi Fox. Just test-drove it. Terrific."

(After me just saying you shouldn't generalize ... guys who smoke pipes can't make up their minds, right? Well, guess what? The near-swagger that guy shut the driver's side door with said it all. This boy knows his vehicles. If that makes me a *selective* generalizer, so be it. It's my typewriter.)

I went over to the Fox, vacantly gazed the interior, checked out the sticker price -- around four grand. I lit a fresh pipe and walked into the showroom. A salesman approached and asked if he could help. I asked if Richard Bailey was around; Richard was the new sales manager at Porsche-Audi and he'd been bigtime helpful to me when I was buying VWs at his previous dealership in Lynn.

The salesman said Richard was off today, but he'd be glad to try to help. Sure. We sat down at his desk. "What can I do for you, sir?" he asked.

"That new Audi Fox out there ... "

"Great machine."

"What colors does it come in?"

He handed me a color swatch pamphlet. I considered the colors for maybe 20 seconds. "I like the British Racing Green," I said. I'd like to get one in British Racing Green. Do you have one on the lot?"

"No, not on the lot. But would you like to take one for a test drive?"

"Not really. I don't know much about cars. They all seem great on a test drive. But I could tell the guy who test drove the one out there knows his cars, and he said it's terrific. So I'd like to order one."

As the salesman's writing up the order, he has an expression on his face halfway between "This boy's a whackbird. He'll back out before it's over." and "Fairy Tales Can Come True." Even after I gave him a deposit check and I'm shaking his hand to leave, his face is a question mark.

They called me when the British Racing Green Fox came in. I did the deal. I loved the car. The time I spent at the Porsche-Audi dealership the day I bought the Fox might have been as much as 15 minutes -- including the time it took to light a fresh pipe on the way out.

, ,

When I finished telling the story, the salesman said, "Sir, would you like to take the Samurai for a ... *test drive*?" He was damn near drooling.

I grinned, turned, and relit my pipe on the way out -- freeing him up to return his feet to his desk.

The Write Stuff

For reasons directly attributable to my headstrong fight to do right by my talented creative department gang, I got my ass (and the rest of me) fired from Wilson, Haight & Welch the end of June , 1974. But thanks to that three months' severance pay I had written into a letter of agreement, I had a six-week window prior to Labor Day weekend, to take a crack at writing the novel I'd always said I was going to write -- and I'd give it my best shot while vacationing with my family in Maine. The extra-incentive I had was that good friend and top Doubleday editor Herman Gollob said he'd give me his opinion if I sent him samples of my work-in-progress.

The week before our departure to Maine, I weaponized Robert Frost's Connect-a-Dot M.O. -- furiously scribbling notes on 3 x 5 cards. Characters, scenes, bits of dialogue, plot twists. More than a hundred 3 x 5s contemplated, moved about, re-recontemplated, ultimately triaged in order of appearance. Stowed in a cheapo plastic case, ready for the trip north, awaiting their moment in the sun -- make that, typewriter.

Friday July 19th: Nancy and I pack ourselves, kids, lady beagle Charlie and 3.9 tons of clothes and gear we'll never use into our Volkswagen Squareback pretense at a station wagon and tool 300 miles, with a stop in Ellsworth for groceries and the liquor store before the last leg, to Harrington, then onto the five-mile stretch of macadam on Ripley Point Road, then the Maine equivalent of the Baja 500 along the last five miles of boulders-ruts-and-dirt road till we park at the crest of the hill and unload stuff forty trips up and down the toe-stubbing gloom of the 75 feet of the tree-rooted path to the unelectrified former boathouse which serves as our bunkhouse -- with a propane stove-kitchen, chemical toilet and rainwater shower -- on the 50-acres-and-a-beach portion of the 150-acre Dana family property.

It was a productive six weeks. I wouldn't do it again, though; for the simple reason that I'm a sybaritic slut. I need creature comforts. Nothing fancy. The basics: electric lights, flush toilets, hot showers. Every morning, I gladly drove the Baja to the campground, where I was positively *thrilled* to pay $2 for the sweet balm of a hot shower.

And I had the adventure -- writing the novel. My daily routine: get up, drive the eleven miles to the vast metropolis of Harrington. Have coffee-and at the seven-stool diner, hit the campground; clean up. Back down Ripley Road, to the turnoff which brought me to the tiny cabin which was off the beaten path, but on the Dana property. This is where my typewriter lived. This is where Robert Frost's file cards lived. This is where I wrote.

I wrote from about 10 to 3 every day, scarce ever taking my eyes from the page. Might as well have been in a closet. I turned out about

90 typewritten pages in a couple weeks and Special-Deliveryed them to Herman before he went on vacation.

His reply was encouraging: "The novel is professional and facile. It's funny without being smart-alecky and self-conscious, and it's touching without drawing a heavy bow across the old heart strings. You're unquestionably a novelist (got a good ear there, Bob)."

Unquestionably a novelist. Wow. From Herman Gollob. Double wow.

ALL DAMN DAY!

Back to the typewriter, at maximum rpms. Come we now to Judgment Day, which is to say the day which may hold the key to the rest of my life.

Novelist? Or Everyman? Which will I be?

It all depends whether or not I get to the Harrington post office by 4 o'clock, the Wednesday before Labor Day weekend so I can Special Delivery it. If I get it to Herman who's on vacation on Martha's Vineyard before the weekend, he'll read it, and give me a quick verdict the following week -- he knows I have crucial decisions to make.

Come we now to the typing of the last words of the single-spaced, 179-page manuscript of *The Perfect Movie*: "Movies are for real," Eddie concluded. *"Life* is the perfect movie."

It's 3:15. It'll take us at least 20 minutes to get to the post office. Nancy, Rich, Kate, Charlie the beagle and I pile into the Squareback. It's a day of furious heat. My blood pressure is volcanic. Pen in hand, I'm trying to edit between bumps as Nancy drives. Not a half-mile underway, just fifty yards ahead of us at the bottom of the steep hill, looms impending doom.

The oldest lobsterman in Maine, driving the oldest pickup known to metal, pulls onto the narrow dirt road. Doing minus-four-miles-an-hour.

The volcano erupts: I am now straitjacket material. *If* I live that long. Somehow, 2.3 eternities later by exact count, the oldest pickup in the world makes it to the top of the steepest hill on the dirt part of ripply Ripley Point road. There, like a crown. A teetering crown

-- hesitating, gasping for air, confused, threatening to back down.

Thank God Nancy has the patience I lack. She waits at the bottom -- otherwise we'd have been squirreling the road, grasping at dirt and ruts mid-hill, ultimately surrendering to off-road, waiting for the pickup to make up its mind. We finally make the crest, tailing along at minus-four. No room to pass. I'm a one-man madhouse. Raving. "Nancy, give him the horn! Make him move over, let us pass!"

"Bob, be patient."

"Nancy, my whole summer will be wasted! My whole *future* will be wasted! We're running out of time! Doesn't he *understand* ... honk the horn, damnit!" She won't. I reach across, sound the horn, long, loud, successive. Nothing. In fact, our speed-if-*speed*-it-could-be-called maybe now reduced to minus-*five* -- to allow the oldest lobsterman in Maine to scratch its bird-shaped head over the mysterious ruckus behind it.

Repeat horn. Now I throw in my best impersonation of a guy having a heart attack combined with an epileptic fit just in case the bird is checking his rearview mirror. Raised in my seat, clutching my head, bobbing and weaving, thrashing my head side to side. Maybe he'll think it's a medical emergency and pull over.

Apparently not. He holds his ground. And pace -- if such it can be called.

A tangible evidence for the existence of God occurs when the dirt road admits to an end and the oldest-ever pickup in the world now even pulls over. It is impossible for this climactic moment to pass without comment -- this is biblical.

As we draw parallel, the bird head fires the first shout. And with great force, for a bird: "WHAT'S YER GODDAM RUSH, YA GODDAM FOOL?!," the bird head shrieks.

Not to be outlouded, I blast, "GOTTA GET TO THE *POST* OFFICE!"

"THE *POST* OFFICE, EH? YA GODDAM FOOL, YA HAD *ALL DAMN DAY* TA GET TA THE *POST* OFFICE!"

The bird did have its point.

Forgettable Idea

A low-budget puzzle reminiscent of the "HELLUVA GREAT GUY" contest: Mike Grasko's business, Office Cleaning Company. He wanted to hit a target audience of 100 office managers of local companies, the decision makers in the hiring and firing of cleaning services. The key selling point was, in a sense, a negative, Mike said: "The office manager *never* has to call you to complain. The president's wastebasket never forgets to be emptied. No dust on the blinds. The better job we do, the less he's even aware that we exist."

I devised a formal invitation format; all elements produced on high-quality stationery. The envelope with no printing on it was hand addressed to the office manager. Inside, a printed one-fold invitation; a smaller RSVP card imprinted with "Please contact me" and name and address lines for the respondent to fill in; and an Office Cleaning Company-addressed, stamped envelope for the RSVP card.

The formal-invitation format teased recipients into opening the envelope. The message on the front of the invitation pulled the trigger:

You are most cordially invited
to forget us.

The message inside the invitation played off 'forget': "The best cleaning service is one that's forgettable ... 21 years' experience, enthusiastic references ... Hire us. Then happily forget us." The invitation was mailed to 175 office managers. It pulled 93 RSVP-card responses, which for a piece about forgetting is reasonably memorable.

Sparkling Idea

Now that I'm on my own, I don't have to just prospect for clients by way of my existing portfolio. I have the luxury of reversing the process – coming up with ideas first, then seeking out clients who might buy. Snappy one-liners for a quality jeweler were raining my brain one night. I bypassed the Kleenex box this time, went downstairs and used a for-real pad. In the morning, I called Jack Van Dell, owner of two popular, high-end jewelry stores, one in Marblehead, the other in Beverly Farms. I asked if I could come by and share an idea I had.

I described the graphic format for a campaign of small space (4" x 4") ads. "Reversed out type (white letters against black background). Subliminally suggesting the way you display jewelry against black velvet with your customers." Then I showed him the one-liners. He flipped. How much, he asked. $7500 for my ideas, production charges at cost.

I signed on Paul Ciavara who I'd worked with in Boston, to freelance the design. He came up with a tasty look, featuring an elegant Art Deco typeface. The ads ran in local papers -- people began to look for them, wondering what was coming next.

A sampling of the ads: GIVE YOUR BUNNY A CARAT. WE FOUND YOUR RING. HAVE YOUR GRANDFATHER FIXED - Expert clock & watch repair. THE EMERALD AISLE (ran St. Patrick's Day). 4TH OF JULY SPARKLERS (ran on 4th). OWN A PIECE OF THE ROCK - Use our layaway plan.

I entered the Van Dell campaign in Design 1, formerly the Boston Art Directors show, and it was awarded one of only six Gold Medals (for Advertising) in the awards presentation in March (just four months after I'd gone into business on my own). A blow-up of the GIVE YOUR BUNNY A CARAT ad was featured in a full-page Design 1 pictorial in the *Boston Globe* the next day. The campaign won other regional and national awards in the coming year. I was not only making a good living, I was having fun doing it -- my way.

Fun

How about this, Bob. Create something to commemorate your first year in business: A piece suggesting Baker might be a savvy, fun guy to work with. I did a takeoff on those slick annual reports for big corporations and institutions. Elegantly presented, four-color multi-page brochures -- wall-to-wall with numbers, charts and gray blocks of text camouflaging the past year and waffling the future.

My annual report was black-and-white on a single 9"x 12"sheet of sturdy gloss-finish stock. On the front: "Baker Advertising First Annual Report." With a wry grin, people would flip it, expecting the back to be blank, like those gag books with such as *Humble*

Politicians on the cover and blank pages inside.

But the back is chock-a-block: panoramic photo of Marblehead harbor spans the top; then text recounting highlights of my inaugural year: "It's been a series of events one dreams of. Like it's a Saturday in October and I'm headed for a football game with favorite friends. It's been like that. Best told to you over a long cool drink sometime." Then comes my signature, above my title: President/Maintenance Engineer.

Plus: photo of me in my rocking chair, talking on phone (Caption: "Executive executive area"); photo of my spool 'conference' table, wall of ads and mementos in background (Caption: "Executive conference area"). Two photos side by side -- *exact* same picture of me (Caption, photo at left: "Chief executive"; at right: "Fulltime staff").

Some spice: photo of a comely bare-nekkid maiden perched on a rock beneath a waterfall(Caption: "Annual company outing interlude").

Truth in advertising: again, same two photos of me, side by side. (Set into the two photos, "FINANCIAL REPORT" Photo on left, captioned, "Assets"; on right, "Liabilities".)

I printed 250 copies of my first annual report, gave it to locals, sent it to agency pals in Boston, clients I'd worked with before, marketing directors of companies I wanted to get projects from. For the most part, the piece was well received, particularly by fellow creatives. There were, of course, naysayers. "That piece will turn off a lot of potential clients, y'know."

"Yes, I do know. It'll turn off *exactly* the kind of people I *wouldn't* want to work for. Or with. Dryballs. People like you."

I entered the piece in the big One Show advertising awards competition in New York. Lo and behold, it was accepted. A year later it was published, along with 829 other winning entries, in a massive 500-page tome which, though it cost $40, could also serve as a doorstop.

No-flah Zone

The phone's ringing as I walk into the office about 7:30 one morning: "Hello."

"Bob, thisizforriepreedown'nausttexas," the voice rat-a-tats.

"Huh?" The voice slows: "Ah said, 'This is Forrie Preece down in Austin, Texas.' Y'll have ta excuse me, Bob. Been up half the night, readin' that annual report a yours in the One Show book with a magnifyin' glass. Man, that is one terrific piece. Y'know, I got a one-man shop like yours. The Good Right Arm, I call it. We'll have ta get together sometime. Whyn't you come down ta Austin sometime. Y'll love Austin. Real happenin' place."

"Forrie, I don't fly."

"Ah well, we'll fix that sometime. Let's stay in touch, OK?"

Forrie, God bless him, did stay in touch. Every now and then the phone'd ring and its good old Forrie at the other end. Christmas cards, phone calls and the occasional note. His signoff always suggested I come to Austin -- that I'd fall in love with Austin. We finally met when he came to Boston for a trade show some years back. And then another visit, this time with his terrific wife, Linda Ball -- and another great get-together. "Getcha ta Austin one a these days, Bob," he'd always say.

About 20 years ago, a phone call: "Bob, I'm on the committee for our Austin advertising awards show. We do it up right. Lahk ta getcha down here ta be one a the judges, and we'd have some fun while we're at it."

"Forrie, I don't fly."

"Bob, we're gonna putcha up at the best hotel. Wahn and dahn ya. Treatcha like a dang *king*, man."

"Forrie, I don't fly."

"Bob, in addition ta coverin' your expenses, we're payin' you a $1000 honorarium, man!"

"Forrie, I really don't fly."

In conspiratorial voice: "Getcha laid, man."

"Forrie, I don't fly."

"Ah guess you *don't*, Bob! Ah sure guess you *don't*!"

Tips for Success

Another of many free-to-be-me moments. Summer of '76 answering machine message from Jib Ellis, advertising columnist for the Boston Herald American. He'd heard I was picking up some business and he'd call me back tomorrow to interview me. The article ran August 2nd:

"

Baker's American dream comes true

Baker Booming in M'head: BOB BAKER ... in this our Bicentennial year ... has pulled off the American dream in historic Marblehead. His one-man agency now counts billings in excess of $500,000.

Baker started working for himself two years ago on the humble premise of a brief, three-sentence philosophy: "Be a genius. Work hard. Stay loose."

... etc., etc., etc. -- and it ended ...

Yes, Virginia, there is a Jerry Della Femina. (A reference to the legendary Madison Avenue creative whiz.)

"

I double up in laughter every time I read "Be a genius. Work hard. Stay loose." Of all the gall. I'd actually jotted it down before he called back, and figured I'd toss it out there on the longest-shot chance he'd ever use it. I couldn't believe I got away with it. What fun.

Jack Be Nimble

I got some good comments on the article, but my favorite exchange was with Jack Connors.

(One more quick bit about Jack. In addition to heading up one of the top ad agencies in the country, he was a power broker mover and shaker held in such esteem that a 2010 *Boston Magazine* cover story was headlined, "Is Jack Connors the Last King of Boston?" And yet, to this day, he's the same down-to-earth, mischievous guy he was in the yarn we now return to ...)

Couple days after that Herald article the phone rings -- when I pick it up the voice at the other end says, with some urgency, "Hey Bob, Jack Connors ... are you near a *phone*?!"

I'm thinking how great it is to be getting a call from Jack, and I don't think twice about being asked if I'm near a phone: "Yes, yes I am, Jack ... "

"You asshole," he said.

After my laughter subsided, he went on to congratulate me on the article and small successes. Then he said, "Bob, why don't you add some people, get yourself an account executive or two and increase your income?"

I am not making this up. I did script "Be a genius ... " in advance of my interview with Jib Ellis of the Herald American. But there's no way I could've anticipated Jack's suggestion, and delivered the following -- what I consider -- epiphany, *and* without missing a beat. It just popped into my bean, and I spoke it:

"Jack," I said, "I've just come up with this theory, which I'm going to present to the Harvard B School some day. I'm one person, right?"

"Right."

"Which means I'm a 100% equivalent of myself ... right?"

"Right."

"So if I go out and try to add another person ... you're never going to find a 100% equivalent of yourself, right?

"Let's say, I get lucky, and I find a *90%* equivalent of myself -- meaning that, for the two of us to equal 200% ... I now have to function at *110%*!"

He hooted.

Now the payoff popped into my head: "Then, if you add *another* person ... you've got office gossip!"

He laughed. But he also had the last laugh -- on me. When he signed off, he got me again. "Watch your fingers, Bob ... I'm gonna slam the phone down now!"

Freedom to ...

In previous stages of life, I'd *worked at* jobs I held. Outside the job, I was *playing* the game of life -- revisiting and exploring the worlds of imagination and ideas I'd known as a kid on Center Road in Old Greenwich. Until I went out on my own I'd only gotten to 'play' on a few occasions:

• 1963, when I was at Little, Brown, I had that idea for a university press which would specialize in publishing first fiction.

• January 1969, at Ingalls Advertising. An idea for a whole new industry: Books on Tape. I sent a writeup to Cheeb Everitt, Managing Editor at Little, Brown, asking him to forward it to the appropriate people at Time, Inc., the then-parent company of Little, Brown. In a June, 1969 letter to me, Everitt wrote, "the Time, Inc. barony" looked into it, said it would never fly; would require too many cassettes per book.

Nowadays, when someone mentions "listening to" a book, swords pierce my heart -- AudioBooks today is a mega-billion-$ industry worldwide.

•

Once on my own, I had all kinds of freedom. It began with the novel I wrote in '74 in Maine.

• In 1976, I created and taught an Idea Workshop course in the Marblehead Community Education program -- "Idea-making as a practical art."

The next couple of years were devoted to business and family. But with divorce in '78, I'm the loner again -- the idea kid on Center Road. The imagination of yesteryear *bursts* to life and runs wildfire. Ideas and writings of all kind and dimension *un*related to the business at hand *force* themselves on me. But I don't just daydream, blink and return to the advertising project I'm working on at the moment. I immediately plant the seed: grab Magic Marker, thumbnail sketch; write title, concept or product name, make notes.

I finish the ad project, making way for my latest idea child. Pound away at the writeup or novel; art-direct the logo or product design. Call someone who knows someone who can maybe advance the idea. Copyright what can be copyrighted or initiate a trademark process. Chase the project by mail, phone, personal contact; for weeks, months, in some cases, years, until, exhausted, I fall on my bed of thorns and pray for rest; only to be seduced by a new and even more voluptuous vixen vision. I've chased more than 40 such moonbeams. Just to mention some here --

• MagaBooks, publishing full-length books in magazine format, *with* advertising. Another whole new industry. Idea came to me 1980, started chasing it full-bore in '88 -- with good counsel from publishing guru Paul McLaughlin. It's where book publishing *should* be today -- and will be.

• The graphic novel, *"nothing new."* Started in '81, finished, '93. Sitting there still, with George Brewer's powerful artwork, a half-dozen copies ... in *dummy* form. Sent a copy to John Updike. His note said he thought it "an ingenious jape."

• In '80, I was handling the advertising for the State of Vermont and as I'm driving to Montpelier, the light bulb goes on. Around that time (1977), New York State was doing the incredibly popular "I Love New York" campaign, with a graphic heart substituted for the word "Love." It struck me that Vermont already has the "ve" of "love" in its name, and you could say "I Love Vermont" in shorthand ... I LOVERMONT. Sold it to the Vermont Chamber of Commerce, substituted a graphic heart for the "O" in "LOVE" and they stuck I LOVERMONT on everything under the sun. I've seen it in countless knockoffs ever since. If I had a nickel for everything it's on ....

• In '91 I wrote a 70,000 word Marblehead novel, *Reflections in O'Mara's Mirror*. O'Mara's is a fictionalized version of Maddie's bar. The mirror over the bar has witnessed virtually every life experience imaginable. Top New York editor Herman Gollob liked it enough to say he thought it would be perfect for Jimmy Breslin's editor, Cork Smith. I couldn't track Cork Smith down to send it to him -- frustrating.

• In '99, I came up with an idea for a Marblehead Naval Memorial, gained official U.S. copyright of the the unique design, and approval for siting of it at the lighthouse at the mouth of the harbor on Marblehead Neck. When the potential for the memorial to turn that pristine site into a tourist carnival suddenly occurred to me, I thanked the Board of Park and Rec and with withdrew my proposal for that venue.

• One of my favorite pursuits was *Life Sentences*, a collection of single-sentence slices of life, begun in '94. Here's another of the four I sent to John Updike, of which he said, "I really liked them. Persevere, and the Lord may provide." Here's one:

All Dressed Up

Stechner had just told me I'm the new Creative Director at the agency as the result of his efficient semi-golden handshake goodbye to Kirk an hour or so before and my head's on champagne at the idea and I do thirteen revolutions of the revolving door out 729 and find my way to The Fives to celebrate and the bar is empty of any sympaticos to drown my ego in but I choke a pair of Daniels down and slide over to The Semblance and at the bar there's only Rigby who's easily in his low 60s and is a loser so I do a counter-revolution and out because even though his head was pointed in my direction he never saw me through the blear, but right next door is Scintilla so I'm there working on my third and the whole time my only words are with the lady bartender who's with the Alvin Ailey dancers and has a body that won't quit but professes to Buddhism so when I tell her about the 'Creative Director' thing she starts to expound in Zen, so just for the halibut I decide to head back to 729 and ceremonially move my shit into Kirk's 'ex' corner office, and as I pass his, heading towards mine, I give a lustful look in, and there's Kirk sitting behind the desk and I say hi but he says nothing back so I just continue on my way towards my office but something seemed funny so I went back and went in and there was blood still streaming like tears from his right temple down his neck and soaking the blue collar of his two-tone shirt like a Rorshach test and he was holding a silver-framed picture of his wife and three kids so it looked out at you and they were all good-looking as hell and dressed preppy with nice smiles and it wasn't more than three hours ago he'd sat with Stechner.

That Bird Could Fly

One of the ad campaigns I take greatest pride in was the one I created for Marblehead Savings Bank in the late '80s. The campaign consisted of ninety or more ads and collateral pieces over a span of five years. All of them had catchy headlines and a look that featured a lot of white space.

But it was the idea I had about a month into the first year that sparked the campaign and became the bank's identification happily ever after. The idea was a simple symbol: the silhouette of a seagull in flight, which designer extraordinaire, Geoff Hodgkinson, rendered to elegant perfection. That bird not only was a punctuation mark in the white space of every ad and bank communication, it found its way onto every form of bank merchandise imaginable: from ceramics and watch faces to license plates and men's ties.

The ultimate compliment came one evening when I was at the bar of Flynnie's in Marblehead, and Hill Holliday Creative Director Don Easdon, who was co-creator of the Clio Award for the top advertising campaign in the country for John Hancock life insurance that year, tapped me on the shoulder.

"I've seen a lot of advertisng in my day," he said. "That campaign you're doing for little old Marblehead Savings Bank here is the best bank advertising I've ever seen."

For a guy who's not big on flying, I was suddenly up there with the gull when he said that.

Bookmaking

Hints and glints of *The Garbage Collector* had been rattling my brain since 1984 -- the story of a reclusive garbage collector in a small town in western Connecticut in the '50s. The wrinkle: through his ritual screening of the week's trash, he'd know more than a little about everyone in town. But I was missing an important piece of the puzzle: the actual storyline.

The storyline and cast of characters for *The Garbage Collector* dawned on me in the small hours of the morning, Monday, November 13th, 1989. What's more, it triggered an internal debate which went like this: "Nice going. Finally figured it out. So what happens next? So start writing it. You mean *chipping away* at it ... an hour here, hour there ... maybe five hours a week, max. At that rate, maybe finish in a year-plus ... then send it off to agents and publishers and wait another whole six months for a rejec ... er, response."

The Lone Eagle kid from Center Road in Old Greenwich jumped in: "Get with it! You've got a story you're dying to tell. You've written manuscripts up the gazoo; here's your chance to produce a *book*. Write and publish it yourself! You've got enough in the bank to cover you for five or six months. Burn your butt, write it, slap it between covers. At worst, it's a legacy. Not everybody has a legacy. Your kids can hold up a copy: 'My dad wrote this. Maybe it's not the greatest book ever written; maybe it is. No matter what: my dad wrote a book ... here it is.' "

That's all it took. I tore into it. I had no major advertising projects in the works, I chased none; I even turned business opportunities down. In a matter of days, I'd developed a routine. Get up at 5:30. Out for breakfast, a chance to chat -- start day on a human note. Come back, read newspaper; start writing about 8:30. Write till 2-ish, when I call it a writing day: out for long lunch. Take breaks along the way. No way I can write five-plus hours nonstop. Check PO box around 10; run errand or two. Chuff on my pipe as I write. In a writing ritual borrowed from no less than Winston Churchill, I partake of a matched set of Canadian Mist highballs en route. (Ira Stein, my writer character in the book calls it "Irish Ink"). My real-time working the keyboard is 3 1/2 hours a day max ... in my case, Bob.

Suddenly I realize I need more pages, at least another short book. Which was when the photo of Susan Minot come-hithered from the book jacket of *Lust*, a collection of her stories. What if I were to set out to win knockout Susan Minot away from her husband/ lover/Sugar Daddy. Not only that, the next-F. Scott Hemingtwain of American letters that I am, I have the weapon of seduction at my very fingertips. The index finger fingertips with which I type.

Thus the premise of *The Winning of Susan Minot*, is that I, a writer, shall win the affection of she who is a writer through the medium of -- what else? -- my writings. The beauty part is most of the writings I'll use I've already written. All I need do is plug 'em in.

I begin *Susan Minot* by divulging my scheme of seduction to the reader. Followed by a story; then, "And if that doesn't win her, how about this?" ... another story. Then a poem, a character sketch, another story and the excerpt from my Marblehead novel which won Best of Show in Fiction at the Marblehead Arts Festival. Interspersed between each piece, is a line in the "And if *that* didn't win her, how about this?" vein.

I finished the 37,000 word manuscript of the two novellas February 23rd, 1990 -- 103 days after Word One. Now comes the hard part: turning a manuscript into a for-real book. The way to accomplish that if you're a person as totally inept at production as I am is to have good friends who are totally ept at production.

In consultation with Gil Laurie, longtime friend and veteran print production manager, I'd determined the ideal package would be a 6" x 9" *Yankee Magazine* format. I was shooting for April Fools', my favorite day of the year, as publication day. Due to a power outage, copies of the book weren't delivered till April 13th. Still, it was only 5 months from the start. Better yet, it's Friday the 13th *and* Good Friday, a bonus far as I'm concerned: I'm Catholic, 13's my favorite number, I've often had good luck on Friday the 13th ... win/win/win.

•

The next chapter in the adventure: I'd decided to sell copies of the book myself, not through bookstores -- I'd direct potential buyers to the "About the Author" section on the back cover:

" "

Bob Baker is widely unpublished: his works have not appeared in *The New Yorker*, the *Atlantic*, nor *Harper's*. He has never been nominated for the National Book Award, the Pulitzer Prize nor the Nobel. To his knowledge.

His favorite pastimes include playing solitaire with a marked deck, waving at birds and breathing. He lives in Marblehead, the only place for a human being to live.

" "

When asked the price, I'd say, "A signed copy is $25. Unsigned is 27 ... I have a very low sense of self-worth. And for a buck extra, you don't have to read it."

In the course of writing, spreading the word, and selling the book, I began to accumulate stories.

• The opening sentences of *The Garbage Collector*: "Uncommon warm for early May. Even the bees are out."

It was uncommon warm for February 2nd, 1990, too; almost 80 degrees, in fact. I'd just finished writing a scene which involved a bee alighting on a woman's cheek, and I wanted to run it by Linda Nighswander who'd read part of the manuscript. When I arrived at the house, Linda was outside, seated on the wrought iron bench in the garden, enjoying the warmth.

As I handed her the manuscript, a bee landed on her cheek.

• *Folio: The Magazine for Magazine Management* ran an article and picture of the book in its September 1, 1990 issue, giving a nice plug to my MagaBooks concept. (As did *ADWEEK*, but the *Folio* audience was even more appropriate to my mission.)

• A letter from brilliant friend, the inimitable George Brewer, of whom it was once said, "George Brewer not only marches to a different drummer, he *ate* the drum!":

‘ ‘

Bob, Your novel in magazine form is a 4-bell ringer. Though I'm no novelist, I offer you some sentences which can be useful in your future works:

'Has it occurred to you, Inspector, the killer could be right here in this room?'

'As he entered her, Lyman noticed his sinuses had cleared.'

' ... Are you a university man, Bob?'

Use them wisely, Bob. For what is a novel? A lattuce (sic) work of sentences, made up of words that when put together, raise man to the highest level. Make mine novels, Bob. And you write them. For once there was a man who wrote words. And the people came. And the people read. And there was light! -- George

’ ’

• I'd hoped to get some kind of response from Susan Minot herself -- not for romance, but to inspire playful interchange, thinking it might get some publicity and elicit interest from publishers. My problem was I couldn't figure out how to approach her. That problem was solved at the Sand Bar one day. Tap on shoulder, look around: tall, good-looking blond guy, about 30, smiling: "Heard you talking about your book. I'm Susan Minot's cousin, John Kelly."

John, who was living and working in Marblehead at the time, thought the idea was a hoot. I gave him a copy of the book and one he said he'd get to Susan, along with a note to her, which began: "We have much in common, you and I. You have much, and I am common." Never heard from her, no surprise. John later told me the author Louis Auchincloss, a relative or close family friend (I forget which), read it, and pronounced it well done.

•

Firms like Xlibris came along in the late 1990s with high-tech systems making it a breeze for anyone to self-publish. Amazon and others came on the scene soon after. I did it *all* the way – writing, design, production, promotion, sales – in 1990. All I lacked was a covered wagon.

Instant Fun with Polaroid

Polaroid, which was headquartered in Cambridge, was a terrific client I did a number of special projects for in the late '70s. In addition to paying top dollar, they really liked my ideas, and were super fun people to work with. In one mammoth assignment, for their MiniPortrait camera which travel agents used for passport pictures, they asked me to come up with other small-format picture product ideas. I created several products, a favorite being a 3" x 5" accordion-fold Friendship Album housing up to 10 MiniPortrait pics of favorite friends for the teenage market -- my rudimentary version of Facebook, you could say.

You Never Know -- A Twofer

#1: In 1978, my one-man ad agency was invited to compete with seven Boston mega-agencies for the New England Regional Commission travel account -- a federally funded project promoting tourism for all six New England states. The $650,000 budget was a drop in the bucket to the big guys; but the account presented the opportunity to showcase creativity in a sexy product category (tourism), and for a whole *region*, which moved the bigs to assign top creative teams to the pitch. ($650,000 was Fort Knox as far as the entirety of Baker Advertising (yours truly) was concerned, which inspired me to put my top creative team (me) on the pitch.)

The assignment: create a 'response piece' to a coupon ad. Typically, the response piece would be a free brochure. Thus, one would assume the slickest brochure, featuring cleverest slogan, would win. I assumed the best *idea* would win. A brochure, by itself, was not an *idea*. I asked myself what would move me to fill out a coupon and send for something related to traveling New England -- other than clever slogan/free slick brochure?

What could I actually *use* to help me travel New England? How about a map? Absolutely. A free road map of New England would be *useful*. Up until about a year previous the big oil companies provided gas stations racks of *free* maps -- now (1978) they're charging *a buck apiece* for what used to be *free*!

I had a road map of all six New England states dummied up, drove to the Parker House in Boston the day of the pitch, presented the *free* New England road map idea to the six state travel directors and three private sector members of the Commission, shed jacket and tie and drove back to Marblehead. Late that afternoon, I got a call from Gabrielle Breuer, NERCOM's liaison with the agencies. She invited me back to the Parker House for a drink.

Drinks arrive, she clinks her glass to mine: "The news, Bob, is, you *won* the account ... but you didn't get it. Everybody else did slick brochures with catchy slogans. They voted, and you -- your *idea* -- won. Nobody was even close. But Joe Grandmaison, Executive Director of the Commission said, 'Hey, hold on, everybody! How can I justify to Washington putting $650,000 in federal money through a one-man ad agency up in Marblehead. We have to vote again.' So they did. Hill Holliday got it."

One a them boomerang-o-tangs: You won ... but you lost.

•

BUT! A year later, I get a call from Joe Grandmaison. Members of the Commission, the state travel directors, were pressuring him to revisit the map idea; would I come meet with him later in the week

-- they wanted to move the account to Baker Advertising. The *entire* staff of Baker Advertising hung up the phone and made quick work of an entire bottle of champagne before noon. All by his/my-entire-Lone Eagle self.

NERCOM scheduled an advertising section to run in the May 11, 1980 edition of the New York Times Magazine. The Big Question: "What is Mr. B going to create to engage readers' attention all the way through to the NERCOM coupon ad at the end of the section?"

Mr. B decides to do an "infotainment" advertisement (before the term existed). A 3,000-word article running the 8-page section. "New England: Reminiscences of a Forty-Year Adventure. By R.F. Baker." I recount growing up in Connecticut; vacationing Maine ("Maine wasn't created, it was carved -- by dazzling strokes of nature."); living in Massachusetts ("Marblehead, a craggy seacoast village beyond fascination, is where I make my home, where I shall forever be at home."); strolling the Cliff Walk in Newport; the beauties of Vermont.

The free-map offer pulled 97,000-plus replies, which meant the cost-per-inquiry of the $103,000 section was just a little over $1, an *extremely* efficient CPI by travel industry standards. That response got Baker Advertising reappointed for the following year.

#2: One response got the entire staff of Baker Advertising 'requited'.

A week after the section ran, a letter in my PO box: "Bob Baker, Marblehead MA 01945." "Dear Bob Baker: I read with fascination your article in the Times Sunday, and can't help but wonder if you're the same Bob Baker I met 20 years ago. You lived in Greenwich, and came to Bedford and you and I and my date had drinks together. You and I had a long talk. Things in the article make it sound like you're the person I met then. If so, I'd love to hear from you. If I have the wrong person, please excuse the mistake. Janet Wilton Holmes."

Wow. Janet Wilton, a very pretty blonde with a brain on her shoulders. We sat in the car and talked till morning. Nothing beyond caressing -- but there was chemistry. I visited recently divorced Janet in Connecticut. She spent a weekend in Marblehead. We had a good time making up for lost time.

It pays to advertise.

● ● ●

•

5

Characters

Humanity i love you because you are
perpetually putting the secret of life
in your pants and forgetting it's there
and sitting down on it

e.e. cummings

• • •

Grunch Then

"During the nineteen-fifties, Greenwich was an ideal place to be a teen-ager. An expensive version of a small town, vast country estates which grew vaster with each passing mile; properties large and valuable, zoning laws tough, and with enough clout from its citizens -- many of them heads of giant corporate interests in New York City -- to keep it that way.

Where social life was concerned, Greenwich was no small town at all: it was tremendous."

-- *Haywire*, Brooke Hayward (1977)

•

Look magazine declared at the time that Greenwich, Connecticut (pop. 40,000) was "The Richest Town in America." (My father guffawed at this, allowing as how Look's worthy abacus twerpers had conveniently 'omitted to include' his income in arriving at this determination.)

•

With all that money to burn, the air was rather stuffy, 'Society' rather closed.

The clock was still wound to the Jazz Age, it seemed. Always two in the morning of the party Lindy Hopping on since the Twenties. The Twenties were The Last Great Time, maybe even The Best of All Possible Times on the American social scene, so why not continue the party! Why in hell not.

Kick off them heels, kick up your heels. "Charleston, Charleston ... da dada Charleston"

Liquor and lipstick, flavors of the night. Crystal and Dixie, sounds in the night. F. Scott-chins, flying ties; Clara-Bow puckers, dare-ya eyes, flicking skirts -- around and around and around and a ... Teeth teethteethteethteethteethteeth-by-Ipana, around and a ...

Scarce notice of an oddball drop-in or so along the sweet long night of this bash without end. You know, that Crash Depression WorldWar fellow, or his like ...

"Probly jus a fren a Tad's er somebuhhhy else'szz maybe." Bother. Da dadada Charleston.

Serious concerns? This very drink. Those very lips.

•

That was the feel of Greenwich then. One long stretch of one long 'serious' party. The world -- the whirl -- according to Greenwich that we young folk would understand as understood as we grew on into it.

Even those who weren't invited understood. It couldn't be helped. It was both pervasive and invasive. If you chose to breathe, you necessarily inhaled cologne.

•

For a teenager on the wrong side of the social ladder in Greenwich in the 1950s to arrive on the Vacation Dance List was comparable at the time to a colored person "passing" for white. Not that in either case the individual necessarily sought out said result. Sometimes, it just ... happened.

•

You rubbed elbows with it enough to come to know its parts, its language, the unspoken Code. Eyes and ears did the spade work for you -- osmosis did the rest: Peck & Peck, Carroll Reed, Trimingham, Brooks Brothers, J. Press and Chipp spun their Chrysler Town & Countrys, T-Birds and MGs downcountry to Greenwich Avenue this fine October Saturday morn, to mingle with my 16-year old self attired in second-tier preppy: Bloomingdales khakis, blue button down shirt and khakis, Van Driver charcoal crewneck sweater, Bass Weejuns (no pennies, tacky). I'd walked across the Post Road from our apartment in the Chateau Lafayette and stood daydreaming there among the gleaming assemblage of pocket knives at Kerr's hardware, occasionally distracted by the clack and race of the money cars along the brass-tubed pneumatic railway to and from the counter and the alchemist upstairs who penned receipts with one hand, while turning hundreds and fifties into fives, ones and pennies with the other.

The north country couples came to Kerr's first on Saturday morning. For necessaries. For oddments. Kerr's had one of most anything. Costly, but who's counting.

One of the gardeners misplaced his pruning shears. Mave the cook is fed up to here with the can opener which "surely come over on the Mayflower with the family silver" and "is hardly sharp enough now to dent a pudding at best." Patrick the chauffeur's list includes a half dozen chamois cloths and Simoniz for the three cars (none of which was, or would ever be, a "Jew canoe" -- a Cadillac, in the biting language of most of the anti-all-except-us aristocracy). The cleaning woman requires Butcher's furniture polish and a new wet mop for the third floor baths. A Phillips screwdriver and a pound bag of tenpenny nails for the fixer-upper man, as the children call him (offspring were 'children' then and there; only the low-class, no-class or goats produced 'kids').

Mister takes a fancy to that quite ingenious English Rolls razor with the askew blade and its very own strop in its very own stainless case -- sure to retain its virginity along with the regiment of other virginal ingenuities stacked in orderly fashion on the top shelf of his bath closet. Mrs. picks up three tubes of shuttlecocks for family badminton and a very nice pair of garden gloves in a rosebud pattern and that hammered copper vase which will show off dried flowers so nicely in the library ... or the den. Yes, of course, the den. We use the den.

Patrick will pick it all up Monday, except for Mr. and Mrs.' purchases, which they'll take with them.

I who'd purchased nothing, save with my eyes, would now amble catty-corner across the street to the Putnam Barber Shop to have my whiffle trued up.

The whiffle cut was uniform of the day for men's hair: close on the sides and back, longer on top, parted on the side, combed straight across to lie flat in front. Not that the look was suddenly 'in' -- it had simply never gone out. A continuance of the Twenties.

(Should you ask for such as a 'whiffle' today, the barber will stare at you. Then, assuming that your mouth has recently been Novocained by the dentist, he'll ask if you'd mind writing the funny word down. You write it down. Sure enough, it reads as he'd heard. So describe it, he says. Describe it you do. "Oh," he'll toss off, "that's sort of a cross between what we call an Ivy Leaguer and what we call a boys' regular." If, based on that confidence-builder, you give him the go, be assured that your entire head will end up looking as if you'd indeed just come from the dentist.)

Wealth

The Putnam Barber shop was a great listening post. Since the 1890's, Greenwich had been famous for famous people, very important people, very wealthy people: the decade of the Fifties was a heyday. If the boys with legacied seats on The Exchange or those who ruled the towers of uptown Manhattan hadn't time to squeeze in a haircut in the city during the week, they hit the Putnam Saturday morning.

Henry Fonda, Leland Hayward the Broadway producer, President-to-be George H.W. Bush, William Buckley, Jr. -- they all lived in Greenwich then, got their hair cut at the Putnam now and again. I was never there when they were there; or at least I didn't know who they were if I was ever there when they were there. Radio was the medium then, television was yet to make it to Webster's dictionary. Faces were faces, voices rang bells.

But I do know who Sam Pryor is, and Sam's here today. Just two chairs away in the #1 chair, having his hair cut and being talked to death between snips by Mike.

Mike the owner wore his hair slicked back like the legendary movie Romeo, Rudolf Valentino, and he'd have been flattered to death if you picked up on an even greater resemblance. Valentino would not. Mike spoke fluent what-my-father-called *fromage debris*. It was the only French expression I remember Dad using and I wasn't word-for-word sure what it meant. But from the disdain on Dad's face when he said it, along with the brushing-away-crumbs sweep of his hand, it's a cinch to gather its implication: "blah-diddy blah blah ."

My guy, Angie, though, didn't just cut a good hair, he was a study in serenity. He uttered scarce a word between "What'll she be, Mr. Bobba?" and "Thank you, Mr. Bobba"

Angie's silence gave me clear listening throughout the cut.

Sam Pryor was among the legions of drowsy giants in Greenwich. The kind not famous; not famous in the Life magazine sense. Nobody'd shell out that 20 cents to look at a magazine filled with pictures and 250-word capsules of guys like Sam. If he suddenly lost all his marbles and decided to walk a tightrope between the Eiffel Tower and the Arc de Triomphe -- yes, *then* he'd make Life. With pictures, of course. Otherwise, he's stuck with being famous in the great gray yawn of the Wall Street Journal, along with the other drowsy giants.

Sam was stuck with being at the top of a large corporation and having a lot of money. Sam Pryor headed up Pan American Airlines at the time. He had a grand home, The Pryory, on Field Point Circle in Greenwich. A mammoth, real-live amphibious plane bobbed out there in a front yard so lovely it also even had a name: Long Island Sound. I don't know if Sam was from Oklahoma, or maybe Texas, but he had a touch of that twang, and a lot of that way about him. Weathered tan face. Solid build. Shorter than John Wayne, but who ever wasn't. Savvy at rest. Easy grin. But at the same time, "Prefer you not to stretch me, son," that grin made clear.

There'd come a momentary settling of barber Mike's incessant *fromage*. Sam's telling Mike about a location he's scouted out on one of the Hawaiian Islands, the site of a proposed "spread" he's planning to build for himself and the "little woman."

"Yeah, Mike, so first I get me my pilot to fly me all the hell and gone all over the island. Unspoiled terrain as far as ya c'n see. Beautiful country, just abs'lutely beautiful. Then I saw it. River snakin' down the mountain through all this lush jungle-type green. Not a man-made thing in sight. The river makes 'er way down a succession of waterfalls. Seven of em, I counted. Each more powerful than the last. Beautiful sight. Last one ... just took your breath away it's sa beautiful. Beside it's a plateau, mostly overgrown. But basically she's flat.

"So we had to fly us back to the field and swap the plane for a 'copter. (A *helicopter* in 1952; but then Sam did have Pan Am at his disposal.) Found us a place to put her down on that plateau. Quite a sight when we get out and look around. Quite a sight. Buncha work to clear us a good road to get to building and making it civilized enough. Lots and lotsa 'copter work, 'course. Quite the sight, though. Easy with that razor, Mike."

"Cert'ly, Mistera Pryor. Wow-a. She soundsa vairrry so pretty."

•

Sam Pryor's home was situated on 100 acres adjacent to the Seven Sacred Pools on the Maui paradise of Kipahulu. He later sold part of the land to his friend Charles Lindbergh, the aviation legend who made the first solo transatlantic flight in 1927 -- an achievement Pryor arranged funding for. Pryor and Lindbergh are buried near each other in a churchyard cemetery there that the two of them cleared by hand.

Runnin' with Rocky

The name Fawcett was as big as they come in Greenwich in the '50s. Fawcett Publications published *True*, the macho men's magazine, along with the highly successful *Marvel Comics*. Fawcett Publications, with its four-story building on Fawcett Place at the foot of Greenwich Avenue, employed 725 people.

We get a feel for the Fawcett boys from Brooke Hayward's memoir, *Haywire*: "Bill (Brooke's brother) and Peter Fonda had fallen in with the Fawcett brothers, a wild crowd. The Fawcetts had substantial property nearby." And: "Rocky Fawcett would throw pebbles at my window in the middle of the night. He'd climb up the tree by the side of the house, I'd wriggle out the casement, and we'd recline side by side on the sloping shingles of the roof until dawn, Rocky with a six-pack of beer and I with my heart in my mouth."

I encounter the very same Rocky Fawcett as we're both leaving a raging Happiness Boys' keg party in Riverside at about 2 in the a.m.

one time. His gleaming fire engine red MG-TD is parked next to my aging gray elephant on wheels, and we get kidding about something. One quip leads to another, and as he's hopping into his MG, he says, "How'd you like to come run the bases at Bruce Park with me?"

"Is that a joke?" I asked.

"Nah. It's fun. Meet me at the softball diamond there. I'll show you." When I get to Bruce Park in Greenwich, he shouts for me to park my vehicle and hop in. He churchkeys a Bud for each of us, puts the MG in gear, over the curb onto the grass, idles at home plate, points toward first base.

"OK, we're gonna circle the bases. You keep time on the second hand of your watch. My best was 5 seconds, with Fonda that time. All right ... " revs the engine ... "*GO!*" The MG *churns* the basepaths -- literally -- carving out gobs of dirt and sod. First, second, third, home. Roughly 8 seconds, according to my trusty Timex.

Again: first, second, third, home. 7 seconds

Again. 6.

SIREN !

The cops took us to the station and actually popped us into a cell for a half hour. Rocky used his dime to call his father. He said I wouldn't need to waste mine. His father never came down, either. Roger Fawcett jingled Chief Gleason at home and the chief jingled the desk guy. The desk guy gave us a very strange lecture because it was more about how much his wife and sister-in-law just loved the shit out of working at Fawcett Publications than it was about the Grand Canyon we'd dug on the softball diamond at Bruce Park.

Mr. Fawcett paid to fix the diamond. The best part was my dad never found out about it.

J.P. Was OK

1962, NYC: I met Uncle Russell, my mother's brother, for lunch at Two Park. A bachelor in his early 50s, Uncle Russ was iron-gray handsome with piercing dark eyes. Smart dresser, autocratic mien (a self-professed snob), leprechaun humor.

(I still have a 1928 engraved invitation from Mom's collection of memorabilia: "To meet/ Governor-elect and Mrs. Franklin D.

Roosevelt/Mr. J. Russell Carney requests the pleasure of your company/on Thursday the thirteenth of December from four until six/at the Savoy Plaza, New York")

After lunch, we took a walk. As we're passing the Morgan Library, a magnificent treasury of world art built by financial wizard J.P. Morgan, Uncle Russ declaimed, in his Park Avenue stage voice, "You *know*, your Grandfather *Car*ney had a *won*derful experience in J.P.'s *man*sion. Father, who was a stockbroker, was hit hard in one of those godawful financial *up*roars of the 1890's. He went to J.P.'s mansion, it was Sunday. The butler asked Father to state his business. Father presented his business card and asked to speak with Mr. Morgan. The butler returned, escorted Father to the library. J.P. asked Father the reason for his visit. Father said he'd like to borrow $3000. Morgan looked at Father and said, 'You appear to be an honorable man, Mr. *Car*ney.' He handed Father a promisory form, which Father signed. J.P. wrote out a check, and then ... asked if your grandfather would like a ride home in his -- Morgan's -- *car*riage. It caused a neighborhood *fuss* when Father stepped out of J.P. *Mor*gan's *car*riage that *Sun*day afternoon."

(As far-fetched as Uncle Russ's story of J.P. Morgan lending grandfather Carney 3 grand based on his "appear(ing) to be an honorable man" might seem, I quote from Jean Strouse in her *Morgan: American Financier*, relative to Morgan's appearance before a House of Representatives investigatory body. Chief Counsel Untermeyer asked Morgan if loans were made "to certain men because it is believed they have money back of them." Morgan said, "No sir. It is because people believe in the man." Untermeyer: "And he might not be worth anything?" Morgan: "He might not have anything. The first thing I adjudge is character. I have known a man to come into my office, and I have given him a check for a million dollars when I knew they (sic) had not a cent in the world. But a man I do not trust would not get money from me on all the bonds in Christendom.")

A Dumb Ending

I used my ascension to editorial at *Harper's* in 1961 as leverage to 'work the room.'

One of many good things about Jack Fischer was his range of interests. He had an almost childlike curiosity and willingness to explore all sorts of possibilities. No surprise then, that in conversation one day, when I let drop that I'd like to take a shot at doing a movie review column for *Harper's*, he told me to give it a go -- without bothering to ask what my purported qualifications were. If, he'd asked, though, I'd only have had to cite the hundred or more movies I saw with Mom in Stamford in my grammar school Friday afternoon years; the Existential viewings with The-Girl-in-Profile at the Pickwick those several Sundays in my teens; my major-distraction-by-a-majorette at the Pickwick one other Sunday; the first weekends in New York when I hit back-to-back double features, Saturday *and* Sunday. I could easily validate my deep understanding of the international film canon.

Fischer wrote a letter of endorsement to movie distributors, and I received an invite to my first screening -- *Guns of the Trees*. Shot in black-and-white, it artsy-craftsily brooded nonstop. I didn't bother trying a write-up: I had no idea what I'd seen. The auteur/director was Jonas Mekas, movie critic for the *Village Voice* and self-anointed Godfather of Avant-Garde Film.

I called Mekas and said I was in editorial at *Harper's* and we were thinking about doing a review column, and could I meet him for lunch or a cocktail. He said he didn't do lunches, and especially didn't do *"cocktails"* -- sneer, sneer. He said he'd meet for coffee, so we did -- in a drab cellar-dwelling cafe in the Village. Mekas was slightly built, with receding hairline and ashen-gray complexion. He wore a loose-fitting, quite wrinkled, ashen-gray sweater. We didn't hit it off to the extreme. He was a Lithuanian who'd spent a good deal of time in post-World War II displaced persons' camps before coming to America. His view of the world and life itself was diametrically darker than that of the shiny face in the Brooks Brothers suit sitting across from him. He did the talking. Amend that: he did the almost inaudible, sometimes-indecipherable Slavic-accent-mumbled *pronouncementing*. Above and beyond the fact that I seriously hated coffee back then, I always-and-ever despise being *expounded to* -- especially by anyone who feels entitled to expound *down* to me. A half hour of this, I thanked His Omniscience for His unsolicited wisdom, flipped a 5er on the table and ascended from the depths of ashen-gray to a *wow*-welcoming sky of cobalt-Disney-blue.

That quickly, I'd begun, middled and 'The End'-ed my career as film critic for *Harper's*. And ... that gladly.

Wry on Rye

Little, Brown published *The Catcher in the Rye* in 1951. I was 16 at the time, and for a number of years it was my bible. In some ways, it still is -- so much rings true.

Publishing in the '60s was ever so discreet, polite. Superlatives earned frowny faces. 'Marketing' had to do with a trip to the grocery store -- lamb chops, bread by Pepperidge Farm and don't forget the tea biscuits, Millicent. That was marketing. 'Advertising' was a 'necessity,' one supposed. But to be kept in its ticky-tacky place. Not to be too 'noticeable.'

The 'place' for the advertising department at Little, Brown was an overgrown closet, the fourth floor attic. There was sufficient dust adrift that space to have filmed "The Grapes of Wrath" there.

I'm an earlybird. It's 7-ish of a Tuesday morn in February; no one's around. I climb to the attic to explore. I pull out a file cabinet drawer labeled "Authors' Statements." (An Author's Statement is a background questionnaire used for ads and book jacket blurbs.)

It may be cold up here in The Dust Bowl, but I've a sudden-acquired coat of sweat, because -- maybe, maybe, maaaybe ... *Salinger*?

My eyes jump the alphabet ... *SALINGER*! Handwritten on the form, next to "Title of This Work": *The Catcher in the Rye*. Every other answer on the form is erased from memory now; erased by the stunning impact of Salinger's response to a question to this effect: "What Was Your Intent in Writing This Book?"

Now mine is a better than pretty-good memory, particularly for things of interest to me. But I cannot tell you whether Salinger's handwriting was cramped, sprawling, scrawling, printy or florid. And I surely can't guarantee that I've got his answer word-for-word, either. I didn't have the good sense to write it down.

But, at worst, I'm within a hair. What follows is definitely 'the message.'

"What Was Your Intent in Writing This Book?

"That it never be put on a shelf beyond the reach of a twelve-year-old."

The thought of 'appropriating' that literary treasure would never have crossed my mind. But if photocopying were anything but as alchemic and unavailable as it was in 1963, I'd have definitely made a copy and framed it.

(As validation of my recall of Salinger's Author's Statement remark, I came across this in Kenneth Slawenski's 2010 *J.D. Salinger* biography: "Little, Brown issued a limited publicity release, in which J.D. Salinger was quoted ' … all my best friends are children. It's almost unbearable for me to realize that my book will be kept on a shelf out of their reach.' ")

Slaughter of The Innocent

Arthur Thornhill, Senior, Little, Brown's publisher, was hardly 'traditional,' as publishers of silver-spoon publishing houses went at the time. There was no tweed in Senior's bloodline. Senior came up the hard way, as a drummer,' a salesman -- lugging outsized black-leather cases stone-heavy with textbooks around far-flung cow colleges for 20 years before powering his way to the top. Senior was all business: a growl on his face and in his voice. Fools were not suffered -- they were disemboweled alive.

My boss, Randy Williams, had me sit in on a Friday morning advertising meeting in Senior's office one time. The Franklin Spier agency from New York would be presenting a proposed ad to run in a booksellers' publication. Absent this Friday was the head account exec, a veteran of the Senior wars, a guy who knew how to 'deal' with Senior -- to whatever degree anyone knew how to deal with Senior.

In the head account executive's stead today is the junior A.E. He's been in attendance before; he knows what can happen. But when this rosy-cheeked, profusely perspiring young man stands to present the ad, a strange thing happens: a beatific, almost-cherubic look overspreads Senior's face. I begin to feel somewhat relieved, because I'd heard about Senior's tantrums. (I was later informed by a veteran

Senior-watcher that Senior's Vienna Choir Boy look, though rarely seen, was the absolute *worst* of all possible omens: "He's setting you up for the kill. That's his pussycat face, his Bengal tiger-pussycat face.")

The young account executive proceeds to read the proposed copy for the ad promoting Samuel Eliot Morison's *Two-Ocean War*. He read the headline first. Apparently the junior account executive had decided the best defense was a good offense, because, despite his obvious nervousness, he read the headline with considerable bravura.

"They'll Be Coming into Your Store in Droves for This One!" he boldly declaimed.

Deathly calm.

Explosion. Senior's face is scarlet; his fist crashes the table. "*Droves?*" he croons; "*Droves?*" he growls; "*DROVES?!*" he bellows at the top of his lungs. "What the hell is a *DROVE?!*" Can you tell me what a *DROVE* looks like, Sonny? Can *any*one in this *room* tell me what the hell a *DROVE* looks like? I've never seen a drove. Look out the window there, Sonny ... do you see anything out there that resembles ... even *remotely* resembles ... a ... *drove?*"

As a theatrical moment, it was comic. As evidence of what we do for job security, it was pathetic, tragic. No one -- my cowardly self included -- raised even a whisper in the guy's defense. Seven of us sat there cowed cowardly dumb as Senior clawed him to shreds.

Moment of Genius

Gene Haley rekindled a happy thought as I was thinking about my Story Street digs just now. Gene rented a room on the first floor. He wasn't as wee as a leprechaun, but other than size, that's what he was. The memory which popped to mind bears me out.

We're sitting in the cave, having a drink, just Gene and I. It's a cold gray Saturday in December; there's a fire going, our conversation has gone to quiet.

Of a sudden, out of the blue, and apropos of nothing at all, Gene elevates his full 5'7" self from the chair. He hunches over and launches into a half-assed jig -- more shuffle than jig. A twinkle in his eye, his face rubberizes till it's all grin. He sings out as adenoidally as he possibly can: "Oh I can't sing/And I can't dance/But I've got a mustache in my pants."

And sits back down.

I tried to get him to do it at parties, but he said he'd only do it when the mood struck him -- when there was no logic for it, no reason to do it at all. Except that it was the time to be doing it.

I'd give anything to have it on film. It was a holy moment. It'd do the world good.

Town Character

My wife Nancy's mother had a wonderful cousin named Ray Ellis. They grew up together in Iowa -- though Ray pronounced it more towards "Aahwah." But the country boy twang emanating from this handsome, solidly built fellow in his late fifties I met at our wedding reception doesn't fool me in the least. This boy is electric.

We only chatted a few minutes, but as we're exchanging goodbyes, Ray says, "Now you two promise you'll come visit us in Marblehead soon's you get a chance. Trific place, Marblehead. Abslutely trific. Promise us now ... OK?"

•

Late spring, 1965. Nancy calls the Ellises to see if we can come visit. Gwin suggests we drive up Saturday, check out rental possibilities first, then stop by their house afterward for "cocktails on the porch." Most of the ride to Marblehead is not inspiring. The coast is flat, flat, flat. But my spirits rise as we near the town of Swampscott. The crag begins, the coast is rockbound. This is strength; it feels good.

Atlantic Avenue, leading into Marblehead is pleasant, but nothing you'd write an anthem about. A commercial district of shops and restaurants adds nothing. So far, Ray Ellis' "abslutely trific place" is abslutely inevident. Sign says 'Real Estate.' We park, enter the storefront office where sits behind an aged desk a large woman in her fifties who it would seem has put on her lipstick this morning without benefit of mirror -- there's almost as much red *above* her upper lip as upon it.

This theme of casual disarray is continued throughout the rest of her person and costume. Her gray hair appears clean and not unmanaged -- just mismanaged. If you're a betting person you'll wager the smock dress she's wearing is black -- and you'll win; because that's indeed how it started life; and black can be said to predominate. But ash of the cigarette variety has assigned the bosom of the dress a leoparding of gray, with liberal doses of gray on the skirt as well. She wearing neither heels nor flats on the feet she withdrew from the top of the desk as we walked in. Her carpet slippers do -- in a way -- coordinate with her dress: a sizable good deal of their surface generally inclines almost pretty much nearly close to on the verge of an approximation of in the somewhere somewhat vicinity of black.

You'll not be surprised to learn that a lit cigarette is caught between her lips. The cigarette acts as a baton, conducting the syllables as she speaks: "Hiya, kids, I'm Betty Clement. Can I do for ya today?"

As she speaks, I'm drawn to her eyes. They're bright, playful, certain. "Hey, I know I'm right. But let's have some fun with you ... before I get my way," they proclaim. I tell Betty we'd like to check out Marblehead, and, maybe, some apartments. Would she be willing to show us around?

"Ya come to the right goddam person all right. Most real estaters'd give ya a map and tell ya go do your own explorin' first. But what the hell, it's slow season, and I can use a change a scene. Might's well take my car; you can sightsee while I drive. Your VW there looks like a goddam glove compartment on wheels. Lemme grapple my weeds first."

She opens a desk drawer, ousts a carton of Camels, grabs a pack, strips the cellophane, flips it in the vicinity of the wastebasket in the corner -- she wasn't off by much.

Nancy and I both hop into the front seat of Betty's in need of a body shop, hulking, maroon Pontiac -- a quick look tells us the back is serving as an attic. A tumble of cardboard boxes filled with papers, pair of high rubber boots, clam rake, electric Schaefer beer sign and cat's scratching post form the tip of this archaeological iceberg.

"Gotta make quick stop first," she says before she hits the ignition and Operation Rolling Thunder gets underway. The thunder might have to do with the muffler, or corrosion thereof. Since Nancy's next to Betty, she can maybe make out what Betty's saying. I can't.

Finally, by craning my head in Betty's direction, listening hard, and following intently the movement of the cigarette baton bobbing her lips, I can at least get a sense of her words.

The noise is cataclysmic. People stare at us. A young mother hoists her little boy from the stroller and comforts him. An elderly woman hobbles after a skittering small dog.

When Betty turns off the engine after pulling into the ramshackle two-pump gas station, she says, "Time for a new muffler maybe."

"What'll it be, Miss Clements?" the empty-faced teenaged attendant asks.

"It's Clement, Stubby. Check the radiator."

He pops the hood, checks the radiator, adds water, slams the hood. "Anything else, Miss Clements?"

"Clement, I said. Tires. Haven't checked em in a while."

"Sure thing, Miss C."

She points to the undistinguished brick building across the street. "High school," she says, lighting a fresh Camel from the other, which she proceeds to give a ladylike twerp out the window.

The boy reappears at her window. "Tires all set, Miss Clements. Anything else?"

"That's all ... it's 'Clement,' I said."

"No gas?"

"Not till you get your prices back in line. Tell your father I said so, too. Tell him hi from me, too."

"OK, Miss C."

"Nice boy," she says, before re-detonating Armageddon.

The thunder seems to have diminished, because I'm able to make out most of what Betty's saying now. Servicing the radiator and tires must have appeased the Muffler God. Either that, or I'm getting good at baton reading.

"Got a mix of everything here. History up the gazoo. High life, low life. Town's started by low life. 1629. Rowdy fishermen from England. Come over, built their shacks and dinky matchbox boats held together with oakum and a prayer that shipped out 300 miles to the Grand Banks in storms they'd no right to come back from ... which a lot didn't. The ones that made it back, before they went to sea again, drank up a rum squall, to forget the ones that didn't.

"Here we are on the causeway to Marblehead Neck, where the moneybags live."

The Pontiac rolls to a stop. "Postcard" is the word. On the right, a mile of rocky beach, the skyline of Boston toylike in the distance. To the left, a mile-long harbor strewn with big kids' toys: a hundred stiletto-hulled, tall-masted yachts, a hundred sizable power boats and motorboats -- scores of work boats and fishing boats. Filling the horizon dead ahead, grand homes on a rock-based peninsula, separated from sea walls at harbor's edge by swaths of manicured lawn. "Trific" is beginning to kick in.

"Y'ain't seen the half of it, boys and girls. Still early now; boats just starting to plop in. Fourth a July, that harbor's up to her gills -- 1900 boats.

"This is the outside loop of Marblehead Neck ... the ocean views. Look between the houses, you can see on out to Portugal. Just the Atlantic between you and there.

"This town's all rock. Might's well be Maine in Massachusetts. The first English called it *Marble*head, cuz they thought it was marble rock. It's not. They told us in school it's porphyritic rock. Honestly, the most useless damn things that stick in your head. Anyway, *Marble*head sure as hell beats *Porphyritic*-head."

Attempts to see Portugal are not rewarded. Fleeting patches of blue-black ocean tease our eyes from gaps between homes and trees.

The car stops and we get out. We follow Betty along a pathway. "From that rock, you can check out Portugal."

Nancy and I ascend the easy grade of the giant rock to the top. Immediately before us, the vast Atlantic, under a fair blue sky, sails all the way to Portugal.

Wow.

Despite 70-degree temperature, a shiver runs through me.

•

In the car again, Betty tells us that most of the 15-to-20-room homes on Marblehead Neck started out as "summer cottages."

"Late 1800s, the rich birds who lived in Boston in the winter packed their families and servants and white suits and dresses into trunks and plopped em in these 'cottages' for the summer. Then they built the yacht clubs to yacht from. And wear their white suits and dresses for dinner, and tuxedos and gowns for dances. And then shutter it up and take the whole parade back to Boston come Labor Day. Poppa came out by carriage or train on weekends. In the ' 40s, people started winterizing em. Now they're year 'round.

"Here we are at the end of the Neck. That's the lighthouse. Different, huh?" Structure. Eiffel Tower. The skeleton of a lighthouse, painted dark green. The spine, a cast-iron cylinder fifteen feet in diameter, shoots ninety feet above the rock to support a platform which serves as pedestal for the beacon's housing. The housing is octagonal, the windows through which the beacon shines are octagonal. The effect is Victorian -- a gazebo in the sky.

Entering the lighthouse parking lot, Betty says, "We won't get out. Never get ya back in the car." She's right about that. Another postcard. Beyond the expanse of blue-black water, occasionally flecked with white hull, white sail, maybe ten miles up the coast, great homes perched on the rock, the white spire of a church, islands of rock -- the nearest island, a quarter-mile from us, a half-mile long, a small compound of wooden buildings, thicket of trees, thin crescent of tan-sand beach. That's Children's Island. Summer camp for Marblehead kids. They ferry out in the morning and learn to tie knots, swim and toast marshmallows and get sunburns. Come back late afternoon, mostly in one piece, worn to a frazzle, ready for bed.

"Past the lighthouse there ... that's Fort Sewall. "Across the harbor, a promontory surmounted with earthen ramparts. "1814, couple British ships're chasing the *Constitution* -- you know, 'Old Ironsides' from grammar school. Ironsides is in trouble, and the boys from Marblehead man the cannons at Fort Sewall to shelter Ironsides in the harbor. The Brits skedaddle. We saved her.

"Birthplace a the American Navy, too. You remember George Washington? The time he crossed the Delaware? Guess who's rowin' the goddam boat? Who else? Buncha Marblehead rowdies. Georgie boy'd still be standin' there pickin' his wooden teeth -- stuck on wrong side the river. We'd all be speaking British today if not for Marblehead."

We recross the causeway, repass Betty's office and enter a house-scape which is a confusion of shifting planes and alleys and angles and obliques and verticals and dips and rises and interrupted sight lines and sudden openings and tucked-aways. "Houses grew up from the water," she says, as we drive by extents of antique houses so close to each other, they seem joined. "From the harbor. Had to be handy to the water, 'cause that's ordinarily the best place to keep your boat to fish from, you see ... the water. Heh heh.

"There's about 800 houses in Old Town. More than 300 were built fifty or more years before the Revolutionary War or fifty years after. That's why it's called 'Old' Town.

"*That*," she says, "*that* is the *real* town hall. Maddie's Sail Loft. Where everybody hangs out, sooner or later ... and often, too. Moneybags from the Neck, carpenters, bankers, plumbers, pilots, stewardesses. Up-and-comers like you people, hotshot sailors, rat's asses, live wires ... it's the Great Mixing Pot, Maddie's is. Everybody goes there, not just for the food -- but the drinks. Cocktail shaker glasses loaded with cocktail and couple ice cubes. With that mixing of drinks and upper-and-lower-caliber elbows in a small crowded space all at once -- you gotta be respectful of each other, no matter what the caliber of the elbow.

"So if a guy from the Neck gets uppity with a plumber standing next him at Maddie's one night, the snoot will get a phone-slam when he calls that plumber on a Sunday in February when the toilets in his mansion back up. Same for every other plumber in town ... word travels quick here. Works other way, too. The Neck guy was OK with the plumber at Maddie's, plumber'll slug his coffee, slap his galoshes on and de-clog the guy's hoppers.

"Plenty gets done -- or not done -- at Maddie's. I'll show you couple possible rental places ... *if* you like what you've seen so far, that is. What say?"

Trific. Abslutely trific.

Neither apartment Betty showed us was right. Both too small. Betty says apartments are scarce. "You young folks all seem to be moving here at once."

When we asked directions to Peaches Point, Betty said, "It's another pretty swell area. Like the Neck."

Driving up the Ellis'es driveway on Bradlee Road, the sprawling Tudor speaks eloquently for itself. Ray and Gwin pop out and greet us as if we're long-lost friends. As we settle into drinks on the porch next to Gwin's greenhouse and I gaze past the lawn and pier and absorb virtually the same view up the coast we'd seen from the lighthouse, I feel every bit the Gatsby I aspired to in my Greenwich days.

Ray, it turns out, is a senior partner at Choate, Hall & Stewart, the quite-Brahmin Boston law firm. The Ellises are members of the quite-quite-Brahmin Myopia Hunt Club in Hamilton, and the similarly elite Eastern Yacht Club in Marblehead.

But Greenwich-sounding resume aside, and most impressively, the Ellises are salt of the earth human beings who major in the art of generosity -- as would be evidenced by their many acts of kindness to Nancy and me throughout the years -- including putting son Rich and I up in their guest quarters and treating us like royalty during Nancy's time in the hospital when daughter Kate was born.

Ray was a masterful storyteller, too. Most amazing was the story he told me of the visit of an iconic national figure and his wife soon after a momentous event in American history.

It's a story that should be told in full sometime soon, by Ellis family and friends who were there. They can fill in the details and tell it right, do it up proud. It's a vibrantly alive, Marblehead-caliber story worth hearing in full.

Ray and Gwin Ellis and Marblehead ... trific. Abslutely trific.

Tall Man

Ed Sissman was leading a triple life: successful ad man; literary eminence; cancer warrior. Ed stepped down as Creative Director at

K&E, the position I was hired for, because lymphoma was taking its toll. But he continued to work: he'd come to the office as many days a week as his strength would allow.

Ed was tall in stature, probably 6'2" or so. But he was tall in other ways as well. As respected as he was in the realm of advertising, Ed was a *giant* in the world of letters. Under his *nom de plume*, L.E. Sissman, Ed wrote "Bystander," a column of observations on the human condition in the *Atlantic Monthly*. His poems appeared regularly in *The New Yorker,* the *Atlantic* and other top-tier publications. L.E. "Ed" Sissman's fans included John Updike ("(Sissman) is, of course, a marvel."); James Dickey, himself a great poet, maybe better known as the author of *Deliverance*: ("(Sissman's) work glows with a kind of deep and generous wit."); the brilliant humorist S.J. Perelman ("A man of dazzling talent.").

Add to those who admired his words, Bob Baker. Add to those who held him in highest regard as a human being, Bob Baker. It was Ed, God bless him, who saved me -- from my clueless self. He easily could have come in couple days a week, nodded good morning to me, smoked his pipe, toyed with a New England Merchants Bank ad job order (Ed *owned* the NEMB account), popped to the Harvard Club for lunch, back to K&E for another pipe, grab the trolley at 4:30. But ... this is Ed Sissman. The ultimate man of grace.

I'm my usual early bird self. Ed's his usual early bird self. I smoke a pipe. Ed smokes a pipe. We sit in my -- his former -- office and shoot the baloney over coffee and tobacco in the 7:30 to 8:30 time slot, before anyone else is around. And he fills me in. And I listen. And

we start to get to know each other. And he eases me down easily from my (self-perceived) illustriousness. And he listens to me. And we get to know each other -- as friends. And though there's no such thing as Immaculate Creative Directorshipness, Ed provides me in his unassuming way as close as there is to an indoctrination.

What's more, this man who has every reason in the world not to need to, treats me as if I'm somewhat important, pretty OK. When his book *Scattered Returns* is published, he invites Nancy and me to the publication cocktail party which is held in the offices of the *Atlantic Monthly*. And over drinks and cheese and crackers at the party we get to mingle with such as the stormcloud-haughty poet Robert Lowell and the extremely affable John Updike and his delightful then-wife Mary.

I had a brief conversation with Updike. There was a genuineness about him; he made it seem as if we're a couple of fellow human beings having a chat. I told him I'd seen the recently released film version of his American classic, *Rabbit Run*, and thought the opening was one of the best ever: middle-aged, down-on-himself, down-in-the-dumps Rabbit Angstrom exits a low-rent bar, lights a butt, slouches along, coat slung on shoulder, happens on teenagers in game of playground basketball, flicks the cigarette, jumps into the game, plays like a teenage kid for a minute or so, quits the scene running full out -- *yanks* the pack of butts from his pocket, chucks it to the winds. Updike said he hadn't seen the film yet, but liked the sound of that opening.

As further evidence of Ed Sissman's graciousness, he asked me a favor. (Another of Dad's truisms: "If you want to show someone friendship ... ask them a favor." As surprising as it may sound, the premise is as basic as this: "I trust you. I'm not too proud or too important to say I need your help, even if you have to say no.")

Ed had been asked to emcee the Club of Odd Volumes "Bawdy Night," a holiday season dinner gathering of the cream of New England literati. The assignment this year was limericks, filthy limericks -- the raunchier, the better, he said (though in literate voice of course). Ed allowed that, though poet he is, the limerick is not his native tongue. If I, with a bit of Irish in me, might have a limerick thought or two, he'll gladly entertain them.

I gave him several, and he used two. He said they went over well. I only remember one:

> In these days of conscienceless sex,
> we're reminded of Oedipus Rex.
> He found it no bother to diddle his mother,
> then on to the relative next.

•

I was presented The L.E. Sissman Award by the Advertising Club of Boston, at the Hatch Awards in 1994 -- awarded annually to the person who "successfully combined a career in advertising with excellence in the arts, while reflecting the *joie de vivre*, skill and unflinching professionalism of Ed Sissman." Ed, the accomplished ad man and towering presence on the American literary scene, died in 1976. The meaningfulness of the award itself, along with the fact that the one-and-only Jack Connors nominated me for it, made this an especially proud moment for me.

Stick It!

Even though I wasn't a hockey fan, I knew enough about him to be a Bobby Orr fan. But then other than the occasional Bantu tribesman minding his goats in the green hills of Africa, it seemed everybody in the '70s was a Bobby Orr fan.

Thus it was more than a little exciting to know this late-September, 1970, day I'd be meeting the guy who immortalized himself last May 10th with his mythic "airborne" Stanley Cup-winning goal against the St. Louis Blues.

K&E had signed Bobby to act as spokesman for B&M beef stew commercials, and we're to meet him in the locker room at the Boston Garden after practice, to audio-tape his readings of the script -- to get a feel for his delivery.

The "we" in the stands watching practice that day in late September are my humble (justifiably) self and three exalted (the only kind) account executive Suits. When practice ends, we sit there till we're called to the locker room. Orr's in civvies, seated on a bench in front of his locker, laughing and chatting it up with Derek Sanderson.

We get introduced all around, and Head Suit, with the solemnity of the Archbishop of Canterbury, droningly imparts our mission to Orr. Head Suit sets the tape recorder whirring on the bench and hands him the script. Bobby grabs the mic and with no hesitation delivers three readings, all of which were ballpark (make that, *rink*), each of which, with minimal coaching, is better than the previous.

Now he volunteers to give one more reading – his interpretation. We gladly agree. Easing into his patented boyish grin, Bobby improvs the payoff: "And so kids, be sure to ask your mom to serve you up some of that B&M beef stew for supper tonight ... it'll make ya shit!"

Even the Suits broke up.

From the second we left the locker room, along the passageway, and continuing down the plateaus of steps exiting the Garden, my exclamation points dart the rafters: "Wow! What a guy! Not a phony bone in his body! Wow! What a fun guy! Wow!"

"Hey Baker, relax ... OK? What're you, some kind of *hero*-worshipper or something?" volunteers a Suit. "You're just a hero-worshipper, Baker," echoes another.

"You're right. I'm a hero-worshipper. "Damn right I am," I admit, as I fire off another fusillade of !!!!!!!!!s.

We're on the last tier of steps -- I'm on my 49th! A voice from behind us, resonant with idolatry, sings out, "You the guys who just interviewed *Bobby Orr*!?"

We swivel our heads to get a reading on just how threatening this whack-job at our backs might be. It's *Orr*, skipping down the steps, a 360 grin orbiting his face. He passes us, with a wave and "See ya at the TV thing," he fast-walks the parking lot to his car.

His ability to poke fun at himself ... superstar.

Despite insistent spewing of "hero-worshipper!"s from the three Suits, I'm fast-walking four steps ahead of them, to maybe catch Bobby's car as he pulls out of the lot, give him a wave -- and maybe catch a wave back.

Fate is with me. I arrive at the lane juncture of the parking lot as his brown Cadillac comes along. I begin my wave. He stops the car. Lowers the window.

The three Suits have almost caught up with me. But I'm still a step closer ... to the window.

"Any you guys want one a my old practice sticks?" Orr asks, as he reaches into the back and hands forth the stick.

To the guy closest to the window. Who thanks him a lot.

He smiles. "See ya guys." Drives off.

The three Suits now attempt to fast-talk the guy who was closest to the window. "OK guys," says the Head Suit. "Let's all flip coins ... or throw fingers ... see who gets the stick ... "

"Hero-worshipper, huh?" says the guy who'd been closest to the window -- and who now cradles the Victoriaville Pro hockey stick with white tape for grip on its handle, Orr's trademark single band of one-inch black tape at the 'sweet spot' of its blade, and "4 B. Orr" imprinted on its shaft, as if it were the sacred sword, Excalibur. Which, in a way, it is.

"Hero-worshipper, huh? Guess what, shitbirds ... fuck you."

•

*Foot*note. When we were making the commercial, I asked Bobby what he attributed his success on the ice to. Without hesitation, he said, "Fast feet." And, he added, " I don't wear socks. Skates fit like a glove. Feel the ice better. Better control."

The Medium Is Definitely the Message

So some of us socialite types decide that a pretty good farewell party which is jollying itself in the board room at K&E one 6:30 p.m. could maybe jolly itself more jollily in the more party-friendly environs of a fellow worker's pad up there on Beacon Hill.

We make our way pad-ward, and flagons of booze, wine and beer find their way into welcoming hands, and funny cigarettes are shared by some. The tunes are on, and everyone's having a time anywhere from mellow to high.

I have occasion to hit the john. So I shut the door to the tiny bathroom, and stand before the hopper. Thumbtacked upon the wall above the hopper there, before my wondering eyes appears a bright-colored cardboard sign, in ye-olde-sampler-style format -- acquired at a 'head shop,' most likely:

IF IT FEELS GOOD ... DO IT

Something feels good to me. So I *do* the *it* which feels good to me. I remove the tacks, slide the 8" x 14" placard under the cover of my navy blue crewneck sweater, and rejoint ... er, re*join* ... the party.

I still have the sign.

It feels good.

Johnny Music

We rented a cottage at Bonnie Oaks on Lake Morey in Vermont one weekend in June, 1970. Nancy, five-year-old Rich, eight-month-old Kate and I arrived late Friday afternoon, grabbed supper around 6 and headed over to the building which served as a glorified rec room: replete with TV, pool table, card tables.

Two guys were playing chess. I asked if I could take on the winner. I hadn't played more than a dozen times since I was 12, not long after Mom taught me the game. But I did enjoy it whenever I got the chance.

The winner turned out to be a white-haired guy with a 'Brooklyn' face -- think Walter Matthau. "Next victim," he said.

This guy by the name of Johnny Marks did not beat me. He bloody well *torched* me. "Check ... *mate*, Mister Man!" in about 4.2 minutes. We played a couple more games, and we both har-de-harred a lot -- mostly over the ineptitude of Mister Man. At blessed last, having sated his blood lust, this Johnny Marks guy said, "Bob, why don't you and your wife and kids come over for a drink. We have a house down the road here on the lake."

So we hopped in our car and went down to Johnny's place and met his wife and they fixed drinks, and we settled into the comfortably cluttered living room with a sizable window on the lake.

I asked Johnny what he did. "I'm a songwriter, the old-fashioned Tin Pan Alley kind. We used to turn out songs like the Chinese turn out babies," he said. He went over to a veteran upright piano, parked himself on the bench and proceeded to ripple the keys. "Yeah," he said, "I wrote *this* 30 years ago, which you never heard of ...

dinky donky dinky donky

"And then I wrote *this* maybe 15 years ago, which you never heard of either ...

dinky donky dinky donky

"But then I wrote ... *this* ...

bum bum ba bum pa bum bum ... bumpa bum ba pum ba pum

We've all heard it once or twice: "Rudolph, the Red-Nosed Reindeer."

As we're leaving, Johnny invites us down to New York "to play chess some time." The chess part was obviously a polite facade. Just one helluva nice guy.

Quality Guy

Sometime in 1969, we meet another New Kid in the Old Town. Pete Hart. Pete is handsome, bright and personable; his star is on the ascent in management of the accounting firm of Price-Waterhouse. Best of all, Pete Hart is the part Gary Cooper always played, the downhome-honest goodguy. Except that Pete Hart isn't *acting* the downhome-honest goodguy part. Pete Hart's the real deal. In every best sense. Over the course of a party or several, Pete and I find we enjoy each other's take on life, and we become best of friends.

Years later, Pete calls me one time with word that other pals of his have use of a place on Nantucket for a duck hunting weekend in November -- would I maybe be interested?Sure 'nuff. I drove to Woods Hole that Friday, rode the ferry to Nantucket, rented a Jeep and picked up Pete, John and Arna Jensen and Pepper Frazier at the airport.

The "bonus" here is that Pepper Frazier's the son of the man who, far as I'm concerned, could well have been the reincarnation of F. Scott Fitzgerald. Pepper's dad, George Frazier, legendary Boston columnist, was a spellbinding raconteur with velvet wit who mirrored Fitzgerald in -- Frazier's favorite word, *duende* ... a charismatic style. (From Charles Fountain's biography, *Another Man's Poison*: after a booze-fueled scene, Frazier's wife Mimsi tells him she wants a divorce: "But Mimsi," George said, "we *can't* get a divorce. We're the young Scott Fitzgeralds!")

We stayed at Frazier's small-but-elegant red-brick townhouse near the center of Nantucket. The bar stayed open all weekend for me. *And* the two long-stemmed blonde Texas beauties who arrived Friday night to come visit l'il ol' Peppah dahlin'.

The other guys did go duck hunting in the chill black *quack* (heh) of dawn Saturday and Sunday, but I felt it my bounden duty to jam with the Yellow Roses who were drinking Jack Daniels, as I accompanied them on my JB and soda. The guys came back late afternoon and we all did have a lively good time. Pure as snowflakes, far as John and I were concerned, but Pete, Arna and Pepper had the benefit of singlehood at the time, so who knows?

I reveled in the Scott Fitzgerald weekend. I particularly enjoyed not firing a shot. Other than the occasional JB.

Mean

The man I'll call Manny Kagan here who was head art director at one Boston ad agency in my days on the scene was ill famed for his sadistic ways -- of particular note, his M.O. in dismissing someone.

He'd invite the object of dismissal into his office at 4:45 Friday afternoon. Without inviting the victim to take a seat, Manny grabs a layout pad and a Magic Marker and doodles a sketch of flames. He shows the victim the doodle. "Know what that is?" Manny asks.

"Fire," mutters the victim. With an expressive arch of his eyebrows, Lenny says, "That's right."

"What about it?" says the victim.

"That's what you are," Lenny says -- pointing to the sketch, his eyebrows frozen in arch.

"That's what I am."

"Yes. You are that."

"What do you mean I am 'that'? You mean I'm ... I'm ... *fire*?"

"That's right. Grab your stuff and see Louise about the paperwork and two weeks pay. She'll mail it to you. Shut the door on the way out, OK?"

You Never Know

Early on in business on my own. Rap on door; in walks thirtyish guy who introduces himself as Joe Desmond (not his real name).

Chiropractor, new in Marblehead. How much would I charge to do a brochure? I say creative fee will be $250, which is lowball, giving another rookie a break. I explain production and printing costs will be extra. Joe says, "Do it."

Few days later, I present proposed copy and a rough layout, which Joe approves. I get estimates on production and printing -- 550, which includes my fee. Joe says, "Go." The printed brochures are delivered to Desmond, and I send him a bill. More than a month later, he sends me a check for $300, which I use to pay the designer and printer. Now we're down to the $250 he owes me, which I bill him for. And which I bill him a month later for. And a month later-later for. Which inspires him to send me $75. So I bill him again, for the $175 balance.

Nothing. Month later, I re-bill him. He sends me another $75. As a matter of principle, I kept billing him for that $100 balance for almost another year -- till I hear one day he's vacated town for parts unknown. So I wrote it off to 'lesson learned.'

Eight years later, on the morning of -- God's truth -- *Christmas Eve*, I pull into Lenny Frost's Shell station around 7:30. A car pulling away from the pumps as I'm coming in does a U-ey. Guy gets out of the car and comes over. I roll down the window -- he says, "I'm Joe Desmond. How much I owe you ... a hundred, right?"

I gape at him, dumbfounded. He pulls a wad from his pocket, peels five 20s. "I'm sorry," he says. Gets back in his car and drives off.

A few months later, I had reason to recount the story to Randy Goodwin, president of the National Grand Bank. "I wished I'd known Desmond was in town," Randy said, "he still owes me 30 grand."

It's' Routine

My weekday startup routine when I first went out in business for myself: Hit a local breakfast place around 6:30. Sass around with Carla, a dark-haired magnificently configured spitfire -- ordering up one of my usual unusual concoctions for breakfast, like a cheeseburger. Carla, who'd dubbed me "It," would snarl into the kitchen, "Guess what *It* wants for breakfast this morning? A *cheeeese*burger!" Turning to me, "And how would *It* like *It*'s *cheeeeseburger* cooked?" she'd ask. "Medium rare, thank you very much, Carla," I meekly reply. "*It* says It wants It's cheeseburger medium *raaare*," she snarls with renewed vigor.

One of my best takes with Carla was the morning I went in and she sauces up across the counter from me. Instead of the usual loose white blouse, today it seems, she's wearing a tight-fitting hot pink sweater which makes the distinction between the male and female of our species immediately and doubly apparent.

"Gee, Carla, that's a nice pair of sweaters you've got on there," I remarked.

"Shut up, It," she said. "Whaddya want?"

I sit there, my eyes fixed on the hot pink sweaters, and I sputter, "Gee, Carla, I dunno. How 'bout? Oh, I don't know. Don't know why I say this, but I's thinkin' maybe ... how about ... how about, like ... two ... *milks*?"

She swats my forehead with the order pad.

On the way out, I meet her at the usual cash register, she hands me the usual check. I hand her my Mobil card. She says, "You can't use that here, stupid!"

"Why not? I got *gas*, didn't I?"

"Gimme the money, and get the hell out! And don't come back till next time, OK? Mister *Itttttt*!"

•

After breakfast, it's time for my aerobic drive around Marblehead Neck. What is aerobic driving, you ask?

Simply put, aerobic driving is a series of calorie-burning/muscle-toning exercises you perform while driving your car. Pressure on accelerator. Lifting of foot to apply pressure to brake. Glancing out windows, turning head laterally side to side to catch scenery. Uptilt of jaw and raising of eyes to check out rearview mirror. The surprising expenditure of energy it takes for all that, *and* manipulate the wheel (even with power steering), all the while keeping the vehicle steady-as-she-goes throughout the entire 2-mile oval circuit of Marblehead Neck.

Muscles tingling, I'm only slightly gasping for breath and I'm ready now to face the day.

FURNACE

In '75, I teamed up with a terrific media-savvy guy named Steve Decatur who lived in Marblehead who'd also gone out on his own. Steve handled the planning and placement on media-related accounts and we worked out a split on media commissions.

Everyone has idiosyncrasies. Steve has some of the best.

On entering his condo office on Cliff Street one winter's day, a memo pad note on the rug FURNACE stares up at me. When I ask about it, Steve says it's there to remind him to turn down the heat when he heads home at night.

Stopping by his office a couple weeks' later, the FURNACE note's in residence there on the rug. But/and, as I go to leave, there's another FURNACE note taped to the door.

"What's the story, Steve?"

"At first the one on the rug did the trick, but then I got so used to it ... " He chuckled sheepishly.

On the way to breakfast the next morning, I stop my vehicle in front of the Decaturs' Gregory Street home. The Boston Globe is there on the porch step. I adhere a yellow Post-It note to the wrapper ...

Sailing

Part of the Hood Sailmakers story has to do with my work on the advertising account. The subtext has to do with sailing mythology.

Calvin Coolidge said, "The chief business of the American people is business." The chief business of Marblehead is sailing. Marblehead has been the "Yachting Capital of America" since the 1890s. 1900 boats of all size and description fill the mile-long harbor the summer long. Marblehead sailors have won virtually every major national and international sailing competition, most notably the Holy Grail of yachting, the America's Cup. Six yacht clubs rim the harbor, including one specifically devoted to sailing programs for youngsters. Yacht yards, marine architects and surveyors, boat builders, marine supply stores, yacht brokers, sailmakers occupied 73 listings in the white pages of the Marblehead phone book in the '70s.

Hood Sailmakers was the premier name in U.S. sailmaking when I was appointed their advertising agency of record in 1975, and Ted Hood himself was the top sailor in the world, having skippered the 12 meter Courageous to victory in the America's Cup in 1974.

"sail" "thirble" 'smorf"

A standout memory was the iron-gray Friday morning in December, 1976 -- I did say *December*! Hood marketing director at the time and super sailor, Robbie Doyle called: "Meet me in 20 minutes at the

landing, we're going out to watch the two Teds match race the 12s."
(Translation: Meet him at the town landing so we could buzz out in
a power boat beyond the harbor to watch Ted Hood and Ted Turner,
brassballed head of CCN and husband of movie star Jane Fonda, try
out new sails on 12 meter boats in match-race conditions. Hood was
at the helm of Independence; Turner, sporting his signature blue and
white train engineer's cap, manned the helm of Courageous -- the
boat Turner would sail to victory in the America's Cup the following
summer.)

I didn't say it, but I was sure as shit thinking, "You gotta be
kidding, Robbie!" I knew he wasn't. So I grabbed a $30 heavy-duty
slicker at the marine supply store handy to the town landing -- it
could be damp out there on the brine.

We jumped into the 17' Boston Whaler and cast off. Said event
signified the end of my innards -- and sanity -- for the next however
too long it was. For the next however too long it was the Tinker
Toy Whaler body-slammed the arctic Atlantic. Over wave crests
the height of Everest, occasionally I'd get a glimpse of one of the
12s; every once in a while I even saw them both. Over the roar of
the engine and the thunderous WHUMP of the hull against the
sea, occasionally I'd catch a word from Robbie -- "sail" "Ted" "new"
"thirble" "smorf." Whenever we got back to the landing, I felt like an
astronaut returning to earth -- only better. I could have kissed the
frozen dock, I was so glad it was over.

I tell that story to seriously-into-pain, diehard sailors -- which is
the only kind there is -- and they look at me in awe. As if I was
blessed to be on the same ocean with, and allowed to have the shit
beat out of me, while intermittently granted the Beatific Vision of
The Two Teds Match Racing 12s ... *plus* ... throw in a snot-icicling
December day as a *bonus*! "Wow! You were one lucky guy!" sailors
say when I reach the end of the story. I'd get nowhere arguing to
the contrary with that masochistic breed, so I just give em a John
Wayne, "Yeh."

Start with a Trifecta ... Then Quit

Every now and then, I have to haul out my other "Sailing Icons" story -- to accompany the tale of the two Teds.

The summer of '52 was my second year lifeguarding at Rocky Point Beach Club in Old Greenwich. We'd belonged there since I was a little kid. My parents enjoyed it; I was never big on it. I did the Sunday morning swimming meets in my kidhood, because in those unenlightened days of yore, kids did what they were told to do -- and I was told to.

I never took sailing lessons, though; because I wasn't told to -- and I had zero interest. Which is why it knocked me twelve ways to Sunday when George Reichhelm stopped by the lifeguard chair one day and said, "Would you be my crew for Junior Day at Larchmont Race Week next week?"

Consider the reasons for my shock:

• George Reichhelm was the coolest guy in all of Greenwich. George Reichhelm was a natural born winner. A hero in my book. For one thing, he looked the part. Wiry, chiseled features, falcon's eyes. Never took a lesson in anything. A natural: kicked serious ass at whatever crossed his path. Club swimming championships, crosstown football games, poker, unattainable babes -- you name it, George snagged the W. When it came to sailing, he was the coolest guy in the country. The previous summer, he'd skippered the Rocky Point team to victory in the Sears Cup, the United States' National Junior Sailing Championship. (I should note here, too, that Robbie Doyle was *twice* a Sears Cup-winning skipper -- and later founded his own world-class sailmaking company, Doyle Sails.)

• George said we'd be sailing Skip Etchells' *Shillalah*, the boat Skip and his wife Mary (O'Toole) Etchells had won the Worlds Star Championships in in 1951 -- their other Star was *Shamrock*. (That statement is ripe with sailing iconography. Skip Etchells, a giant of a man,, was one of the founders of Rocky Point. He was also one of yachting's premier designers. In 1967, Skip introduced what became one of the gold standards of contemporary racing sailboats, the Etchells -- the big, fast, stable sloop described by America's Cup victor, Dennis Conner, as "the world's best racing class." The slightly smaller Star boat, originated in 1911, has always been one of the most popular 'racing machines' for competitive sailors.)

I had no illusions whatsoever about George's invitation. It was getting close to deadline, and his regular crew was likely unavailable -- he needed somebody to make an attempt at working the jib and whatever else -- as per the skipper's orders. But the way George asked, and the fact that he'd always gone out of his way to be nice to me, where most of the other kids when I was growing up had treated me as an outsider -- I said "Sure." With enthusiasm.

The following Wednesday, I met George at Rocky Point at 6 a.m. -- flat calm Long Island Sound, and pea soup fog. We rowed out to the beat up old launch, which of course, had no intention whatsoever of starting. Which meant that George had to fuss and tinker and "you *fucker*" it until it finally gasped into submission to ignition. We grabbed *Shillalah* off her mooring and George somehow miracled our way through the soup -- which of course lifted the minute Larchmont Yacht Club hove into view.

On the way to Larchmont, George demonstrated yet another aspect of his larger-than-lifeness. No bottle opener to snap the caps from our bottles of Coke -- George pried them off with his teeth.

In the race itself, I was a clunkburger crew, made none the better by a busted winch on the starboard side. (That's about the extent of my salty vocabulary -- "winch" & "starboard.") We didn't finish last. But thanks to me, we weren't far off. George, to his everlasting credit, didn't sweat it. We had a bunch of laughs, and we caught a fast-stepping, Grunch-caliber dance at the club that night. Larchmont Yacht Club had this incredible party room: The Pandemonium -- is that the best name ever, or what!?

I danced with a girl in a blue and white polka dot dress who I fell in love with. Lost that one, too.

That story, iconically seasoned with "Skip Etchells", "World Star Championship boat" and "Sears Cup-winning skipper," gets a nod of respect from even the crustiest salts I share it with. I end saying I never raced again for the obvious reason it's an impossible act to follow.

woo-woo

I'm a woo-woo magnet. A "woo-woo" was son Rich's and my nickname for an amazing Twilight Zone-caliber coincidence connecting two or more entities. Synchronicity is another word for it.

Example of a major woo-woo -- totally verifiable, I still have the letter: 1999. John Updike's *New Yorker* piece about uncanny experiences in his life inspired me to send him a piece I'd written about an 'uncanny' experience in my own life.

Less than a week later I received a reply. I'd been fortunate enough to have received *five* brief notes from the man famous for the line, "Gods do not answer letters" in the past, but this was almost a typewritten-page long. I decided to count the words of text -- just so I could brag: "John Updike? *The* John Updike? Well, *The* John Updike, he took the trouble to write me a ... *245* (as it turned out)-word letter! How 'bout that?!"

I made a photocopy of the letter and began counting, writing the count in pencil next to each word -- here I underline the woo-woo connections:

"

Dear (1) Bob (2) Baker (3):
I (4) read (5) it (6) all (7), through (8) the (9) <u>uncanny</u> (10) bit (11) on (12) page (13) 12 (14) and (15) the (16) Cambridge (17) color (18) on (19) 25 (20). I (21) believe (22) my (23) first (24) wife's (25) sister's (26) beau (27) -- my (28) future (29) brother-in-law (30) -- lived (31) on (32) Story (33) Street (34), which (35) was (36) indeed (37) a (38) choice (39) location (40). And (41) I (42) used (43) to (44) speak (45) to (46) that (47) class (48) in (49) publishing (50) when (51) Doily (52) Venn (53) ran (54) it (55), way (56) back (57). As (58) to (59) your (60) ms. (61) itself (62), you're (63) <u>64</u> (64) and (65) I'm (66) <u>67</u> (67) ...

"

What are the odds? In a letter about things <u>uncanny</u>, Updike's reference to my age at the time -- <u>64</u>, which I'd mentioned in my letter to him -- and his age -- <u>67</u> -- are the spot-on *64*th and *67*th words!

Coincidence? Of course. But more. Woo-woos of varying degrees of *im*probability spring up and hit me in the head like stepping on a rake, and with such frequency I've come to believe something's going on. Something extra-normal, paranormal, even supernatural.

Often I sense a 'message' aboard. A sign. God letting me know he's with me, on the same wavelength; endorsing something I'm thinking about doing, validating a decision, or just plain encouraging me.

(I should note, too, that, in addition to this long -- and *uncanny* -- response from literary 'god' John Updike, the fact that it was my *6th* letter from him, is a delicious counterpoint to the ending of "Hub Fans Bid Kid Adieu," his iconic October 22nd, 1960 *New Yorker* profile on Red Sox legend Ted Williams' last at bat -- a home run. Updike's too-cool-for-school last sentence tossed off Williams' non-response to the frenzied acclaim of the fans as he circled the bases, saying, "Gods do not answer letters." Couldn't prove it by this letter-getter -- a great man, John Up.)

Bar Car Train of Thought

Something reminded me of a deliciously insane W.C. Fields line: "I make it a habit to never drink anything stronger than gin before breakfast," he said. *Which* reminded me of a line on the same *track* as Fields': "He built a bar in the back of his car, and he's driving himself to drink." *Which* reminded me of a story in the '70s when I was partnered with Chet Sawtelle to play a tennis match against a Beach Club team in Swampscott. It was a bright Sunday morning made the brighter by Chet's classic Rolls Corniche we rode to Swampscott in. We finished our match about 9:30, having been swiftly reduced to rubble by our Beach Club opponents. Chet, a most courtly (p.i) gentleman in his late 60s, asked our worthy massacrers, "Would you gentlemen care for a libation?" The stunned *"Huh?!"* look that covered the faces of the Beach Club guys (and me) was eased when one of the Beach guys says, "A drink? Sure." (figuring maybe Chet had a cooler with a couple of six-packs in the trunk). We ambled over to the car. Chet popped the trunk, and ... *Wow!* There to our wondering eyes appeared a fully stocked, elegantly crafted mini bar built into the trunk of the Corniche! When I say fully-stocked, I mean racks of nips of every flavor of liquor imaginable, mixers, silver ice bucket and tongs, shakers, cooler of beer ... you get the picture.

Humanity

As numbing as my divorce was in 1978, it caused me to see life in general, and Marblehead in particular, in a new light -- the light of Earth. Ten years in the stratosphere of Boston advertising and 3 1/2 years dabbling at the craft in Marblehead had done nothing to rid me of the air of 'aboveness' acquired in my Gatsby days in Greenwich.

To make matters worse, I did -- *we* did -- belong to the elite Eastern Yacht Club on the Neck, and its winter-months' cousin, the Gut 'n Feathers badminton club in downtown Marblehead. Many of our friends belonged to a yacht club, or the Beach Club in neighboring Swampscott.

None of us were snobs. We intermingled with townies and contractors at Maddie's and at Midget Football fundraisers at the Gerry 5 VFA. But we pretty much hung with the executives-in-Boston kind when it came to house parties.

The thing about divorce was that, short of the wife being an adulteress, the husband was instantly the 'odd man out' on the social scene -- as in s-h-u-n-n-e-d. Thus d-i-v-o-r-c-e morphed me from member of The Club Crowd into a sullen sudden applicant for membership in the fraternity of The Bar Crowd.

Acceptance was far from automatic. I had to learn to stop reciting my resume: "The Story of Bob the Magnificent in New York at Cote Basque East & Among the Glitterati of Boston Ad-dom." I had to learn to shut up and listen. And open my eyes.

So I did that: I listened and watched -- and shut up. And, eventually, I got accepted. There wasn't a ceremony or anything. It occurred gradually over time. I happened onto some colorful fabulously wonderful characters and good stories along the way -- on and off the bar scene. We were all players in the Marblehead troupe of *The Human Comedy*.

Linc

Linc Hawkes is a damned hard guy to tackle with a typewriter. Rowdy, inventive, coarse, precise, quick, generous, irrepressible, funny, feisty, bawdy, clever, mischievous -- that's a start.

Linc could do most anything with his hands. Even more with his mind. His genius factory there on a half-acre of land next to Redd's Pond was unvarnished, full to over, and rarely still. A series of worksheds connected to the more substantial main building housed hundreds of his makings and himself. A small ancient barn clung for its life out back.

Linc carved signs; built an organ and taught himself to play the fugues of Bach on it. He made furniture; built boats; put a house on skids and rafted it across the pond; fished; ran a sawmill; had a sign out front of his place, "Antiques Made to Order -- Up to 300 Years Old"; wrote poetry not of the Emily Dickinson sort but of the filthy sort; near drowned himself a million times over in towering rum squalls which took days to subside; raised his own vegetables; raged against developers trying to trash his beloved "Marblehead Town"; taught himself to paint a pretty fair landscape; cooked up his own booze; recited books from memory, spun a good yarn, croaked raunchy songs; motored the town in later years in his weathered red convertible, scally cap at its usual rakish angle, usual Camel cigarette adangle a corner of his mouth, the buxom, not-unattractive live-in blonde in her 30s at his side.

Kept a cow and a bull. Inspired by a blast or seven of hooch, he walked Humpy the bull to the Town House on Election Day one year, to introduce Humpy to the politicians. Then promenaded Humpy down State Street to Stan Sacks' antique store, seeking to enter in and re-enact the saying, "like a bull in a china shop." Stan Sacks thought that wasn't such a good idea, so Linc walked Humpy across the street and into the Landing Pub. Refused to leave until he (Linc) was served. Said he could care less if the bull was thirsty, but he (Linc) was -- and they'd damn well better serve him. They damn well did.

Before exiting the Landing, Humpy deemed it appropriate to leave a souvenir.

Linc came by my place once to check out some tools I'd found in an old junk shop in Maine some time back. I told him he could have any he wanted, no charge. We chatted a few, and then -- I don't know how it came up -- he said, with a twinkle in his eye, "Y'know, I been thinkin' 'bout makin' love ta my cow one a these times. Only thing is, ya got such a long way ta go ta kiss her goodnight."

He winked. Though Linc was in his mid-60s at the time, it didn't matter: I was looking at a fresh-faced kid named Huck Finn.

&

Chip Percy, master bartender and co-owner of the Three Cod Tavern, told me another one about Linc. It seems, back in the 1970s, a fellow by the name of Newt Clemson wanted Linc to do some carpentry for him on a Sunday. Linc said he'd do it, and gave Newt his price, and said that because it was a Sunday, Linc required what he called a 'Sunday' bonus. "What would that be?" Newt asked. "I need you to pick me up a clam plate from Dill's before I start work. Tell em it's for me. It'll cost you 5 bucks." Newt agreed, and on Sunday morning he called Dill's Restaurant and ordered a clam plate for Linc Hawkes. He went to Dill's, asked for the clam plate for Linc Hawkes, paid the $5, and they told him to go round to the back door, where he was handed a quart of gin in a brown paper bag. (You couldn't buy bottled liquor or packaged goods on Sundays at the time.)

Oops

Ed Samson was a mountainous macho guy who ingested Mount Gay Rum and red meat -- in quantity. If he used the word "liberal," it was usually in tandem with "perverts" -- and more spat than spoken. As is often the case, Ed had his soft-hearted side, mainly as related to wife Jen and daughter Amy. But in the main, Ed was Alpha Male.

Ed told this one on himself when we were in Jake Cassidy's one time: Into Ed's yacht brokerage office one morning walks a guy who browses the boat listings on the corkboards, and informs Ed there's one he'd like to look at. Ed says it's in a boatyard up in Beverly, and for the guy to follow him and Ed'll show it to him.

Ed has Jen's car for the day, his ride's in the shop. Guy gets in his car and follows Ed to Beverly. Ed exits Jen's car, walks around back to meet the guy -- who pulled up behind him.

Ed notices a sticker on the back bumper of Jen's car which is new: SO MANY MEN, SO LITTLE TIME.

One $4 Ring, Priceless.

The store near State Street on Washington had been closed for years. Frozen in time in the window display, the trappings of a drug store/variety store, circa the 1950s. Lipsticks and mirrors and fountain pens and razors and scissors and clocks and junk jewelry and perfumes and fine soaps and pins in motley array.

And dust and spider webs and dead flies.

Gazing through the window on even the brightest day revealed only a soda fountain looming one wall, and glass display cases and shelving against the other.

Miracle of miracles, driving by one Saturday morning I look, and ... *Sesame!* ... the door she is open! I pull over and enter. First thing to greet my senses is the musty smell of an old attic. Though it's sunny outside, it takes a few seconds to adjust to the half-light.

On entrance, a figure seated behind a glass case in the darkest recess of the room rises and moves towards me -- in labored step. A prunefaced gnome of a woman cloaked in a brown serape. She peers up at me through the filthy lenses of horn-rimmed glasses; then, as if disgusted by what she's seen, clams shut the lids.

"Can I ... can I look around?"

Her "Yes" is high-pitched, drawn out -- Wicked-Witch-ish (say *that* 10 times fast).

"Are things for ... are you selling things?"

"Yes." Eyelids part.

"How long you been closed?"

"54."

"54 years?"

"1954."

"Oh ... am I your first customer?"

"Yes."

On the verge of coming down with the bends from the depth and intensity of our conversation, I somehow manage to summon the strength to tear myself away and explore Aladdin's Cave. What does it hold? What gems will I unearth?

Aladdin's Cave replicated the window on the Cave. Standard variety store fare.

I did mine one gem, though: I plucked the graduation ring from its tangled nest of pins and earrings in the costume jewelry case. It caught my attention because it seemed so out of place. What the hell was a man's ring doing in a henhouse? What school or college designation did it bear? Did somebody hock it for beer money or to pay the electric bill?

There must be a story here. And there was. It was typical enough at first glance: gold-plate ring, blue glass stone, elaborate eagle escutcheon. Now ... what school?

Therein the story which makes it priceless: Imprinted on the base-metal oval framing the blue glass stone, two words: HIGH SCHOOL.

Not MARBLEHEAD HIGH SCHOOL, not BOSTON LATIN HIGH SCHOOL, not GREATER SOUTHWESTERN ABNORMAL HIGH SCHOOL.

Just plain old HIGH SCHOOL! Why would this store stock such a ring? Who would buy such a ring? Why would anyone want such a ring?

Here's my scenario: The store stocked such rings because they'd sold a number of such rings. They'd sold such rings to young men in their early twenties who should have graduated from high school -- but hadn't. Young men in their early twenties who should have graduated from high school -- but hadn't -- *who* wanted to impress female girls of the opposite gender.

Sweet.

I had to have it. "Four dollars," the enchanted-enchanting crone informed me.

Not a perfect fit, so I've wrapped tape around the skinny part. I only wear it on special occasions; I call it my good luck ring. It's one of my favorite possessions. Because it's a story.

Hiro's the Hero Here-o

Hiro Naka is a terrific Japanese guy I played tennis with in the '90s. When I say Japanese, I mean 'Japanese executive working in the United States.' Hiro was a good tennis player with a good sense of humor. All too often, he'd slide a sly shot by me where I least expected it, which occasioned me to introduce him (by explanation, and then necessarily frequent usage) to the term "Pearl Harbor" -- shorthand descriptive for the Japanese "sneak attack" which got us into World War II.

Hiro caught me off guard so often that I was "Pearl Harbor, Hiro!"-ing him left and right. And he'd laugh his "Ha, Bob!" with great delight. One day, out of nowhere, I pulled off a sorta sly shot of my own -- and won the point.

Hiro put a mock-serious face on, looked at me, said, "Bob Harbor, Bob! Bob Harbor."

We both cracked up.

Breakfasts with Joe

It is not true that Joe Dever invented breakfast. Or that he was the inspiration for calling a cup of coffee "a cuppa joe."

Joe was, however, the undisputed overlord of the local breakfast scene in recent years. His rise to power in that arena wouldn't have been immediately apparent -- especially in light of his previous career. Until his retirement in '05, Joseph I. Dever was First Justice of the Lynn District Court, widely acclaimed for his evenhandedness and advocacy of alternative sentencing.

Even when he was still presiding over the court in Lynn, though, Joe was slowly but surely building his empire, his breakfastdom -- recruiting his capos at the Shipyard Galley, where I first met him early mornings in the 1990s.

The Shipyard was presided over by the very sensitive, semi-mental -- sorry, I meant 'sentimental' -- Russ, the perennial winner of the Miss Congeniality ... *Not!* award at the Bad Hash Slingers of America Convention held annually in Unnatural Acts, Iowa. When you knees-knockingly approached the counter to whimper your order, Russ's

"What the f-bomb do *you* want!" would trigger barks of maniacal laughter from the assembled congregation of Russophiles, including the likes of Joe, Chip Randall, Fred Lausier, Fraffie Welch, Dave Rodgers, Don Flynn, Phil Cash, Butch Morgan and Skip Lyons.

It was at the Shipyard that I got caught up in the magic of Joe Dever. The beauty of off-duty Joe Dever was that, no matter how serious the conversation, there was always the imp champing the bit behind the grin tickling his lips -- craving the least opening to explode in laughter. He was my kind of guy from the getgo, and we became the best of friends. (I was only one of many. As attested to by the outpouring of eulogies and tributes at the time of his departure, Joe Dever probably had more honest-to-God best friends than whatever the Facebook version record is.)

I was honored to have been Joe's guest at his Clover Club Christmas party once, and his retirement party. But easily the best times were the maybe 50 or so occasions in recent years when Joe would take a break from his pals at Dunkin, Starbucks and the Driftwood, and I'd pick him up at 6 and we'd shoot to Maria's Place in Salem for breakfast.

The stories we swapped. When Joe was in the Air Force reserve, at a commemoration of the atomic bomb drop on Nagasaki, Major General Charles Sweeney, who'd actually piloted the plane, had the abhorrent bad taste to have the band open the ceremony with "I'll Be Seeing You in All the Old Familiar Places." (Sounds like a clip from *Dr. Strangelove*.)

Joe made the mistake of sharing a story having to with his uncle, Paul Dever, who was Governor of Massachusetts from 1949 to 1953. It happened that the impossibly-cute Hollywood child movie star of the day, Margaret O'Brien, was in Boston for an event one time, and Joe, who was her age, had been her escort 'date' for a state function of some sort.

The next time Joe and I hit Maria's, when Joe got in the car, I handed him an envelope addressed to him at my address -- in as feminine handwriting as I'd been able to fake. As I handed it to Joe, I said, "I don't know how this got to me by mistake. It's a damn good thing."

Joe pulled the note from the envelope and broke up as he read it aloud, "Dearest Joe, All these years later and I still achingly miss your burning kisses! Margaret O." Then, with a wink, he suggested I get myself a lawyer.

One of the best bits of all was the charade repeated over-and-over once we got to Maria's and the waitress came by to take our orders.

I'd tell Joe to go first, and Joe, who had had some medical issues, but was allowed a Maria's now and then (I'd asked his son), went through the same hilarious script each time: "I'd like a medium orange juice. And two dropped eggs. No butter on the wheat toast. Wheat toast. Absolutely no butter. And thennnn ... (mischief plays his little-boy face) ... and thennnn, I'm going to ruin it all with an order of sausage paddies ... please???" -- he'd look at the waitress questioningly, and then me. I'd smile.

The waitress wrote. A little boy grinned. Life was good.

Very good.

Joe Dever did not invent breakfast -- he merely perfected it.

The Jones Mobius

Mister Jones was an unnoticeable man.

When I had my office on the second floor of Graves Yacht Yards in the 1970s, I'd have lunch three-four days a week at the Landing Pub, and every time, Mr. Jones would 'quiet' his way through the pub door at 12:45, give or take. It was long after I'd been lunching there before I really took notice of him -- and only then through comic incident.

Mary Hulbert, the bartender, and I were the sole inhabitants of the pub this one day. The door from the dining room corridor swings open. Ushers forth in poke-step, a stooped gray little man, probably late '70s, wearing a threadbare gray suit, blotting his thin reddish nose with a small wad of toilet paper, as he poke-steps towards the exit.

All of which would've continued his anonymity but for the stream of white being lifted and dragged in trail with every lift and step of his left foot -- a five-foot length of toilet paper adhered itself to the heel of his left shoe. I'm a study in mixed emotions at the sight of this sad little sniffling man and his ludicrous baggage. I have to stifle laughter begging release. A quick gesture, and I share my discovery with Mary.

When the outer door closed behind him, we both broke into hoots of laughter, and rushed to the window to follow his progress. The toilet paper had survived guillotining by the doors, and trailed him in insolent banner as he crossed Front Street and out of view up State Street.

"Who is he?"

"That's Mr. Jones, he's a widower. He comes every day, has lunch out in the dining room. Been doing it for years. Comes all the way from Newton by bus ... *two* buses."

"That's a couple hours each way."

"Probably. The waitresses all love him ... he has his own table out there."

"Anything else?"

"Nope. Just that he's a very nice man."

In the time it took Mary to tell me that, I'd gone from comic pity to highest admiration. This is a Man. As long as there's a day, there's a Grail. The fact it's as unbejeweled a Grail as the Landing mattered not: it was important it be pursued.

Important to me as well. From then on, I'd go out of my way: "Hi, Mr. Jones" and "Bye, Mr. Jones" as he came and went, always with highest respect.

On Christmas Eve one year, Mary said, "Come into the dining room with me. We all chipped in and we're giving Mr. Jones a present ... his very own mug for the one beer he has at lunch every day."

I followed her to the dining room. Mr. Jones, the lone patron, was gazing straight ahead -- it was hard to tell whether he was fixed on the stone-cold harborscape outside, or a warm memory in the deep of him.

Three waitresses and Mary approached his table. Mary handed him the gift, wrapped in white tissue, tied with red ribbon, a card tucked beneath the ribbon. "This is for you, Mr. Jones ... because you're our very favorite customer."

He looked up as though woken up. "Oh ... oh," he cooed in his sweet tenor voice.

"Open it, Mr. Jones. You can read the card on the way home on the bus."

It must have taken him three minutes, but finally he raised the silver cup forth, much as a priest raising on high the Chalice of Communion. "Oh ... oh ... oh," he sighed as he took in the splendor of his gift -- the physical manifestation of his Grail.

"Look, Mr. Jones, it's even got your name on it, 'Mr. Jones' -- it'll be right here for you when you come to lunch every day."

"Oh ... Mercy!" -- he began to sob in little soft gulps. He fetched for his napkin to dab his eyes, but he'd forgotten to remove his glasses, and so was only pat-pat-patting at the lenses, while the tears streamed down his cheeks.

Mary helped him off with his glasses and we all sang "For He's a Jolly Good Fellow" to him.

Soon thereafter, I switched lunch places and hadn't seen Mr. Jones in ages,. So I assumed he'd passed away.

&

You knew right away there was something special about Chris Jones.

It's daughter Kate's fourth birthday party and the kids are hopping about, having a mad old time, giggling, screaming and rending asunder.

Little Chris Jones is an island of calm there in the corner. You are immediately compelled to his eyes. They are disproportionate to his fragile face. They are great and round and dark and bright and full and empty all at the same time. These eyes do not blink. They do not wonder. They know.

The next time I was aware of Chris Jones, he was about 14.

10:30 on the morning of a school day, down the driveway of the high school veers and glides a skeletal, drab-clad figure on a skateboard. Despite the grace of the brief arcs being carved, it's to the figure's head my eyes are compelled. A skull: head shaved almost to the bone -- and shiny. Cheekbones forcing at shiny skin, mouth firmset, hollow, *knowing* eyes.

Chris Jones, maybe? Still marching -- skateboarding here -- to the distant drummer?

That evening, I described the skateboarder to Kate, and asked if it could've been Chris Jones. It was, and he also *was* a drummer, it turns out. "Yep, that's Chris. 'Cept now he's Bones. He's a wicked good drummer, with Straw Dogs. They even play in Boston and they're even going to make an album."

"He's a strange-looking little guy. What's he like?"

"Oh, he's just himself, Dad. He shaves his head and he's into his music and his skateboard and he's quiet a lot ... he's neat. And when he plays his drums all these wild things start happening ... he is so good, Dad."

Thereafter, I saw him often. I'd be driving along and there above the horizon of approaching car tops would glide the shining skull. Bones on his skateboard, entranced and entrancing -- at one with his cosmos, alone only to those who envied him.

For me, it was always a joyous sight: this so-old boy who seemed to know Beyond, passing in seamless flow slowed machines with big wheels, upon a board with little wheels which was a toy.

I don't know why, but it made me chuckle every time.

Bones Jones was killed in a car crash, May 1, 1986.

There is always shock at the passing of a young person. For those who knew him, though, the loss of Bones Jones wasn't just the loss of a good person, it was a loss of connection to the ether -- other things, other places. In a sense, the loss of this one little person meant a loss of freedom. The freedom to be here and somewhere very far away at the very same time.

The day after Bones Jones died, 'Bones Lives' appeared in white graffiti on the black bridge at the Marblehead/Salem town line. It was immediately painted over, per town ordinance and process.

To reappear the next morning, per passion and allegiance of friends.

The game of cat-and-mouse continued for a while until ... the graffiti ceased, and life moved on. Bones had apparently been consigned to memory.

But not: because he was to reappear a year later. I put together a small (one column wide, 3" high) memorial ad to run in the

Marblehead Reporter on the anniversary of his death. The message, lettered graffiti-style in white, against a black background: 'Bones Lives.'

Coming out of designer Geoff Hodgkinson's studio, on my way to deliver the finished ad to the Reporter, I caught sight of an old man walking along the sidewalk across the street.

A more stooped, more little man in a threadbare gray suit. Mr. Jones. Just poking and stepping along. To the Landing, no doubt.

Exception to Catch-1629

A 10-item decree forbidding such as wanton re-gifting of fruitcakes and the killing of your parents on Sunday was handed down by Moses in the year of God-knows-when. The date of the Decree of Marblehead, however, is known: 1629, the year the town was established.

The Decree has been passed down from generation to generation: "Ya ain't born in Marblehead, ya ain't a Marbleheader."

Inasmuch as the only hospital in Marblehead, the Mary Alley, closed its maternity ward in the mid-1960s, the only way to become an official Marbleheader thereafter was if your pappy was handy at boiling water and momma didn't mind ruining a perfectly good set of Honeysuckle Rose Springmaids. Otherwise, you got yourself outfitted in swaddling clothes in a place called Not Marblehead.

I was more than a little envious of for-real Marbleheaders. Particularly after my divorce, when the feeling of 'not-belonging' consumed me. I was running with a happy tribe of Townies, in the midst of one of my favorite songs: "I've Fallen in with Evil Companions and I'm Having a Wonderful Time." I'd have given a lot to belong; to be able to call myself "a Marbleheader."

One of my favorite 'evils' was a born-Marbleheader by the name of Jackson Tremblay. Jack Tremblay and I swapped stories and laughs at the Barnacle bar many a spiritually enriching afternoon.

Jack could cover a lot of ground. He'd range from the Louis L'Amour six-gun saga he's reading to a finger-jabbing outcry against bigotry to the interesting notion that peanut butter's the ultimate topping for a baked potato.

We'd be talking away and hours'd pass like seconds. Then, out of the blue, he'd look off in the distance, and almost sigh it: "Time to go ... time to go." Next thing you know, he's out the door. It always seemed he left too early, leaving us wanting more ...

We're in the Barnacle one day, and I've been going on about the town. Jack interrupts me: "Too bad you're not a Marbleheader, Bob." He excuses himself, and heads for the john.

Minutes later, I'm staring straight ahead, looking through the dining room to the window on the harbor. I feel something soft come to rest on my head. I look back, and up, and in Jack's raised hand is a toilet brush -- which he proceeds to gently lower to tap the something soft (which turns out to be a roll of toilet paper).

Tap, tap, tap: "I hereby proclaim you, Robert F. Baker, an official Marbleheader ... and only a Marbleheader can so confer this honor."

We broke into hoots of laughter; joking about how it was appropriate that my head was 'marble' and the ceremonial materials came from the 'head.' But I was truly honored -- I could tell he really meant it.

The only possible witnesses to Jack's proclamation that day were *non*-witnesses -- a bartender who was paying more attention to a waitress who was paying more attention to a soap opera.

But it really did happen. Tuesday, November 18th, 1986. I marked it on my calendar.

Man of His Word

To say Jimmy Buresh was a free spirit would be on par with saying there are quite a few people in China. He and I are in Jake Cassidy's one time and he mentions he's headed for Colorado to ski-bum for however long he felt like it. "Sounds great, Jim. Hey, send me a postcard. I get a kick out of postcards."

Jim looks at me, and with all the earnestness of a guy talking to his mother on her deathbed, says, "Bobby, I don't do postcards. I never sent a single postcard my entire life."

"Well, good," I said. "This can be a first. I like firsts. Let me be the first person Jimmy Buresh ever sent a postcard to in his entire life. How 'bout it?" He looks at me: "No way." Then he laughed. "OK, I will. Maybe."

A month later, into Jake's he comes, and I hit him with, "So Jimmy, where's the postcard you said you were gonna send me? Guess I was wrong, old buddy, huh?"

He reaches into his inner jacket pocket, pulls out a postcard, hands it to me. On the front: aerial shot of a skier carving his way down a slope. The address section in back: "Bob Baker, Marblehead." The message section says, "Your friend, Jim"

"Nobody has stamps out there," he said. I bought him a well deserved drink.

Killer

"I want a drink and I want it NOW!" -- his instruction as he took his usual post at the corner of the bar.

Arm's length from the bar, the fingers of his left hand fanned on the bar, his right hand raising the Tiparillo cigar like a maestro's baton s-l-o-w-l-y to his lips, his wit and proclamations punctuated with a growled "Bucko" to the guys and the "Darlin' "all but crooned to the ladies -- that voice from the bowels of the earth made Killer more the 9' 5" that he wasn't than the 5' 9" that he was.

He once told me if you wanted to drop from sight, all you had to do was, as he put it -- with a wink and a shrug -- "Make an honest mistake." Just transpose two of the numbers in your Social Security number when you're filling out forms. All of a sudden, the person on the form isn't the real you, it's someone else. And the real you can't be held responsible for failures to comply with the law perpetrated by the honest-mistake you; because the honest-mistake you isn't on file with Social Security -- so he or she is untraceable.

That's how it went according to Killer's theory, at least. I never felt the need to put it in practice, and I'm pretty sure he didn't either. It's just one of the infinity of ingenious ideas, schemes, tricks, shortcuts and insights that he toyed with, before gliding on to the mischievously inspired next.

It's no wonder the subject of confused identity would be of interest to him. His own father sowed the seeds, after all. As a concession to his mother, the Kane boy was called Robert Michael on the birth certificate. But his father, a devotee of Buck Rogers comics, 'transposed' Robert Michael to "Killer" -- after arch villain Killer Kane in the hugely popular strip of the '30s. Needless to say, calling someone weighing 9 pounds who's sucking on a pacifier "Killer"doesn't make a lot of sense. But that's what he was called pretty much from the getgo. At first, it was a bit tongue in cheek, then it caught on -- and stuck. So unless you're the principal of the school or a by-the-book teacher, you'll be calling this Robert Michael kid with the deep raspy voice "Killer" despite the fact he's only six.

There's an old Irish saying I'm about to make up which holds that "To achieve the status of Legendhood you have to have spawned enough colorful stories to amount to a Grand Total. And not a penny less."

Some contributions to Killer's Grand Total:

• He was one of the smartest people I've ever known. Not just book-learning smart; though he was solid in that department. He was lightning-quick when it came to problem-solving. If he didn't have the answer on the tip of his tongue, he'd have it in the time it took to set his eyes adrift in the mirror over the bar, take a quaff or three of beer, interspersed with lazy draws on the Tiparillo. His eyes still lost in the mirror: "I read an article about that in my neighbor's Wall Street Journal he always throws out. Bonds are the way to go." or "That's a job for a guy who knows what he's doing. You want Perry Asher." or "The map makes it *look* faster heading north; but it's 10 minutes quicker if you take the (wink) 'long' cut. Go *south* two miles, then grab 62 west." or "I just figured out why that's impossible ... "

• Killer was, for many of us, search engine and font of sparkling conversation combined. But because the not-infrequent night of excess would occasionally manifest itself in a look of 'unmade bedness' about his person, there were elitists who, at their peril, might mistakenly mistake Killer Kane for the owner of a turnip truck.

One such tilt-nose asked Killer to do patchup work on the interior of his fast-decrepitating chimney. The agreed-upon price was $250; to be paid half up front, half on completion. The front half was paid; Killer completed the work in his usual timely fashion.

Let Killer take it from there: "So I go to collect the buck-and-a-quarter the guy owes me. He comes to the door, tells me come back another time, he's real busy. This is September. I go back three more times -- the guy's real busy 1, real busy 2, real busy 3.

"Sometime late November I get a call from the guy -- he is very unhappy-sounding. He says I totally screwed up his chimney of the fireplace he lit up the night before ... he says his whole new all-white-decorated livin' room got filled with -- heh heh -- smoke and ashes ... poor guy.

"I go over to the house: I tell the guy, 'Hey, I think I can correct the little problem quick as you pay me the buck-and-a-quarter.' He looks at me funny ... but goes to the other room, comes back with the checkbook, starts scribbling me a check on one of those checks with pretty sailboats on it. 'No go, Bucko,' I tell him. 'I want cash. No cash, no splash. Like they say at your boatyard when you go to put your boat in the water every June. Except I want *cash* cash, see.'

"He goes to the other room, and comes back with the one-two-five ... cash. I give him an insincere 'Thank you,' with a nice little wink to go with it. I pop out to my truck, grab the ladder, grab a brick from the truck, get up on the roof, drop Mister brick down Mister chimney, break the pane of glass I mortared in just above the fireplace -- and out of sight -- to completely seal the flue.

"It's one of the greatest sounds in the world, Bucko ... that breaking glass. The sound of money in the bank. Better yet, cash in hand.

"I let him keep the brick. No charge. I guess you could say, I sorta ... *threw* it in -- heh heh."

• Kill was a perpetual motion machine -- such energy, it rubbed off. We're in Maddie's saloon one afternoon. He looks at me, winks the wink: "Bobby, thinking about getting some money together and buying the Blue Kangaroo."

(The Blue Kangaroo was a bar on Atlantic Avenue whose life span was about 2 months-5 days-27 seconds. In addition to its ugly name, its storefront window was consumed by the pop art image of a fluorescent-blue kangaroo. It would've surprised no one to discover it had in fact been painted by a kangaroo, it was that bad.)

The idea sprang into my head. "Killer," I said, "I've got the name for your place. The *Western* Yacht Club."

"How come?" was barely out of his mouth when he said, "Oh, I get it! You got the snobbo *Eastern* Yacht Club over there on the Neck ... Atlantic Avenue's *west* of the Neck ... I like it."

We schemed away. There'd be 'memberships'; the decor would be half-hull boat models and vintage yachting photos on the walls; the distinctive WYC burgee (club flag) hanging over the mirror serving as the bar's logo as well ...

As with many a scheme, it hasn't come to pass. But it's still a begging-to-happen concept for a Marblehead bar ...

• Killer had the all-purpose Yogi Berra-type good reason to do something or try something -- though it was always something no risk: "Might as well," he'd say, "nobody ever died from it, did I?"

• A lady friend of Killer's was throwing a Halloween party and she told him to pass on an invite to any and all he deemed worthy. "Supposed to be a costume party, but I hate those things," he said. "Anyone who'd go out of their way to look more like an idiot than they already are is three bricks shy of a load." We were in sync on that one.

I showed up slightly past the appointed hour, dressed as I'd been when Killer mentioned the party that afternoon -- sweater, striped button-down, jeans, boots.

The hostess opened the door costumed as I-couldn't-quite-figure-what -- a cross between Little Bo Peep and Dracula is about as close as I can come. A look of horror more horrible than even her makeup allowed came over her: "Where ... where's your *costume*?!" she shrieked.

"Got it on," I said, with a smile. "I came as myself -- I came as an asshole." Because I was a friend of Killer's she let me in, but you could tell she was bummed.

Half hour later, doorbell rings, Bo Peep/Dracula opens door. There stands Killer, wearing his roguish grin -- and the same outfit he'd been wearing earlier. "Killer, where the hell's your *costume*?!" she shrieks. "Wearin' it," he says. "Came as myself. Came as an asshole."

We had *not* rehearsed it. Simply a convergence of great assho ... er ... minds.

• Quaffing merrily away in Maddie's gloom-darkened bar cave one glorious July afternoon, I remarked at the beauty of the day. "Too nice a day to be outside!" Killer grinned.

• The back of Killer's RMK General Contractor card: "Rates/ Normal - $12 per hour/If you watch - $15 per hour/If you help - $20 per hour/If you started first, then called me - $30 per hour/ Free estimates grudgingly given"

• One of Killer's ventures was the esteemed Humble Painting company. The story is told of a house exterior Killer was painting in Ipswich while the couple was on vacation. The color, white. Killer decided that in order to speed the process he'd spray paint. The fact that spray painting produces a short-lived inferior finish was of less importance than the fact that the job could be accomplished in one-third the time.

I forget who told me the story, but whoever it was said he had to go to Ipswich to bring Killer something the day Killer was wrapping the job. The guy pulls up to the house, which was out of view of other houses, and there's Killer with a spray cannister, touching up the *bushes* around the house with *green* paint where spraylets of white paint had wafted.

• Killer was one of the founding fathers of The Great Race that night in 1967 when one faction at Maddie's loudmouthed that you could traverse the 17 as-the-crow-flies miles from Watertown to Marblehead faster in a canoe on water than you could by bicycle on land, with the other faction loud*er*mouthing back that bicycle would "sure as shit" be faster. The only way to settle the dispute, of course, was to have at it -- which happened at the crack of midnight and a cannonade of beers at the starting point in Watertown the following Friday. Thus was born a tradition which continued into the early '80s, when it outgrew itself, took on the excesses of Spring Break and got the boot.

At its peak, the race attracted hundreds of entrants to the midnight start and a couple thousand horny boozers to the all-day party that started at dawn. Devereux Beach was the 'finish' line for the contestants -- and not long after, for many of the boozers as well.

There were only two rules governing the race. Rule #1 stated that you could use any form of conveyance to cover the distance from Watertown to Marblehead as long as it wasn't motorized. Rule #2 stated that the first entry to cross the finish line in any given category was automatically disqualified, because ... you had to have *cheated* -- that was Killer's ingeniously mischievous wrinkle.

(Dan Levin crafted a funny piece featuring Killer in the June 23rd, 1975 issue of *Sports Illustrated* on the cockamamie race which drew thousands to the day-and-night-long boozefest after party at the welcoming bars and beaches of Marblehead.)

2nd Is 1st!

My favorite story related to The Great Race had nothing to do with the event itself. In November 1978, I threw a small party at my Baker Advertising office to celebrate the 4th anniversary of being in business on my own. Killer shows up, with his attractive lady of the moment -- introduces me to his date, hands me a vertical object wrapped in red tissue. "Congratulations. You can open it," he says, with his fox-grin that says he's up to his usual.

A trophy about 11" tall, featuring statue of a bare-nekkid guy holding a wreath, standing atop a starburst-decorated metal colyum, mounted on a faux marble base, to which is affixed a plaque reading:

19 - GREAT RACE - 69

CANOE 2ND

"Wow, Killer," I said, "that's really great. Really." I put my hand on his shoulder, and laughed, "But I gotta be honest with ya, Kill. You know how it is with me ... I only settle for first."

"Bobby," he growls, "I gotta remind you, Bobby. Rule number 2 of the Great Race. The first finisher in any category has to have cheated ... so they're automatically disqualified. So there *are no* first place trophies. Top trophy in each category is *second* place. What you've got there ... that *second* place trophy ... is really a *first* place trophy! See what I mean?!"

The trophy stands on display in my creative cave with other most treasured possessions. I love it. I love and miss the guy who gave it to me. Killer got transposed Elsewhere in 1991 -- to, if there's any justice, a seat next to God.

It occurs to me, too, that a bit of logic he'd spout when cautioned against partaking of another Budweiser or seven would make an epitaph he'd savor the irony of.

"Nobody ever died from it, did I?" he'd say.

I could hear his growl of a laugh as I was typing that. I could almost smell the Tiparillo.

F-Fantasy

Jed, who tends to stutter some, told this one on himself at Maddie's one day.

"B-back in my serious drinking days, I came home with a pretty good package on this one time. "I was l-legless, tell the truth.

"I walk in the door and my wife's s-sitting there in the living r-room, and I asked her where the kids were. She said they were already in bed.

" 'G-good,' I s-said, 'I've got a great idea! Why don't you go up to the bedroom, and I'll go up and take a shower ... and while y-you're waiting, you just think of the greatest *f-fantasy* we can act out when I come outta the shower. Make it good and wild, OK?'

"So sh-she goes up and I somehow make it to the shower, and I come out bareass and b-bounce the wall goin' into the bedroom, and there she is under the covers, and there's enough light so I can see she's starin' at me.

"So I say: 'W-well ... so did you th-think of a real g-good f-fantasy?'

" 'Y-yeah,' she says, kind of strong. 'You're .... y-y-you're ... n-not ... *here*! ' "

Amazing Joe

Joe Garland, master storyteller and crafter of intoxicating prose, was doing a signing for the re-issue of *Eastern Point: A Nautical and More or Less Sociable Chronicle of Gloucester's Outer Shield and Inner Sanctum* at Marblehead's Spirit of '76 bookstore in May of '99. I'd called Joe at his home in Gloucester the day before, just to introduce myself -- he sounded like my kind of guy right off. I brought to the signing a copy of the book I'd self-published in 1990, which I'd inscribed to Joe," The title of a venerable old hymn best describes your prose: 'Amazing Grace.'"

I also brought along my weathered copy of the Joe Garland classic, *Boston's Gold Coast -- The North Shore*, published in 1981. Before heading to the store, I spent a few minutes immersing myself in the almost-lyrical prose of the 76-year old Master -- my head nodding approval as I read along. Of a sudden, at the top of page xii in the Preface, a phrase jumped out and all but stabbed me in the eye: "Subscribers pressed equally as hard for inclusion ... "

Good old badassed "equally as." Hadn't I said and written or uttered good old badassed "equally as" a kazillion times in my life, and finally, in the late '50s, gone to the Irish Wall with my then-fiancee Joan over it? She who was an honors English major, graduate of the Radcliffe Publishing Procedures Program and copy editor for a Boston publishing house? She who finally-finally-*finally* convinced me that something was, for example, simply "*as* enjoyable" *or* "*equally* enjoyable," but that badassed old "*equally as* enjoyable" was redundant-dundant-dundant, if you catch my drift-ift-ift.

I wrote "equally as" and the page number on a 3 x 3 note, and paper-clipped it to the page -- intending it as a fun note to myself.

At the bookstore, I introduced myself, and Joe Garland and I hit it off from the getgo. We chatted about writing, had some laughs, and I went on some about my hopes for publication of something I was working on. When I handed Joe his book to sign, he, of-Murphy's Law-course, opened *immediately* to my stupid 3 x 3 page marker!

Even as I'm frantically fumfering apology that it wasn't meant for him to have seen, he is roaring gravelly laughter: "Of course! ... 'equally as' ... That's ... *redundant!*"

He grabs his pen, crosses out 'equally.' Now he's got me hooting along with him and I tell him that consistent with standard publishing procedure, author's changes have to be initialed. With the grin of a mischievous kid, he says, "Of course." Which is why atop page xii of *Boston's Gold Coast* it says "JEG ! !"

As he's flipping back to sign the title page, his mischief is contagious: "You have to use 'equally as' in your inscription, too, Joe," I instruct him. Again the grin. "Of course!"

And so Joe's inscription doth read: "For Bob Baker, equally as talented as the best -- just waiting for that shot (not shit!) Joe Garland 5-29-99"

A day written in indelible ink -- the man, the experience.

Eat a Better Breakfast, Feel Better All Day

One blizzardy February late morning Bob Guy and I walked into Maddie's to see if we could catch a stray bloody Mary or two. The only person there was the owner Kenny's mom, Mother Duncan, who was busy cleaning. We asked if she could fix us up a transfusion and she said "Sure ... be glad ta."

While she was mixing, I got in conversation with her, and asked how old she happened to be. "I'm 84," she said.

"Wow, Mother, you look pretty good for your age," I said -- which she did. "What's your secret?"

"Well, I went to the doctor some years ago, and he told me what to do. So every morning when I get up, I take a spoonful a cod liver oil ... and a shot a bourbon."

It reminded me of W.C. Fields' hilarious line, "I make it a habit never to drink anything stronger than *gin* before breakfast every morning."

Not Happy

Tom Edson was one of the fun regulars in the happening Marblehead bar scene of the '70s into the early '80s -- before DWI requlations put a you-should-pardon-the-pun 'damper' on all the wetness going down.

Tom was plenty smart and successful in his insurance brokerage business to begin with. But having grown up in Harlem, and a black man making a go of it in a frequently unwelcoming world, he also had an edge in the street-savvy department -- which he'd occasionally make evident in some of the great lingo he'd share ... and to the accompaniment of his hearty chuckle.

My all-time favorite was: "Some people are always moanin' and groanin' about how bad the world is *always* treatin' them. Like it's only them, y'know. They go around all the time with a damn cross up their butt.

You know how, if you have a kidney stone, maybe if you drink a lotta water, you can pass it ... cuz it's round? Can't do that with a cross up your butt."

Perry's Stories

Perry Asher is one of the sadly ever-scarcer Marblehead breed: a wonderful hardy lot, equipped with bright wit and straight-on stories.

He tells the one about a Christmas Eve when son Warren was four. Perry's buddy Skid Miller, unbeknownst to Perry, decided to have some fun and dress up in a Santa outfit he had, and come over and surprise Warren.

Perry and his wife were in the cellar putting together a bike for Warren, when there's a knock at the door. Warren opens the door.

Perry recognizing Skid's "Ho ho ho," yells up, "Hi, Skid, we're down cellar. Come on down."

Later, in the kitchen, Skid's having a beer -- Warren says, "I thought Santa likes milk and chocolate chip cookies."

At the doorway when Skid's driving off in his Chevvy wagon, Warren says, "I thought Santa had a sleigh." "He does," Perry said. But one of the runners is broken so he had to borrow Skid's car."

•

Another Christmas Eve, Perry tells Warren it's time for bed. Warren asks if he can open just one present first. Perry says no, go to bed. Warren pleads and pleads. Perry says, "Go to bed."

At the top of the stairs, Warren pleads to open just one present again.

Perry: "Go to bed!"

Finally, Warren SCREAMS at the top of his lungs to his mother, "Ma, can't I open just one present?!"

Perry shouts up, "She can't hear you ... she's opening one of her presents."

That Face

A few years ago, as I'm just inside the entrance of a local medical center, I see an elderly man, walker poised, struggling his way down the last steps of a nearby staircase. His frail body is twisted and his face is contorted -- a woman, maybe his daughter or health aide, is on the stair above and behind him -- she appears concerned.

I'm only steps away. "Can I help you, sir?" I offer. He turns to look at me. There's a twinkle in his eye; his face rubberizes into a grin that's crooked and ear-to-ear, but consumed with radiance. In tenor voice he sings out clear as a bell, "How ya doin', *handsome*!?"

I swear I was looking at the face of God.

I could feel the glow.

•••

•

6

Opened Gifts

We are all walking each other home.

Father Gerry Barry

•••

The Ingrate Gatsby

Although I'd won an academic scholarship to prep school, my academic performance at UConn was in the -- to put it politely -- for-shit range. The recipe for disaster was the fact that I was newly sprung from thirteen years of Catholic school cloister into a world of beer, girls-girls-girls and unlimited cuts.

(It being the 1950s, a lot of the students were veterans of World War II or Korea, hence assumedly mature enough to skip class without being penalized. They were right about the vets, incorrectamundo about this kid.)

Do the Math

My academic performance at UConn can be summed up, as it were, in two words: Math 108.

Freshmen in the College of Arts and Sciences were required to take review courses of high school English and math. No matter how many repeats it might take/it might take/it might take, you had to pass, have at least a barebones D in English 106 and Math 108, before you could -- what's that word? -- *graduate.*

Since I was an English major, English 106 was no problemo. Math 108, on the other hand, had the makings of a problemo. 108 incorporated three disciplines: algebra, trigonometry and calculus. I'd had algebra and trig in high school, and aced them both -- I even got a 98 in trig on the fierce-feared New York State Regents exam.

The catch to Math 108 was that, to pass the course, you had to have a passing grade in *each* segment -- algebra, trigonometry *and* calculus.

The *problem*-problem was I'd never taken calculus, not to mention even heard of the fucker. The *problem-problem*-problem was that whenever an instructor opened his or her maniacally contorted mouth to say something in calculus, horns sprouted from his or her demonically contorted forehead. Calculus was the language of the Devil, far as I was concerned.

I did make an attempt to understand calculus, and on more than one occasion, too. Four/ five times maybe. OK, twice. But it was a foreignmost-of-all foreign language. I couldn't even get started ...

Comes senior year and someone asks what courses I'm taking. "Oh, History 212, English 263, Science 211 and Math 324," I rattle off.

"Wait a second, Baker ... Math 324. *324*? *Three*-hundred numbers are *graduate* course numbers, Baker."

"Usually so," I say. "But in this case, it's just Math 108 ... third time around."

(To the instructor who, in retrospect, even somewhat resembled Mother Teresa, and who at the eleventy-eleventh-hour found it in her compassionate heart to mercy-grade me the D in calculus which gave me the 'pass' in 108 and *eked* me out a diploma, you should know that years' later I wrote a hymn in your honor: "You Are So Beautiful," I called it. Neil Sedaka, among others, covered it, I believe.)

Minus / Plus

Indeed, most of the story of my five-year vacation at UConn could be written in red ink. Waste. Waste of time, waste of money, waste of God-given talent. Lots not to be proud of. My shameful academic *non*-performance; my callous disregard for a loving, totally selfless, *wonderful* father who busted his ass to come up with the money for this ingrate Christ Child's tuition, room and board, *plus* 12 bucks a week spending money, even as -- get this -- throughout his last two years at UConn this ingrate Christ Child is doing the Great Gatsby Great *Pissaway* with an amount of money inherited from loving dead aunts sufficient to support a Connecticut family of four for a year, a whole family of *four*, for a whole *year*, but which instead the Christ Child Gatsby chooses to lavish on himself and a slathering drool of fellow ingrates who near break their arms slapping Christ Child Gatsby on the back and cranking their elbows to the tune of his party booze till Christ Child Gatsby's dead aunts' money runs out and the fellow ingrates pack up their arms and elbows and chase on out into the world beyond Gatsby's place at Andover Lake in search of another ego-driven wallet with a jellyfish spine.

I'd give most anything to be able to take all the bad stuff back or make it go away. At the same time, I can't wallow in it now, just as I didn't wallow in it then.

I worship at the altar of *"Excelsior,"* the motto of the state of New York: "Onward and Upward." For all the minuses of my UConn years there were handholds of hope for the future, some of which become apparent only now, thanks to 20/20 hindsight:

• I learned, for the first time, to 'exist' in a crowd. For periods of time, I did in fact, become part of the crowd -- as in the early, rah-rah stage of fraternity life. This crowd thing was new to me; but I learned to blend in, to 'pass' as one of the crowd when I wanted or felt I had to.

• Of greater relevance, I learned I didn't *need* the crowd. I could sustain myself and be happy in my own world, or bring the world to me when I wanted. I could be all by my lonesome at Andover Lake, or Jay Gatsby at the center of the party at Andover Lake.

• People came into my life then who would become a kind of 'family' to me after college and throughout the rest of my life -- they would be as inspiring and important to me in later years as my own parents had been in my formative years.

The charismatic and witty Wilsons, professor Ken and wife Marilyn, were bright lights admired from afar. I, whose only reason for inclusion in their presence at parties at Echo Lake and Andover Lake and the occasional Sunday evening scotch/cheese-and-crackers salon at the hearth of their A-frame on Separatist Road, was my close friendship with Jim Shaw who was blessed with at least two things which I lacked in the extreme -- intelligence in matters which related to the real world; success in matters which related to the real world. Given my sophomoric attempts at repartee, I'd hardly have expected the Wilsons to have found me worth continuing with once I'd departed the campus for who knows where thereafter. Jim Shaw was a wholehearted guy, one of the bright lights in my life then -- as he and his terrific wife Mary would be throughout the rest of my life.

Bang

Here's another non-hunting story for you.

The general manager of the Boston office of K&E, my boss, was a brilliant marketing guy -- with tastes markedly different from mine. One was guns. A gun was inherent to his after-hours activity as a volunteer on his hometown police force. A gun was inherent to his hobby of hunting.

In November '71, he invited me to go deer hunting with him and two other guys from the agency. Without thinking, I agreed.

The four of us in his four-wheel Whatever to northern New Hampshire, almost to the Canadian border. Settle into log cabin, fire in fireplace, pot of stew on stove, drinks and palaver, and with an "Up at 4!" from the Boss, we hit the hay.

Up at 4. Pitch black, crotch-shrinking cold. Into the four-wheel Whatever, bumpity-bumpity-BUMPITY-bump-bump-BUMPITY-stop. We get out, grab rifles and packs. Boss locks the Whatever. Boss says, "We'll head off in different directions. Meet back here by 3." They all head off, I go about ten yards down the road, find a trail, sidle in, find a broad-trunked tree, set my lever action Winchester 30-30 against the trunk, sit down, rest my back against the trunk, open backpack, grab book. I read and partook of Seagrams 7 from the silver flask I'd purchased for the Vacation Dances back in Grunch days, along with ham-and-cheese-on-rye sandwiches I done brung from home.

At stone-cold 3, we reconvene. BUMPITY-bump-bump-BUMPITY back to the cabin, have drinks, more brung-along stovetop vittles, early to bed: Boss says, "Up at 4! See ya then."

They all get up at 4. I tell Boss, "I'll stay here and guard the cabin." Boss stares me hard like he could plunk a round in my piehole -- 'cept it'd be a waste of a perfeckly good bullet, y'know. So they all hop into the Whatever, and I walk to the nearby downtown, and believe it or not, find a Sunday *New York Times*, and a country store where I get cheddar cheese and crackers and a couple roast beef subs. They come back around 3. No deer, though. Nobody got anything.

But a little over a month later, I got something -- my ass fired. Let me not kid you. Hardly did I get fired because of non-hunting. The *main* reason I got fired was a 100% completely valid reason. The same, as in the case of my firing from Little, Brown: I was not *ever* meant to be an *administrator* -- a memos, meetings, reports, hire and fire, details guy. The Great Light Bulb in the Sky put me on this earth to make light bulbs -- ideas.

As Creative Director, I was creating less and directing (administrating) more -- and half-assedly at best. So Boss was right to fire me. Though surely my gutsy No-Shots-Heard-Round-the-Agency on the hunting expedition hastened my execution.

Boss did one thing wrong, though. It was the *way* he fired me. He bullied me. In telling me I was fired, he also told me there was one agency he *forbade* me to work for. "You are *not* going to Hill Holliday ... *understand*?!" -- with his trigger finger aimed right-up-close in my face.

Hill Holliday was the hot new agency -- headed up by my friend Jack Connors.

I've always despised bullies.

not me

I rub my hands and lick my lips in Machiavellian glee when I recall the followup, the "Shootout at Maison Robert" -- the quintessential "free to be me."

David Herzbrun, the VW "snowplow" legend who hired me to freelance the Dukakis campaign, and who became a forever-after good-good friend, invited me to Boston for lunch. I met him at his office. "Where to?" he asked. I suggested Maison Robert, the white linen restaurant in the old City Hall. I'm no connoisseur of French cuisine, but their menu was more like 'good food with a French touch' -- and the place did sparkle. I'd been there a number of times.

Inasmuch as I was dressed in my liberated-from-corporatedom outfit -- what I called my 'L.L. Bean Punk' look (plaid lumberjack shirt, blue jeans, Timberland boots) -- Dave asked if I thought I'd be allowed into the quite spiff Maison Robert, where the uniform was tie and jacket, as was the regime in all executive-level Boston restaurants at the time.

I told him I'd already broken the dress-code barrier at Maison Robert a couple times -- which I had. (I was also an early-on liberator of Lock-Ober, a bastion of formality second only to the Ritz in Boston back then.)

As the maitre d' is showing us to our table, I feel a tug on the sleeve of my shirt. I look down to see the grinning moon face of the bullnecked bully who fired me not many years before; the same bullneck who poked his bully trigger finger right up in my face and told me where I was bully well *not* going to work next. I was bully well *not* going to work at Hill Holliday, he'd informed me.

Bully boy was with three other account guys from K&E. As opposed to being unnerved, as might be expected, a sudden calm came over me. I turned to the 'legendary' (Volkswagen snow plow commercial) David Herzbrun and introduced him to bully and the other guys. Admiration registered on their faces. Even a contorted version on the bully.

With a nod to them all, I said, "Well, we've gotta get to our table. Good to see you," and went to move along.

I felt another tug on the sleeve of my lumberjack shirt. I'm looking into bully-boy's steely eyes. He says in a grandmotherly -- at the same time, threatening – singsong voice, "Say *Bobbbb*, don't you know you're supposed to wear a tie and jacket in here, *Bobbbb?*"

"Uh uh, mister," I said, "*You* are."

David Herzbrun and I proceeded to our table and a three-martini lunch. It may well have been the best three-martini lunch the world has ever known. I believe we even had some food as well. It was quite good. David insisted on picking up the check, too.

Friend in Deed -- Indeed

Soon after getting word my wife has filed for divorce in 1978 ...

As I'm exiting the White Hen Pantry, I bump into client Ken Linn, owner of Village Decorator. Ken's a smart businessman and an easy guy to like. We've been great friends from the getgo: he even honored me with an invite to his son's bar mitzvah.

Ken makes the mistake of uttering the all-purpose: "How ya doing, Bob?" -- so I tell him.

His face wears sorrow: "Bob, wherever you move, you've got furniture. Everything. You've got it. No charge. We'll take care of it. Don't worry about a thing. Ya hear me, Bob? You're all set. You're all set, Bob, OK?" He chucked me under the chin -- like I was his kid brother -- and walked away. Wow. I could have cried. But I smiled instead -- at the idea that a Ken Linn existed.

I found a neat studio apartment up at Fort Sewall at the mouth of the harbor. Ken Linn provided a sizable sleep couch, two sturdy Harvard beds for the kids, a comfortable sitting chair, folding chairs, a work table; drapes, upholstery, bedcover, bolsters and throw pillows in the colors and fabrics of my choice. All delivered and set up -- no charge. Everything first class -- like God-bless-you Ken Linn.

One of the toughest things was deciding what books to take. I owned 1,000 or so. I had shelf space for about 750. Telling 250 close friends they aren't going to make it onto the lifeboat, is like telling someone they're going to have to leave the house real soon.

But, as they say at Mayflower Cleaners here in Marblehead, "We press on."

Partly Me? Not.

April, 1984. A call from Paul McDermott, former executive director of the Boston Ad Club, asking if we could get together in Marblehead.

At lunch, Paul tells me he's head-hunting for top Boston agency HBM/Creamer: they're looking for a top creative person to also serve as liaison with their key account, Bank of Boston (later Fleet, then Bank of America). Paul had recommended me. The salary's $100,000 -- in the top 5% for creatives in New England at the time.

I told Paul I couldn't imagine relinquishing the freedom I'd enjoyed since going out on my own in '74; but it wouldn't hurt to talk. A week later, I met with HBM Creative Director Mary Moore and showed her my portfolio. Next day, Paul calls: HBM's prepared to offer me the job. I wrestle with my mirror for all of 5 minutes, call Paul, tell him to thank HBM, but I can't see giving up my independence.

Weeks go by, Paul calls again. How about I give HBM four days a week, keep Baker Advertising active; give it a trial run to see if I want to do HBM full time? $6600 a month. The best thing about the offer; it provides me a lifeline to Baker Advertising. I can take a look, and still retain my own clients. What's more, I can return full-time to Baker Advertising with just a month's notice. Tug of war with the Devil: Beelzebub yanking me to Boston with a bunch of money and security. What the hell, I might get in there and decide I like it. On the other hand, I made a contract with myself when I went out on my own. It's not about money. It's about being free to do your things (plural) and *play* the *Game* of Life.

I accepted the offer; gave it my best Monday through Thursday, beginning in June. It was stimulating to be in a swirl of bright-plumed peacocks again, *but* ... acid reflux commute; (strait)jacket and tie; meetings-meetings-meetings; office politics; time sheets (account for every minute); ideas homogenized, compromised; projects advancing at the speed of dark ... Corporate Box.

Admiral of All I Survey at Baker Advertising; I'm just pulling an oar at HBM. Do it their way, or ... I gave HBM a month's notice, expressing my gratitude for the opportunity -- I returned to the ripe brine air of Marblehead in October.

I can't explain why or how four months in the Box and my subsequent escape to freedom triggered a da Vinci explosion, but it sure as hell did. All but a few of the veritable blizzard of ideas and manuscripts mentioned in my Ideas section (and many not mentioned) were created *after* I became a full-time me again.

A Shirt Named Al

Son Richard gave me the greatest gift of all time the Christmas of '89. Despite the fact that Rich was perfectly *ab*normal in the best sense of the word, he could tend to notch it up to the deliciously insane from time to time. His father's son, he.

The gift was bestowed in usual Men-of-Baker-Family fashion. Rich handed me a clump of newspaper, the traditional MoBF gift wrap. Sad to say, though, red tissue paper was taped to the top of the clump, providing un-Bakerly panache. Hey, nobody's perfect. I bit my tongue and whipped the paper off the present: a handsome, dark blue CPO shirt. The kind you'd find at L.L. Bean. "Wow. Nice, Rich. Thanks, pal."

"Naw, Dad, look at the front." Over the right pocket, a patch reading "Kinney R.V.s -- Rt. 1 Arundel, Maine." I pointed to the patch, and hooted.

"Check the other side, Dad." It said "Al." When I finally got the whooping cough laughter under control, I asked where he'd found this treasure. "Building 19. (a chain of 'Good stuff cheap' remaindered goods stores.) There were shirts with other guys' names. But Al had your name on it, if you catch my drift."

I agreed.

The very first time I wore Al, it brought adventure. I christened it two days after Christmas at the Porthole, a usual lunching-liquoring hole for me at the time. Of course, it's like when you buy a new car. If you try to steal around town in your shitbox with a belching muffler, you see everybody you know. But first time out in your spandy new diamond-polished Mercedes-Ferrari, it's either raining elephants or everybody's home restringing their dust mop. Such it was with "Al" at first. *Finally*, a waitress picked up on it, then the bartender, then Tony the busboy, who grooved on it. I was having fun as one after another paid tribute to Al, and I in turn paid tribute to the genius of Rich.

The stir settled and I ordered up a bowl of beef stew. I'm seated at the end stool, the two seats to my left are unoccupied.

A stocky fortyish guy in a three-piece suit plunks down next to me. I'm minding my business eating my stew and two seconds after he's seated, he's minding my business too -- telling me how he's a terrific lawyer specializing in accident cases and how if I'm ever in an accident and even if I'm not really hurt maybe I am really hurt, and he foists his card between spoon and mouth as I'm about to bring spoon to mouth, so I plop the spoon back to the bowl, give a grab to the card and a glare to him and in the process get a glimpse of the knockout blonde in the fur coat who eases into the seat next to him.

Oh well. There but for the grace of the ambulance chaser t'would be me she'd be nexting to. Such is life. Back to minding your stew, Al.

Now the Porthole does not usually tend to attract platoons of guys in three-piece suits to begin with, but I'd never *ever* seen a woman in a fur coat there. Not to mention, a knockout blonde in a fur coat.

The three-piece suiter now becomes the one-piece suitor. He orders another Chablis and tattoos the blonde-fur-piece with jabber and prattle and cards and verbal prancing for ten minutes; finally realizes he's getting nowhere, gulps the Chablis -- out the door, leaving a quarter tip.

"Get over here!"

Huh?

"Get over here!" the knockout is saying to Al-who-is-me, inviting-directing him-who-is-me thither with a lowering of the head and graceful swoop of the hand. Such grace ought not go unrewarded, Al figures.

So over he/me Al moves, orders up a fresh JB and soda and makes friendly words with the friendly knockout in the fur coat.

And friendly she is. And nice. And interesting, too. But most of all, she is friendly. She is touching Al's knee when she is telling Al how she's just ditched the guy who limo-ed her to lunch at the Ritz. She's kissing Al's hand when she's telling Al how she can't stand Yuppies -- like the ambulance vulture whose cards we both now ceremoniously tear asunder and laugh like schoolkids about. She's kissing Al's cheek when she's telling Al she'd once been with the New York Ballet; and when she tells Al she's Jewish and Al -- in all honesty -- tells her he'd always fantasized a Jewish ballerina as the ideal woman, she is kissing Al frequently on and about Al's roseate puckered lips.

Now in the course of all this attention, Al did find it necessary to tell the friendly knockout that he wasn't really Al, but that this shirt was his best Christmas gift ever, and that he was in truth just a lowly advertising slug who also liked to write and drink scotch.

She excused Al his disguise with a flurried buffing of Al's lips with kisses: "That's what attracted me to you. I am so sick of Yuppies! I came here to get away from Yuppies! "I looked down there, saw you eating your beef stew, you had a nice face ... that shirt ... I figured you were a ... a *plumber* ... or something."

That's Al, folks.

Dave Got Me Thinking ... and Doing

It hasn't often happened that I've become the best of friends with a guy who kidnapped me. I'd only been kidnapped once in my life: that time four drunked-up SAE pledges attempted to spirit me from Storrs, Connecticut to a mountain top in New Hampshire one icicle winter's night in the 1950s. One of those pledges was David McKain, who somehow managed to juggle a UConn basketball scholarship with membership in the fraternity, before having the good sense to take up with the beatniks beginning to confuse the campus.

In the early '60s, Dave and I reconnected -- when I was at *Harper's* and he was at *American Heritage*. We laughed about the kidnapping caper and had a couple good get-togethers. Then I lost touch with him.

In 1993, I caught up with him again. He'd added much to his resume since we'd last met: English professor (University of Connecticut's -- 'Outstanding Teacher', 1983); poet (winner, 1990 Ithaca House Poetry Award); winner of the Associated Writing Programs Award for Creative Nonfiction for his memoir, *Spellbound*. His wife, Margaret Gibson, a poet, was actually one of five finalists for the National Book Award in Poetry that year.

David and Margaret came for a three-day visit to Marblehead that summer, and we had a terrific time. As they were leaving, I gave Dave a copy of my self-published book, *The Garbage Collector*.

Shortly thereafter, Dave wrote me: "*The Garbage Collector* has the wit and density of poetry, the closely observed insights of fiction, and the boisterous romp of language sometimes referred to as pure Baker. It's amazing how much the voice is yours: bemused, probing, irreverent -- a voice that brings with it a wry and troubled smile. A Beckett play written by Joyce."

To top it off, based on stories I'd recounted, he suggested I write *The Vacation Dance List*, the account of my odyssey from Greenwich days Gatsby-wannabe to a lightning bolt-decision to become a human being instead: "I feel all of Marblehead is your house and backyard. *The Vacation Dance List* has extraordinary promise, whether you decide to make it narrative or turn it into a novel.

"I was thinking on the way back yesterday how American the story is. I don't know how far into the present you'd take it, but it seems to me your living in Marblehead -- 'in this place no one is important' -- is an important part (maybe the resolution of the struggle) of your story.

"I was thinking of your being an outsider ('a loner', as you put it) in Greenwich, at UConn, and in the workplace ('I got fired from three jobs and after the third time I decided to become my own man.') And then you became your own man.

"Most people don't get to the point where they feel at peace with themselves. They never find a Marblehead -- a community where they feel a part without giving up who they are. I know I haven't found such a place, but I'm still looking. We're all wandering the desert looking for the Promised Land, as the very reverend Haines used to shout. Everything fits, and that's why it's such an exciting story."

•

I took Dave's advice and wrote *The Vacation Dance List*. And although it remains in unpublished-albeit-complete, 100,950-word manuscript form to this day, considering the quality of some of the commentary about it, I count TVDL as one of life's little victories:

• Charles Everitt, literary agent; former head of Pequot Press; former managing editor, Little, Brown; also a Yalie-paradigm of the Greenwich prepsters: "It's bang-on, you've really got something there! You've got me every step of the way!"

• Robert Taylor, editor of the *Boston Globe* book section: "When a Scott Fitzgerald sensibility illumines the '50s the result is Bob Baker's poignant yet comic portrayal of a girl-hungry Gatsby from Greenwich. Like the upper-class kids who populate Whit Stillman's films, Baker's characters are educated in everything but emotional maturity -- and their growing up absurd in Connecticut has a rueful charm."

• I called Bernie Yudain, the retired longtime managing editor of the *Greenwich Time* and otherwise known as "Mr. Greenwich" who I'd never met and asked him he'd be willing to read my manuscript-in-progress to check for factual accuracy and flavor of the town and the era I was writing about. Bernie couldn't have beeen more gracious, and encouraging in his observations along the way: "You capture the spirit, the aura, the physical presence of this place and the time so well. I congratulate you on your perspicacity and your laid-back, funny, yet poignant saga of one man's rite of passage. When a reader can identify with awkward or embarassing moments, you know you're hitting the mark. It's a *movie!*"

Then, to top it off, Bernie devoted his entire Sunday, November 29, 1998 column to my 'novoir,' as I'd dubbed my fictionalized memoir, *The Vacation Dance List: Greenwich, Gatsby, The '50s -- A Memory*. In the course of his enthusiastic 750-word column, headlined "Coming-of-age novel has a Greenwich flavor," Bernie totally knocked my socks off, particularly with the last sentence of the following excerpt from his column: "Baker has a really distinctive voice that really kept me with him. I was delighted to zero in on all the good Greenwich stuff, the appearance of characters I actually knew of, recognition of places, things, the culture and moods of the town. The accuracy is acute. Baker has amazing recall. It all rings true."

•

A parallel story, which plays back to Dave McKain's reference to finding my 'true home' in Marblehead, has to do with a visit to Greenwich I made right after writing *The Vacation Dance List*. I wanted to drive around and kind of scope out where I'd come from, I guess, so I did a Memory Lane circuit of Greenwich first, and then Old Greenwich, by way of Riverside. My last stop was the bungalow on Center Road, the center of the loner kid's world -- where his-my imagination caught fire, where the idea kid was born.

I took a snapshot of the house; I jumped into my car and *flew* back to Marblehead. Home ... where I belong.

•

(In 1997, the Marblehead Chamber of Commerce awarded me an Honorary Lifetime Membership. It was a great to be recognized by my adopted homeland.)

Holding Hands

Peg. I catch my breath whenever I think of her -- which is often.

•

1960. Months had passed, and no reply to my letter seeking to rekindle the flame with Peg, the girl from New Canaan with the maid, the butler, and the 'wonderful' soul. Finally, a letter in our mailbox at the Chateau Lafayette. Her unmistakable handwriting; part print, part script. Dare I hope?

" "

Beloved Bobby:

Behold for I bring you tidings of great joy. For unto me is born a husband and his name will be Jim and his love for me seems like it's going to go on forever and ever. It's hard for me to believe that such a wonderful thing has happened to me, that he actually does want to marry me, and that I'll never know loneliness or real misunderstanding again. Everything is so beautiful and happy all at the same time. And peaceful, too.

Whenever I think about you, I get so sentimental. I've always felt that my friends, not my parents, were the ones who really brought me up, and it's very hard for me to think of a friend who has meant more to me than you. Maybe it's because we got to know each other just as we were beginning to think about more serious things, but I think it's a lot more than that because I remember playing do-you-know in those days and knowing an awful lot of people, most of whom I've completely forgotten.

But you meant so much to me. Do you know when we first started going out together I carefully wrote down what we did and talked about so I could always remember getting close to you? But we were friends right away, right off, and we never bothered to flirt with each other or hide things and we laughed and danced with other people and talked long and deep when we were alone.

I'd never wanted to talk with anybody before then, but we weren't afraid of each other, and you gave me confidence in myself and my own ideas by listening to me so lovingly and you made me feel aware of other people the way you opened yourself so completely to me, so much so that you finally told me there was something of your mother in me which is probably the most important compliment I've ever had.

Bobby, I'm sitting here and I'm so grateful to you and fear to think who I would have been without you. I remember your coming over in the evening in the summer and telling me that my hands felt cool on your sunburned face and we'd try to put together what little each of us knew about God, and what we'd done that day.

Bobby, don't ever leave me, don't ever let me leave you, and when we get together, like we said, no matter if our grandchildren are there, let's hold each other's hands, so we know, just so we know.

Well, the tears are streaming down my face and I've got to stop this because you understand all I'm saying before I say it. You know that I am your loving

Diana

,,

I went to the wedding at "half after four o'clock" at St. Mark's in New Canaan that glorious Saturday in July.

Peggy, luminous, coming down the aisle on Jim's arm, catches sight of me. Her eyes to mine: her mouth forms "Bobby." Jim, who I'd met a month previous and couldn't help but like, winked at me.

She didn't trip, either: I remember thinking that through the mist.

The Dawsons held the reception at their home, underneath two tents of Ringling Brothers' dimension. I got swimmingly drunk, and it was suggested to me by the kindly New Canaan constabulary that, rather than have my car make further mincemeat of the Dawson's lawn in my continuing failed attempts to find exit, it indeed might be a really good idea for me to catch some rest at their nearby hostelry instead.

I awoke Sunday morning in the New Canaan jail. It was a clean well lighted cell. The door was even open.

gone

We stayed in touch through the years. I visited Peg and Jim in their townhouse in Brooklyn Heights when I was working in New York in 1962. She visited wife Nancy and me when we were living in Cambridge in 1964. And, yes, each time before she left, Peg and I'd sit side by side on the couch in conversation with each other and spouse -- and holding hands.

In September of '66, she called. She was going to be in Boston over the weekend and would love to come to Marblehead and say hi. Of course.

We open the door to greet her, she points to her knees: "No Band-Aids! You probably don't recognize me!" Her stay was brief, but -- wonderful. Towards the end, she and I sat on the couch and held hands, as son Richard toddled about, spreading his cheer. Then, "Time to head back to Boston," she said.

•

Wife Nancy was terrific at communicating with our friends. Christmas cards, birthdays and occasions of note, such as birth announcements. As was Peg. Nancy sent the Ritcheys an announcement when daughter Kate was born in October 1969.

After New Year's 1970, we noted that we hadn't heard from the Ritcheys, not even the usual Christmas card. We agreed it seemed strange. After supper one Monday in late January, Nancy said, "I didn't have the heart to show you this over the weekend." She handed me a letter:

" "

Lovejoy, Wasson, Lundgren & Ashton, Attorneys at Law
250 Park Avenue, New York, N.Y. 10017

Re: Estate of James V. Ritchey, III

Dear Mr. Baker:

This is in response to your correspondence to the Ritchey's former address. I've enclosed the account of the accident which appeared in the New York Sunday News, June 15, 1969.

Sincerely, Emilia J. Ariola

There were two enclosures. A news article, and ... an obituary notice. From the news article:

Planes Crash Over Sound; 9 Die

Waterford, Conn., June 14 (UPI) -- Two private planes collided in flight today, exploded and plunged into Long Island Sound, killing nine persons. The crash occurred in poor visibility about 300 yards offshore. (My note: Two couples from California in the first plane.)

The second plane, a Piper Apache based at Linden (NJ) Airport, carried Mr. and Mrs. James V. Ritchey of 77 State Street, Brooklyn, and three children, a boy, 9, and two girls, 3 and 4.

The crash occurred at 11:10 a.m. near Waterford, which is in the Groton-New London area. (My note: They were probably en route to Bailey Island, Maine, where I believe the Ritcheys had a summer place.)

The obituary notice:

RITCHEY, James V. , III, died suddenly, on June 14. Margaret (Peg) Dawson Ritchey, daughter of Mr. and Mrs. Northrop Dawson, James V. Ritchey IV, Elizabeth Barrie Ritchey and Georgia Dawson Ritchey. Memorial services at Trinity Episcopal Church, Southport, Conn., on Wednesday, June 18, at 11 a.m., and at Plymouth Church of the Pilgrims, Brooklyn, N.Y., at 8 p.m., on Thursday, June 19. In lieu of flowers, contributions to the St. Anne's Episcopal School, Pierpont St., Brooklyn, will be greatly appreciated.

, ,

I'll try to be analytical about my feelings, my reaction:

1. Tragedy beyond my ability to comprehend, my ability to absorb, my ability to process: an integral part of me ... *vanished*.

2. I get the news in the cold and dry of an attorney's letter, news article, obituary. Not a human voice. I only learn about it *six months after* the fact. There isn't a single person I know who I can talk with about it, find out more from, and -- more importantly -- share my

-273-

grief with. No one. I feel so helpless, lost.

3. Peg reminds me of my mother in her pure goodness. In a sense, losing her is like losing my mother all over again.

I'm constantly compelled to the letter telling me she's marrying Jim: "Bobby, don't ever leave me, don't ever let me leave you, and when we get together, like we said, no matter if our grandchildren are there, let's hold each other's hands, so we know, just so we know."

Gone. All that goodness, gone. It still hurts. Deep.

Nobody held hands like Peggy did. Or ever will.

Friends Forever

Jim Shaw was a campus god at UConn in the mid-'50s. He was a rugged-handsome World War II veteran going for his masters in English who'd been president of SAE, the fraternity I was an occasional member of, and president of the Student Senate. Even though he was a few years older, and light years' more savvy than I, Jim, probably because of our shared mick sense of humor, took me under his wing and we became friends for life. I was honored to be best man in his wedding and honored to have him be my best man.

It was Jim who initiated my friendship with another pair of forever-pals when he brought me along with him for Sunday afternoon scotch, cheese and crackers salons at the Wilsons' way-cool A-frame tucked into the woods on Separatist Road in Storrs.

•

My relationship with the Wilsons flourished unabated through the years -- Ken, the hotshot young prof who rescued my wastrel student(?) ass in the '50s who went on to become Dean of the College of Arts & Sciences at UConn; Marilyn, his soulmate and coequal in mind and spirit.

We'd gotten together in New York and Boston in the '60s; in Marblehead in the '60s and after; and I'd visited them in Storrs, Connecticut a number of times, including a couple of times right after my divorce when they dressed my psychic wounds and provided me 'family'.

When they visited Marblehead the summer of 1993, Ken handed

me a book he'd just published: *The Columbia Guide to Standard American English* -- Ken's answer to Fowler. (Since 1926, Fowler's *Modern English Usage* had been 'the bible', *the* reference, when it came to appropriate use of language in speech and writing.) From the jacket blurb to Ken's book: "Over 6,500 lively entries, more than any other usage book." Consider Ken on "euphemisms": "Whitening a sepulcher does little to alter what's in it, even when everyone agrees to the paint job."

When I saw my name on the acknowledgments page, I was floored. I asked Ken how I rated such an honor. He grinned and said, "Oh, we've had good words about words over the years, you and I."

&

In March of 2003, I got a call from Marilyn saying Ken had passed away and there would be a memorial service in Storrs at the end of the month if by any chance I could make it.

I wrote a tribute and sent it to Marilyn, in case I couldn't make it. But I did attend, and when I arrived Marilyn asked if I'd read my tribute. There were nine other eulogists, including Marilyn, and I'm pretty sure my shaky delivery was no better than my disastrous rendition of *Religion the Hope of America* in eighth grade ... but I did it for Marilyn and Ken:

" "

A Toast to Ken & Marilyn

I have so many outstanding memories of Ken Wilson throughout our 50 years' of friendship, and every one of them co-stars Marilyn. Which is not surprising: because in so many senses Ken and Marilyn always seemed opposite-gender *replicas* of each other to me -- equal in mind and humor and pride in each other.

My favorite anecdote recalls the time I got to have some fun, *and* at the same time compliment them both. The year was 1997. Ken and Marilyn had come to Marblehead for a stayover en route to Maine. I'd invited some friends for cocktails at the Corinthian Yacht Club to meet the wonderful friends from my happily misspent college days who'd stuck with me throughout the rest of my happily misspent life.

About an hour into cocktail banter, I tinked silverware to glass, and announced I'd like to propose a toast. I hoisted my glass in the direction of Ken and Marilyn, who were standing side by side.

"To the wittiest person I've ever known," I said -- and paused.

"And to her husband, Ken," I added.

Marilyn was a schoolgirl.

Ken was simply beaming. He said to whoever was next to him, "He's right, you know."

•

Ken often signed off his letters, "Be of good cheer."

And so we shall. "Here's to Ken and Marilyn." (I raised my hand in toast.)

, ,

I count myself among the luckiest of aging boys to have had such wonderful friends. I only wish I could *re*-misspend those golden days with them all, all over again.

• • •

•

7

A Surprise Sidekick

You feel mighty free and easy on a raft.

Huck Finn

• • •

Book of Revelation

Ideas by their very nature are a form of surprise. Something that wasn't, suddenly is! As a player of the idea game since forever ago, I was pretty immune to surprise. Which made it all the more, *surprising*, that I got caught by surprise by my bar-style format. It was as if I'd set out to invent checkers and invented chess instead. A glass of water turned out to be vodka. To use a *Mad Men* expression, bar-style "had legs."

When I gave the finished manuscript a test read, the interaction among the stories and anecdotes created a new effect: a *Book of Revelation*. Bar-style enabled me to see, and compare, the different 'me' I was at various stages of my life -- and learn things about myself.

The most amazing revelation came to light when I interrupted reading the manuscript to factor in an overlooked anecdote which had special meaning to me.

Back in the '80s the Advertising Club of Boston asked some of us creative types to describe what it felt like to win a Hatch Award, the Oscars of New England advertising -- the quotes were to be used on a poster for the upcoming event.

My quote, "Barefoot and twelve in a field of sun," had implications beyond the Hatch Awards. I intended it also as a statement -- the euphoria I felt being on my own in business, being my own man ... free ... to be me.

When I revisited my time-worn copy of the Ad Club poster ... *whiplash*. An illustration accompanied each of the half-dozen quotes on the poster. The artist's interpretation of my quote told me *exactly* who I was identifying with in "Barefoot and twelve in a field of sun."

The illustration, a silhouette: ball of sun, guy in straw hat and overalls lying on back, contemplating toes of elevated bare foot in wiggle mode. Lacking only the label: Huck Finn.

Huck.

That's *exactly* who I was calling to mind! *Exactly* who I'd been influenced by and identifying with throughout my life, and particularly in my world of independence since 1974. The *ultimate* free spirit! A kid I'd first encountered centuries ago when I was about seven and rode the raft on the Mississippi with him and his gentle buddy, Jim the slave, in Mark Twain's indelible classic, *The Adventures of Huckleberry Finn*.

I was so *surprised* by this revelation, I had no choice but to immediately devour a copy of *Huckleberry Finn* to try and figure out what it was about Huck that had infiltrated me, immersed itself in me, laid low in my soul till the time was ripe all these years.

How had this raggedy kid who stubbornly forsook regimen come to outlast and vanquish all the larger than life heroes, idols and symbols of 'wannabe' for me at different stages in my life -- Sir Galahad, the Lone Ranger, Lone Eagle (my own invention), the Great Gatsby / Scott Fitzgerald, Holden Caulfield, the genius ad man Bill Bernbach, etc., etc.?

Huck Finn was a different kind of hero -- new to me.

As I sped the pages of *Huckleberry Finn*, Huck's 'heroic' qualities were everywhere in evidence -- in this book of "wonderfulness everywhere you look," as George Saunders put it. Huck's openness; his levelheaded approach to risky adventure; his creativity; gutsiness; incisive 1-2-3 logic; guerrilla mode ingenuity; persuasiveness; playfulness; compassion; selflessness; mischievity; free spirit ... his *un*cool easygoing nature.

What makes Huck different is ... he's a *human* hero. All those terrific qualities, and each sparks to life every now and then -- as needed. Never *all* in play 24/7. Never dominate, *never* override Huck's true self. He's flesh and blood real. A poor country kid with no pretensions. Happily imperfect, happily human. Wow.

That's why I identify with him: free spirit, human.

•

Keith Neilsen tells us in the afterword of the book that Twain's success-oriented Tom Sawyer character grew up to become super-successful Mark Twain in real life. "But," Neilsen adds, "it's easy to imagine that, at night, Mark Twain dreamt of being Huckleberry Finn."

Yes.

ACKNOWLEDGMENTS

Thanks Giving

I could spend forever and a day thanking everybody on this list if I were to do it right. Because for each person there's a different reason -- no matter how slightly different from anyone else on the list.

But since I'm running low on forevers, not to mention days, I'll simply express my gratitude by naming some of the many who have helped me in a meaningful way throughout my life:

To my heroes: Mom and Dad, son Rich, Pete and Mimi Hart, Jack Connors, Roland Merullo, Peg who was Diana -- those to whom this book is dedicated.

To those who have been an extended family to me: Ruthie Deignan, Marie Deignan, Ken and Marilyn Wilson, Mary Grace Mullen, Greg Merrick, Dave McKain, George Brewer, Steve Decatur, Skip Chard, Father Dennis Burns, Grace and Edith Baker.

To Jim and Mary Shaw, Ray and Gwin Ellis, Paul McLaughlin, Judge Joe Dever and son Joe Dever, Ellen Davis, Mildred Callahan, Bernie Yudain, Bob and Brenda Taylor, Herman Gollob, Killer Kane, Suya Quinn, Michael O'Shea, Forrest Preece and Linda Ball, Billbo King, Jayne Comstock, Dan Jensen, George Reichhelm, Pete Schalck, Susan Chandler, Geoff Hodgkinson, Jean Fogle, George Ulrich, Ken Linn, Father Terence Curley, Ney Tejada, Brad Bradshaw, Debbie Smith, Gay Walley, Steve Haesche, Jim Mullen, Andrew Christensen, Ann McGreevy, Rob Carr, Laurel McDonough, Teri McDonough, Marjorie Quinn, Keith Taylor, Roger Wise, Dave D'Alessandro, Susan Moynihan, Andy Fleming, Howard Waldman, Fern Selesnick, Paula Viera, Gene Labonte, Dick Goodenough, Leon Remis, Martha Costello, Rich Campbell, Katherine Wilson Conroy, Julie Livingston, Warren Zimmer, Brian LeClair, Jane Clayton, Dick Finocchio, Doug

Santa Cruz, Cait O'Callaghan, , Amy Bucher, Bob Sharp, Barbara Biele, Paul Downing, Sister John Marie, Colleen Thibault.

A special note of thanks to the most excellent Ted Grant for his numerous generosities in recent years -- most recently in relation to this book; and to design craftsman supreme Mark Sutherland, who shared my graphic vision as if through my own eyes, and whose artful genius made my words become book.

•

It's a given in creating invitations to occasions and acknowledgment sections of books that there will be unintened omissions of the deserving. To those in that category, please forgive me.

•

As they say at Mayflower Cleaners here in Marblehead, "We press on."

• • •

ABOUT THE AUTHOR

At the Lighthouse, 1990

Following *When Life Was Wow!*
Bob Baker will be in play on
branding projects, a novel and
a North Shore road trip idea.

His hobbies include mischief,
spinach bagels with peanut butter
and not being cool.
His favorite form of exercise is
hanging around with good people
who know how to laugh.

He lives in Marblehead,
home to some characters
with character.